Cromosys Publication

Teach
Yourself
Photoshop

NIRANJAN JHA SHOWMAN

Founder - Niranjan Jha Showman

Education and Technology Research Center

Patankar Park, Nallasopara (W), Mumbai. +91-9561450045

Education, Technology, Publication, Healthcare, Newsmedia, Realtor, Filmmaking

www.facebook.com/cromosys

+91-9561450045
Learn Advanced Skills
And Get Job Instantly
GERMAN
Python
FRENCH
C++
SPANISH
Java
ENGLISH
HTML5
RUSSIAN
CSS
JavaScript
Cromosys
Education and Technology Research Center
Nallasopara (W), Mumbai

Learn Web Programming
Demo-Class Free
HTML
CSS
React
JavaScript
Typescript
Bootstrap
Cromosys
20 Years of Experience
Nallasopara (W), Mumbai
+91-9561450045

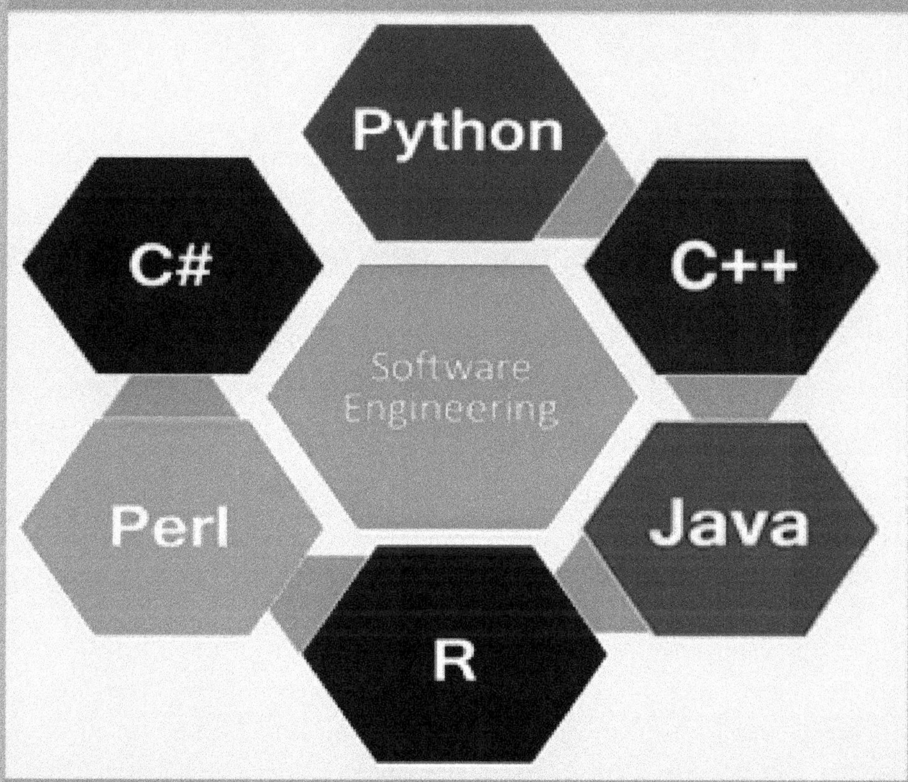

+91-9561450045
Learn Software Engineering
Demo-Class Free
Python
C#
C++
Software Engineering
Perl
Java
R
Cromosys
20 Years of Experience
Nallasopara (W), Mumbai
+91-9561450045

25 Years of Experience
Learn Visual Multimedia

● Animation VFX
● Movie Editing
● Game Development

Cromosys
+91-9561450045
Education and Technology Research Center
Nallasopara (W), Mumbai
www.facebook.com/cromosys

Jobs Available
For Candidates Who Know

German
French
Spanish

Vacancy in Germany, France, Spain

For Hospitality, Engineering, IT Sector
With Free Visa, Airfare and Accommodation

Cromosys

Education and Technology Research Centre
Nallasopara (W), Mumbai
+91-9561450045
20 Years of Experience

+91-9561450045
Foreign Languages Institute
German, French, Spanish
Basic and Advanced - All Levels
3 x 6 = 18 Courses
FRANCHISE
Business Offer
Teaching Materials Provided
We have 1 Million Students Globally
Great Income Assured
Global Exposure
Cromosys
20 Years of Experience
Nallasopara (W), Mumbai
+91-9561450045

Book: Teach Yourself Photoshop
Author: Niranjan Jha Showman
Publisher: Cromosys Corporation
ISBN: Acquired
Date: 2020
Category: Computer Education

Preface

Cromosys Publication's **Teach Yourself Photoshop** book is an optimal quality guide to the beginners and advanced learners. We are the leading book publisher of languages and technology. Our research and education center working for last fifteen years has made tremendous efforts to simplify the learning of Photoshop, and so we assure you that this book will walk you through in the simplest way in your entire course of learning, and will make you a master of this application in just one month of time. This all-inclusive book provides a thorough introduction to the new features of Photoshop CS6 and the latest version, with enhanced cropping options, a new Blur Gallery, and Content-Aware Move Tool. This current edition focuses on the key features and explains the core concepts of raster image editing in Photoshop CS6. The lessons of this book also cover the enhanced features in Photoshop explaining how to use layers to edit an image non-destructively, and introduce techniques, such as cropping, adjusting brightness and contrast, correcting and changing color, and retouching and healing images. The latest Photoshop CS6 version helps you to transform your creative imagination into new and innovative concepts. An easy-to-understand language and step-by-step approach to the concepts that starts from the basics, supplemented with practical examples are some of the features that make this book unique. The content is presented in such a way that it will be equally helpful to the beginners as well as the professionals. The lessons conceived and prepared by us help you start learning from real basic making your move amazing, astonishing, and exhilarating for you. It's cool, simple, and sublime!

Niranjan Jha, the author of this and fifty other books published online, is the founder, owner, and word-coiner of Cromosys Corporation. His dedication in technological and linguistic research is significantly known to millions of people around the world. This book is the creation of his avowed determination to make the learning of Photoshop easy to the people. After you install the application on your system, you just have to follow the instructions of this book doing the same on your computer, and you will see that you are quickly learning everything. Just an hour of practice per day, and in a month of time you'll get a lot of knowledge, tips and tricks to work with this software. This is an unmatchable unique book of its kind that guarantees your success. The lessons are magnificently powerful to bring you into the arena of graphic design. With the industrial growth from the year 2014, the accurate and profound knowledge of this software has influenced millions of minds; therefore we conceived the idea of making this book a guideline to those who want to be perfect in this application starting from real basic. What Photoshop CS6 does, no other software can do. The quick and precise lessons with screenshots will help you enhance your creativity of crafting sophisticated high-quality designs. This book explains the new and improved features in Adobe Photoshop CS6, with the different concepts of color theories, color modes, and color adjustments. You will also learn from this book the fundamentals of vector and raster images and the concepts of smart objects and shapes. Creating and modifying text, including type mask and 3D text with various painting and retouching tools, creating interesting effects using filters and actions, using different ways of refining selections, working with video and creating an animation, saving a Photoshop document for the print and the Web, will make you overwhelmed with joy in Photoshop. It is the need of time and that is why many people have been sharpening their knowledge to be good in this application.

Digital images convey an idea, a story, or large amount of information quickly, which is why they are such prominent aspect of graphic designing. Adobe Photoshop is the most popular industry standard software for graphic designing and image editing. The latest edition, Photoshop CS6 is a major release with a restructured interface, several new features, and several enhancements that will enable you to work faster and more efficiently.

Cromosys, our education and technology research education center, saving human efforts from being wasted, is committed to help you gain profound and contemporary knowledge. The world growing with density has brought enormous opportunity to graphic design talents irrespective of their geographical boundaries. We strongly believe that this book is useful for people working for picture editing, graphics and animation, media houses, and entertainment world. After you start the lesson, you don't need to worry about anything but just follow each and every step carefully. This book is designed to fulfill the instant need of learners in a very economical way, as it is easy to find on Internet and affordable to buy and share. Cromosys, our path-breaking pioneer training institute for Computer Courses, English Speaking, Foreign Languages, and Competition Coaching, is dedicated to enlightening human mind with educational endeavors, and we have been doing the same for last successful fifteen years. And recently we have come up with 'Worldwide Online Teaching System' for languages and technology. We not only hope but believe that your success is in your hand, as this book will take you miles ahead in your expectation. We always respect the views and comments of readers, so for any communication with regards to assistance, enquiry or collaboration, we are always there at your reach as it helps us improve our quality.

Niranjan Jha Showman
Founder: Cromosys Corporation
Web: facebook.com/cromosys
Contact no.   +91-9561450045
Email address: cromosys@yahoo.com

Books by the same author:
Teach Yourself CorelDRAW CS6, Teach Yourself Premiere Pro CS6, Teach Yourself After Effects CS6, Teach Yourself Adobe Flash, Teach Yourself Adobe Dreamweaver, Teach Yourself Autodesk Maya, Teach Yourself Autodesk Combustion, Teach Yourself Autodesk 3ds Max, Teach Yourself Tally ERP 9, English Voice Accent and Pronunciation, English Word Power, English Dictionary of Modern Slang, Teach Yourself Spanish, Teach Yourself French, Teach Yourself German

Cromosys
Education and Technology Research Center
Education, Technology, Publication, Healthcare, Realtor, Filmmaking
Nallasopara (W), Mumbai, India

Caution: All the writing works that include all the educational, non-educational books, novels, and articles of the author Niranjan Jha, are the registered contents of Online Digital Services and also published contents of his registered magazine FACE OFF - Inventing Truth, which carries registration no. MAHENG12112/13/1/2009-TC and the endorsement no. 3244 28/5/2009 with the Ministry of Information and Broadcasting, Govt. of India. Any plagiarism in this regard will attract strict legal action. Any further publication of any of his books requires his written permission. Copyright certificate of this book is attached at the end of this book.

Lesson 1
Introduction

Photoshop CS6 offers some of the most sought after features to edit vectors with improved layer management, and the ability to save in the background and auto recovery. Based on user feedback, all these features are developed. The new layer search feature in Photoshop CS6 allows you to quickly filter through your layer stack under different categories, such as Kind, Name, Effect, Mode, Attribute, and Color. Photoshop CS6 also includes three new blur effects: Field Blur, Iris Blur, and Tilt-Shift.

The Adobe's Mercury Graphics Engine is a new addition to Photoshop CS6. It speeds up the editing tasks using the processor-intensive tools, such as Liquify, Puppet Warp, and Transform. In addition, the compatibility of Photoshop with other software helps you to export Photoshop documents directly into other Adobe software, such as InDesign and Illustrator.

In this chapter, you first learn how to invoke the Photoshop CS6 application. Next, you will learn to explore the new and enhanced features of Photoshop CS6. In addition, you will also learn about the interface elements. Next, you will learn how to create a new document, as well as save the document. You will also learn about commonly used file formats in Photoshop. Next, you will learn about frequently used tools in the Tools panel. You will also learn about screen modes. In addition, you will learn how to navigate in a document and familiarize about guides, grids, and ruler. You will also learn to use Mini Bridge to open a file. In the end, you will learn to close the active document and exit Photoshop CS6. Let's begin the chapter by learning to start the Photoshop CS6 application from your computer.

Starting Photoshop CS6

Photoshop CS6 is available in two separate versions: Photoshop CS6 standard and Photoshop CS6 Extended. Photoshop CS6 Extended includes all the features of Photoshop CS6 standard, with advanced digital imaging capabilities that helps you create and edit 3D and motion based content, such as animations and videos. This book is based on Photoshop CS6 Extended. The software is sold separately, and you may use the free 30-days trial version of the software available at http://www.adobe.com/. The use of the software is subject to the terms of Adobe's license agreement.

Before you begin, ensure that you have installed the software in your computer; in our case, we have installed Photoshop CS6 Extended on the Windows 7 64-bit operating system. To run Photoshop CS6, you need the following system requirements:

- Intel Pentium 4 or AMD Athlon 64 processor
- Microsoft Windows XP with Service Pack 3 or Windows 7 with Service Pack 1
- 1GB of RAM
- 1GB of available hard-disk space for installation
- 1024x768 display (1280x800 recommended) with 16-bit color and 512MB of VRAM
- OpenGL 2.0-capable system
- DVD-ROM drive
- Broadband Internet connection

Keep in mind that additional free space is required during installation. You cannot install on removable flash storage devices. Some Graphics Processing Unit (GPU)-enabled features are not supported on Windows XP.

Similar to most applications, you can start Photoshop CS6 from the Start menu or by double-clicking the Photoshop CS6 icon on the Desktop. Perform the following steps on your computer to start Photoshop CS6 using the Start menu:

1. Click **Start> All Programs> Adobe Master Collection CS6> Adobe Photoshop CS6** from the Start menu on your Desktop screen.

If you have used earlier versions of Photoshop, the first thing you will notice when starting Photoshop CS6 is the icon that has been changed.

Now, the Photoshop CS6 splash screen appears. The splash screen displays the name and the version of Photoshop. After few seconds, the Photoshop CS6 window appears, as shown in picture 1.1.

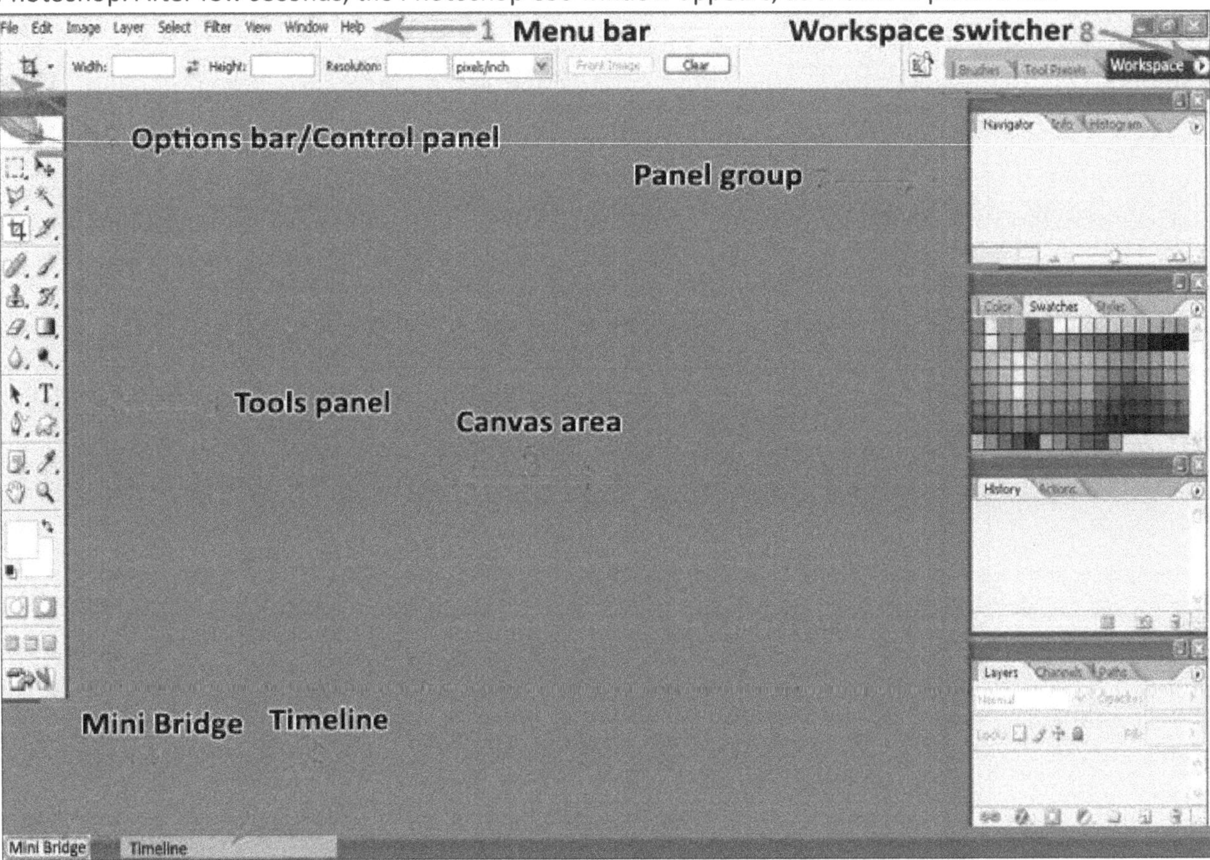

Picture 1.1

As shown in the picture, the default Photoshop CS6 window includes several interface elements, such as panels, menus, options, and the canvas area. The canvas area is where you open and edit images. Now, before exploring the various interface elements, let's briefly learn about the new and advanced features of Photoshop CS6 in the next section.

Overviewing the New Features of Photoshop CS6

There are several new as well as enhanced features included in the latest version of Photoshop. The Photoshop CS6 interface is the first thing you would notice, which is darker as compared to previous versions. The new features include enhanced cropping options, as new Blur Gallery, skintone-aware selections, Content-Aware Move Tool, Adaptive wide-angle lens adjustments, improved auto-adjustments, and various useful video editing tools. These enhancements help you work with Photoshop CS6 faster and more efficiently. This is the list of new and enhanced features in Photoshop CS6:

- **The new dark interface:** Refers to the most prominent feature in Photoshop CS6, the darker interface. The darker tone of the interface helps your images in the canvas stand out against the dark background, so that you can focus more on the image. You can also choose one of four different color themes for your interface that are available in the Preferences dialog box.
- **Background save and auto recovery options:** Enables you to set Photoshop to save your document automatically. This provides a protection against any kind of software crash and if there is a crash, Photoshop will automatically recover the file that you were working on. You can also set Photoshop CS6 to save recovery information at user specified intervals.
- **Content-Aware Move Tool:** Allows you to recompose and blend image selections quickly without making slow and precise selections. In addition to Content-Aware Tool, Photoshop CS6 updates the existing Patch Tool with the Content-Aware option. You can select this option in the Options bar and enables you to replace undesired image elements by blending nearby content seamlessly.
- **New Crop Tool:** Allows you to crop images interactively. When you select Crop Tool, the interactive preview feature is activated, which enables you to visualize the results in a better way. Various options for Crop Tool, such as Straighten and aspect ratio controls are included on the Options bar. The Straighten option straightens an image by drawing a line on it. You can access the current aspect ratio or resolution by right-clicking the image.
- **Drawing Improvements:** Provides additional options, such as Fill, Stroke, stoke width, and stroke type for the line and shape tools. You can apply strokes and fills using the Option bar. These options enable you to create fully vector-based objects in Photoshop. In addition, you can stroke objects with various dashed lines options and fill objects with preset or user-defined gradients, colors, and patterns.
- **The new Adaptive Wide Angle filter:** Corrects lens distortion that appear when you shot using wide-angle lenses. Lens distortion makes objects appear curved in panoramas. This filter automatically fixes distortion or perspective issues in your image. To automatically correct images, the Adaptive Wide Angle filter uses the physical characteristics of individual lenses. You can select this filter by selecting the Adaptive Wide Angle option from the Filter menu.
- **Improved auto corrections:** Allows you to quickly enhance your images using improved Auto feature for Curves, Levels, and Brightness/Contrast. These options provide a better starting point for making adjustments in your images.
- **Blur Gallery:** Enables you to create photographic blur effects using three new blur effects. The new blur filters uses a sample new interface with on-image controls that is all the controls to modify a blur effect appears on the image. When you use these new blur effects, you can preview all blur actions live with the Adobe Mercury Graphics Engine and a modern graphics card. However, Photoshop automatically switches to Central Processing Unit (CPU) mode for older systems.
- **Mercury Graphics Engine:** Provides real-time result while working with memory intensive tools, such as Liquify and Puppet Warp. It also provides faster rendering while working with 3D and allows you to paint more freely, and smoothly resize brush and brush tips in real-time. The Mercury Graphics Engine takes advantage of your computer's graphics processing unit (GPU) and video graphics card to speed up Photoshop's performance.

- **Increased Maximum brush sizes:** Allows you to paint with brush sizes up to 5000 pixels.
- **Erodible brushes:** Draws realistic brush strokes using drawing tips that gradually wear away. You can also create a wider variety of strokes while painting with a static tip by using the new Brush Projection option. You can save brush setting as presets.
- **New Character and Paragraph Styles:** Allows you to create styles and save your favorite styles in one place, and reuse them. You can use paragraph style to effectively manipulate text by creating a set of properties for each style.
- **Properties panel:** Refers to context-sensitive panels that appear when you select certain type of layers, such as masks, adjustments, and video layers.
- **Layer search:** Filters the layer stack based on categories, such as Kind, Name, Effect, Mode, Attribute, and Color.
- **3D Improvement:** Provides an efficient interface, easier workflow, and simplified toolset that allow you to create refined 3D content. When you create a 3D layer, Photoshop sets up an optimal workspace displaying key panels, tools, and the interactive 3D widget automatically. In addition, Photoshop CS6 supports for the industry-standard ways (Y-up) of describing the orientation of objects.

In this section, you have learned about the new and enhanced features with major improvements in Photoshop CS6. After getting familiar with this, let's now learn about the Photoshop CS6 interface in the next section.

Exploring the New Photoshop Interface

The Photoshop CS6 application's interface is where you work on your digital images. Generally, you open or import images into the canvas area and then edit the images using combinations of tools, menu commands, and panel options. By default, the new interface is set to a darker color theme, which makes the image you are working on appear more prominent against the background and helps to focus on the image. The default Photoshop interface includes the Menu bar, Tools panel, Options bar, canvas area, and several panels, such as Color, Adjustments, and Layers (picture 1.1). All these panels are present in groups; you can collapse or expand a panel as per your requirement. You can also make a panel as a floating panel or collapse it into an icon to increase the canvas area. Now, let's discuss the Photoshop CS6 interface elements beginning with the Menu bar.

The Menu Bar

At the top of the Photoshop window, the Menu bar replaces the Application bar in Photoshop CS6. It begins with the Photoshop icon that lets you minimize, maximize, restore, move, or close the application. It also displays the menus, such as File, Edit, Image, and Layer. There are three buttons: Minimize, Restore, and Close that are present at the right-most corner of the Menu bar. The screen mode options that were present in Photoshop CS5 can now be solely accessible using the Windows menu. In addition, the Mini Bridge button is now available as a tab below the canvas area.

The Options Bar

The Options bar or the Control panel is located below the Menu bar. It displays options that help you customize the selected tool in the Tools panel. For instance, if Move Tool is selected in the Tools panel, the options specific to Move Tool appear in the Options bar. The Options bar is separated into different groups by vertical lines; for instance, in case of Move Tool, the Options bar is divided into Tool Preset picker and Align groups. You can move your cursor over any setting to see a pop-up description called a tooltip. A tooltip briefly describes the functionality of a setting.

The Document Window

The Document window appears when you open an image or create a new document. The area of the image displayed inside the Document window is editable. The Document window consists of a Title bar and the image area where all the actions are performed to edit the image. The Title bar contains the tabs for the documents that are currently open and displays the name and format of the document, magnification level, color mode, and bit depth of the document.

If multiple documents are opened, you can switch between documents by clicking their respective tabs. Due to this property, the Document window is also referred as the tabbed Document window. The Status bar is positioned at the bottom of the Document window and displays useful information about the document, such as the current zoom level (24%) and file size of the document.

You can increase or decrease the zoom level of the image by typing the desired value in the text box. The icon next to the current zoom level text box enables file sharing; and appears if you install Photoshop on a network computer and activate the workgroup feature. Next to the icon, the file and image information box displays the file size of the document by default. You can click the right arrow icon to display a dropdown list for the document properties, such as Document Sizes, Document Profile, Document Dimensions, Current Tool, and Efficiency.

Panels

Panels are small adjustable windows that provide the access to common commands and options. For example, creating a layer in the Layers panel or going back to a particular history state in the History panel. By default, these panels are combined into groups known as panel groups and appear to the right side of the Photoshop window. Panel groups are useful as they provide more space to work with. For instance, by default, the Color panel is grouped with the Swatches panel. You can click the name of the tab in which you want to work with, to activate it. Panels in a panel group can be collapsed into tabs or icons, where in the tabs form displays the icons and names and the icons form displays only the icons. Now, let's discuss some guideline that will help you to use panels efficiently while working in Photoshop. You can customize the panel arrangements in the following ways:

- Press the Shift+Tab keys simultaneously for hiding/showing all panels in Photoshop excluding the Tools panel.
- Drag the panel tab to a desired location to undock and make the panels as floating panels. By default, panels are docked into the right side of the Photoshop window.
- Click the icon of the respective panel for display the expanded panel view with commands and options.
- Click the panel icon again or click the double arrows in the title bar for closing the panel.
- Click the panel menu icon at the upper right corner of a panel to open a panel menu.
- You can click the panel name that appears without the tick mark (in the Windows menu to display it) for accessing the hidden panels. By default, Photoshop CS6 displays some panels and hides some panels.

The Tools Panels

The Tools panel displays various icons that represent various tools in Photoshop. These tools are grouped according to their functionalities and used to edit images in Photoshop. By default, the Tools panel appears docked on the left side of the Photoshop window. As a general workflow rule, you select a tool by clicking the respective icon in the Tools panel or pressing the shortcut key assigned to the tool. And then you modify the image with the selected tool. Now let's explore some guidelines that will help you to use the Tools panel efficiently while working in Photoshop CS6:

- Press the V key on the keyboard at any point of time to activate Move Tool.
  - The name and the shortcut key appear in the tooltip when you place your cursor over any tool. For instance, when you place the cursor over Move tool, the tooltip appears as Move Tool (V) where V is the shortcut key for Move Tool.
- Click and hold the mouse-button to open a flyout to access the additional tools.
  - The presence of a small triangle on a tool means that some additional tools are present and hidden under the main tool. For instance, Lasso Tool contains additional tools, such as Polygonal Lasso Tool and Magnetic Lasso Tool.
- Click the double arrows in the title bar of the Tools panel to bring the Tools panel into the two-column view and vice-versa.
  - The Tools panel is in the one-column view by default.
- Click the title bar at the top of the Tools panel to create a floating Tools panel.
  - Dock it back by dragging it to the left side of the workspace.
  - Release when you see a blue vertical bar appear.
- Press the Tab key to hide/show all the panels, including the Tools panel.
- Press the Caps Lock key on the keyboard to change the shape of the pointer for the painting tools to crosshair.
  - To return to the standard cursor, press the Caps Lock key again.

Creating a New Document

You can use the Photoshop CS6 to either edit an existing document or create a new document from scratch. You may want an empty canvas to paint your art or paste a copied section into a new blank document. Photoshop gives you a variety ways to create a new document which appears in the middle of the canvas area.

You can either create a new document using the File> New command or press the shortcut keys, Ctrl+N together. In both cases, the New dialog box opens. The settings here let you specify the document's size, resolution, and color mode, all of which affect the quality and size of the image. Now perform the following steps to create a new document in Photoshop CS6:

1. Select **Start> All Programs> Adobe Master Collection CS6> Adobe Photoshop CS6** from the Start menu to open the Photoshop CS6, if not already open.

2. Choose **File> New** from the Menu bar. The New dialog box appears on your screen, as shown in picture 1.2 below.

3. **Type** a name for the new document in the Name text box. In our case, we have named the document as **First Document**.

4. Type **Width** and **Height** values in their respective text boxes. In our cases, we type **16** for <u>Width</u> and **12** for <u>Height</u>, and selected **Centimeters** as the unit for the dimension, (picture 1.2).

5. Type the **resolution** for the new document in the Resolution text box. In our case, we type **100** and select **Pixels/Centimeter** as the unit from the Resolution dropdown list.

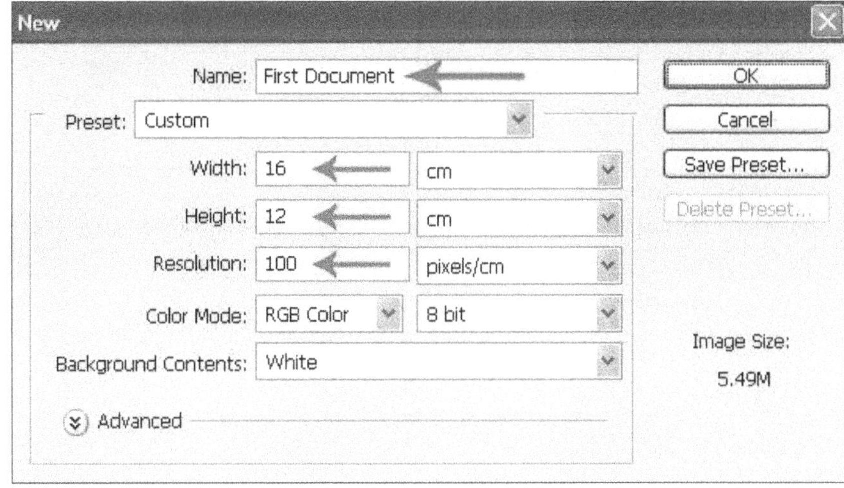

Picture 1.2

You can notice the Color Mode is selected as RGB Color and Background Contents is selected as White by default. You can also set the current settings as a preset by clicking the Save Preset button.

6. Click the **OK** button to create a document with the specified settings. As a result, the new document (First Document) appears in the middle of your canvas area.

You can also optionally set additional options in the Advanced group. There are two options in this group, which are described as follows:

- ☐ **Color Profile:** Assigns a color profile that is the way color looks in a document to the newly created document.
- ☐ **Pixel Aspect Ratio:** Selects an aspect ratio which is the relationship of width to height of a pixel. The default setting Square Pixels is good for print and Web images. Images for digital video may require a non-square aspect ratio, such as D1/DV NTSC.

Photoshop provides presets to create documents for specific purposes, such as Web, film, video, or mobile device. The available presets include U.S. Paper, International Paper, Web, Mobile & Devices, Film & Video, and Photo. When you select a preset, various templates for that preset appear in the Size dropdown list. Templates have predefined dimensions, resolution, and color depth. Let's now learn how to save a document in Photoshop CS6.

Saving a Document

When you create a new document or modify an existing document, you need to save the changes made to the document on your hard drive to be able to work on it later. In case, you accidentally close the Photoshop window without saving the document, Photoshop prompts you to save the changes or discard the changes made to the document. Photoshop gives you a variety ways to save a document. You can either save a document using the File> Save command or press the Ctrl+S keys together. In both cases, the Save As dialog box opens. This dialog box has various options which allow you to save your document in different formats as per your requirements. Perform the following steps to save a document in Photoshop CS6:

1. Select **File**> **Save** from the Menu bar to open the <u>Save As</u> dialog box, as shown in picture 1.3.

2. **Navigate** to the location on your hard drive where you want to save the document. In our case, we select <u>Desktop</u> location.

3. **Type** a name for the document in the <u>File name</u> combo box.

4. **Select** a format in the <u>Format</u> dropdown list to save your document. In our case, we select **Photoshop (*.PSD,*.PDD)** format.

5. Click the **Save** button to save with the specified settings.

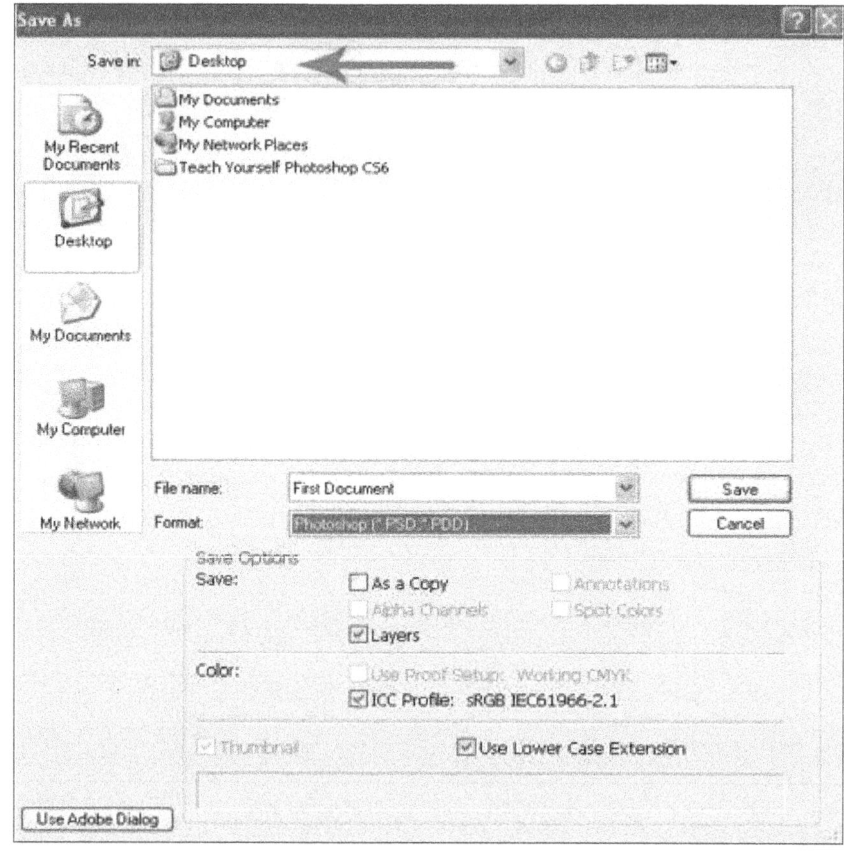

Picture 1.3

As you noticed, we saved the document in the Photoshop format, which is the default format for Photoshop. However, you can also save your documents in other formats, such as Bitmap (BMP), Encapsulated PostScript (EPS), Tagged Image File Format (TIFF), Portable Network Graphics (PNG), Joint Photographic Experts Group (JPEG), Portable Document Format (PDF), and Pixar (PXR). Let's now learn about various file formats in Photoshop CS6.

Exploring File Formats

An important decision needs to be taken while saving a file; that is, choosing the right file format. File format refers to the way the data (that is pixels) is represented in an image, the compression techniques used, and the Photoshop features supported by the formats. For instance, to save documents larger than 2 GB, you must select file formats, such as Large Document Format (PSB), Photoshop Raw, and TIFF. Photoshop supports more than 20 different file formats. The format for a file you select depends on the purpose of the file. For instance, if you want to use the file for Web, the file should be saved in the format that is designed for file compression to reduce the file size. Similarly, if you want to export a file to another application, you should save the file in a format that can run on that application. Before moving to file formats, let's learn about various file compression techniques.

File Compression Techniques

Now, we are going to discuss about file compression techniques. File formats use compression techniques to reduce the file size of raster images. Compressed files use lesser hard disk space or transmission bandwidth as compared to uncompressed files. For instance, an image of 4 megabytes will take more time to download as compared to an image of 1 megabyte. The two types of compression techniques available are as follows:

- **Lossless technique:** Preserves original image detail or color information.
- **Lossy technique:** Removes some image details or color information and reduces file size.

The following are commonly used data compression algorithms:

- **RLE (Run Length Encoding):** Uses lossless compression. This algorithm is supported by some common Windows file formats.
- **LZW (Lemple-Zif-Welch):** Uses lossless compression and supported by TIFF, PDF, GIF, and PostScript language file formats. It is useful for images with large areas of a single color.
- **JPEG:** Uses lossy compression and supported by JPEG, TIFF, PDF, and PostScript language file formats. It is ideal for continuous tone images, such as photographs.
- **CCITT family:** Uses lossless compression techniques for black-and-white images supported by the PDF and PostScript language file formats. (CCITT is an abbreviation for the French spelling of International Telegraph and Telekeyed Consultive Committee.)
- **ZIP:** Uses lossless compression and supported by PDF and TIFF file formats. Likewise, LZW, ZIP compression is useful for images that contain large areas of single color. Let's now discuss the most commonly used file formats in Photoshop.

Photoshop Document

PSD is the native Photoshop file format and offers optimum options for all image-editing tasks in Photoshop. It saves all the details applied to a Photoshop document, such as transparency, layers, adjustment layers, masks, clipping paths, layer styles, blending modes, vector text, and shapes. PSD is the default file format for Photoshop. The native format of Photoshop usually retains software-specific image properties. For instance, you can retain the ability to edit layer styles and text in a Photoshop document only when the image is saved in PSD format. Let's now learn about different file formats supported by Photoshop CS6.

Bitmap

BMP is the cross-platform standard format for Windows operating system that is compatible and supported by the majority of graphics applications. It supports millions of colors in the form of RGB, Indexed Color, Grayscale, and Bitmap Color modes. In uncompressed BMP files, image pixels are stored with a Color depth of 1, 4, 8, 16, 24, or 32 bits per pixel. You will learn more about color modes in the next chapter.

Encapsulated PostScript

EPS is the standard file format for importing and exporting files. EPS can contain both raster and vector images along with text. EPS supports transparency. This file format supports lab, CMYK, RGB color, Grayscale, and Duotone Color modes. This file format does not support alpha channels and clipping paths. As Photoshop users do not use this format much, so recently, EPS is being replaced with the PDF format.

Tagged Image File Format

This is the standard format to exchange raster images between different applications and computers running on different operating systems. It is basically a flexible bitmap image format supported by almost all image editing applications. TIFF can preserve layers, transparency, and smart objects; however, the file size is large.

Pixar

PXR is a raster image format developed by Pixar and used in computer animation production systems. This format stores strokes images as RGB or grayscale bitmaps at a resolution of 8 bits per channel. PXR does not use any kind of compression techniques.

Joint Photographic Experts Group

JPEG stands for Joint Photographic Experts Group, and was named for the organization that developed the format. An advanced variation, JPEG2000 (JP2) graphic file format is being used on the Web and in digital photography. JPEG is commonly used for photograph and images, when you need to keep the file size small and can afford to lose some quality. Saving a file in the JPEG format can lead to loss of data since it discards pixels to reduce the size of a file. JPEG is not suitable for images with text, large blocks of color, or simple shapes, because crisp lines will blur and colors can shift. Only JPEG offer the format options of Baseline, Baseline Optimized, or Progressive, described as follows:

- **Baseline (Standard):** Refers to the JPEG format option that is recognized by all Web browsers. This format option makes the least amount of changes to your image.
- **Baseline Optimized:** Provides optimized color and slightly better compression. This format option compresses the image to save space. It is supported by all modern browsers, but was not supported in the very earliest of Web browsers. It is the best choice for JPEG files today.
- **Progressive:** Creates a JPEG file that displays gradually as it downloads, beginning with a blocked display, and gradually getting clearer as it downloads. On a slow connection, it creates the illusion of faster download.

Portable Document Format

In the year 1993, Adobe Systems created PDF format to exchange documents across applications. This format preserves fonts and page layouts. It also preserves vector and bitmap data based on the EPS imaging models. PDF files also contain text search tools and navigation features. You can also perform minor editing in a PDF file in Adobe Acrobat. Let's now learn how to open an existing Photoshop document.

Opening an Existing Document

In Photoshop, you can open an existing document in different ways. You can select the File> Open command from the Menu bar or press the Ctrl+O keys together. In addition, if you have a blank canvas, you can double-click on the canvas area to open an existing document. All of the ways display the Open dialog box. Photoshop is compatible with a number of file formats, which means that besides Photoshop format, you can open, edit, and saves files from different file formats. Perform the following steps to open an existing document in Photoshop CS6:

1. Select **File> Open** from the Menu bar to open the <u>Open</u> dialog box.

2. **Navigate** to the folder on your hard drive and **select** the file that you want to open in the Open dialog box.

3. Click the **Open** button to open the document in Photoshop window.

As a result, the selected document opens in your Photoshop canvas. Once you open an existing document or file, you can work on it further. Let's now learn about various tools in the Tools panel of Photoshop application.

Working with Tools Panel

As we have already discussed, there are number of tools and commands available in Photoshop's Tools panel, and you use these tools as per your requirements. There are some tools you frequently use while working on a document. These frequently used tools include Move Tool, Quick Selection Tool, Content-Aware Move Tool, Brush Tool, and Type Tool. You can access these tools from the Tools panel. Photoshop displays the most frequently accessed tools and hides other tools for limitation of space. Let's now learn how to display the hidden tools.

Displaying Hidden Tools

The Tools panel, by default, arranges relevant tools in a group. For instance, all the selection tools are grouped into one group while all the type tools are grouped into one group. A small triangle at the lower-right corner of a tool indicates that there are hidden tools. To display the hidden tools, click and hold the tool to display a flyout of all the tools in that group. For instance, when you press and hold Rectangular Marquee Tool, the flyout displays other tools, such as Elliptical Marquee Tool, Single Row Marquee Tool, and Single Column Marquee Tool, as shown in picture 1.4.

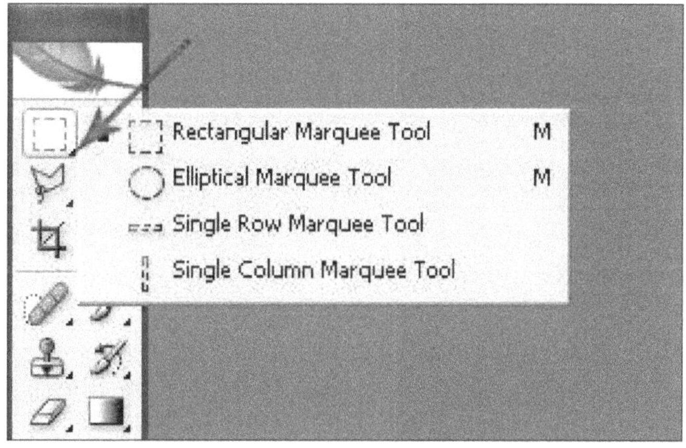

Picture 1.4

After learning how to access the hidden tools, let's now discuss these tools in detail including Content-Aware Move Tool, which is introduced in Photoshop CS6.

Move Tool

Move Tool is used to move selections, layers, or guides from one location to another in the document. You can also use Move Tool to move document among multiple opened documents. Move Tool helps to rearrange different elements in a document; for instance, to move a selection in a Background layer or in the non-Background layers. Background layers are locked layers and appear when you open an image for the first time. You learn more about layers in *Lesson 6: Working with Layers and Masks*. Now, perform the following steps to move a selection in a document:

1. **Open** any Photoshop file (.PSD) file in Photoshop window, as shown in picture 1.5.

2. **Make** a selection using any of the selection tools. In our case, we have made a circular selection using **Elliptical Marquee Tool**, on the word Niranjan Jha, as shown in picture 1.5 with the red arrow.

By the way, you learn more about selections in lesson 5: Making Photoshop Selections.

3. Click **Move Tool** in the Tools panel or press the **V key** on the keyboard to select it.

4. **Click** inside the selection and **drag** the selection to a desired location.

By default, when you move a selection, the original location is filled with the background contents. Keep in mind that when you move the selection, **hold the Alt key** down to create a copy of the selection. Let's now learn about Eyedropper Tool.

Picture 1.5

Eyedropper Tool

Eyedropper Tool allows you to select the Foreground Color or the Background Color. You can pick any color from an opened image. When you click a color, the color is picked as the Foreground Color, if the Set foreground color swatch is active. Similarly, press the Alt key while clicking with Eyedropper Tool to select the Background Color. The keyboard shortcut for Eyedropper Tool is I. Whenever a painting tool is selected (by pressing the Alt key), you can temporarily switch to Eyedropper Tool. The options for Eyedropper Tool appear in the Options bar. These options allow you to specify a single pixel sample (Point Sample), a 3 x 3 Average, or a 5 x 5 Average and so on. The 3 x 3 Average option averages the color of the nearest 3 pixels surrounding the area where you click. You can also change the sample area options by right-clicking anywhere on the image when Eyedropper Tool is active.

You can also select a layer to sample for Eyedropper Tool in the Sample dropdown list. Another option for Eyedropper Tool that appears in the Options bar is Show Sampling Ring, which helps you to select a color with the help of a circular ring. When the Show Sampling Ring check box is selected and you click a color with Eyedropper Tool, a circular ring pops up, as shown in picture 1.6 with the red arrow.

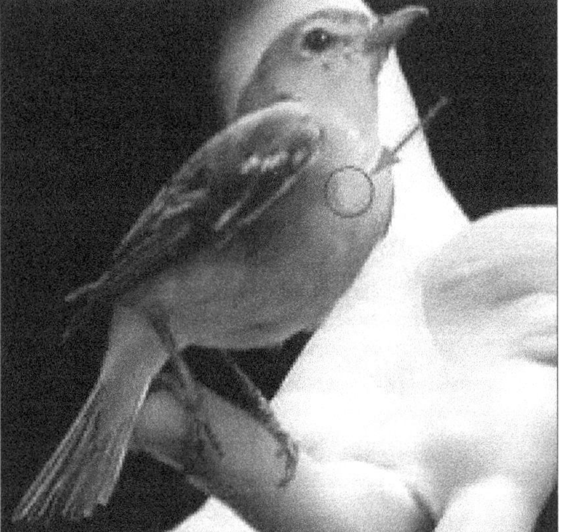

Picture 1.6

As you can see on your screen, the gray ring on the outside is a neutral gray strip that differentiates the color sample from the image. The top half on the inside represents the current sample color and the bottom half is the active color before sampling. It helps when you work on the full screen mode with everything hidden. When Eyedropper Tool is active and you right-click the image while holding down Alt and Shift keys together, a Hue Strip appears. A Hue Strip is a pop-up color picker that helps to select different color shades of the color sample. Let's now learn about Content-Aware Move Tool.

Content-Aware Move Tool
The new Content-Aware Move Tool in Photoshop CS6 allows you to recompose and blend image selections quickly without making precise selections. The advantage of using this tool is that you can quickly select the object you want to move in your document. Photoshop automatically fills the area created after moving the object with surrounding pixels and ensures that new pixels blend well with the surrounding pixels.

Content-Aware Move Tool has two modes, such as Move and Extend that you can find in the Options bar when this is selected. The Move mode is selected by default and allows you to place object selections in completely different locations. It is most effective when the background is similar. On the other hand, the Extend mode allows you to expand or contract object selections. Perform the following steps to use Content-Aware Move Tool:

1. **Open** the image in which you want to use Content-Aware Move Tool.

2. **Click** and **hold** the mouse button down on Spot Healing Brush Tool in the Tools panel to display a flyout.

3. Select **Content-Aware Move Tool** from the flyout.

4. **Drag** a marquee selection with Content-Aware Move Tool around the area on the image that you want to move.

5. **Click** and **drag** the selection to a new position. As a result, Photoshop automatically fills in the hole with matching elements from the existing background.

Using Screen Modes
You can use Photoshop's screen mode feature to view your documents with or without various interface elements, such as Menu bar, Title bar, or Tools panel. Photoshop provides different types of screen modes. You can access the screen mode options from the Tools panel. You can click and hold the Change Screen Mode icon at the bottom of the Tools panel to display available screen modes. Unlike, Photoshop CS5, where screen mode options were located on the Application bar, Photoshop CS6 includes screen mode options on the Tools panel. You can also access screen mode options from the View menu by selecting View> Screen Mode.

There are three screen mode options, such as Standard Screen Mode, Full Screen Mode With Menu Bar, and Full Screen Mode. By default, the Standard Screen Mode option is selected. Let's discuss these screen mode options in detail in the following sections.

Standard Screen Mode

This is the default mode of viewing your document in Photoshop. In Standard Screen Mode, documents appear in its standard form. In this mode, an image is displayed with all screen elements, such as Menu bar, Document window, Tools panel, and panel groups. To view an image in Standard Screen Mode, click the Change Screen Mode icon on the Tools panel and then select the Standard Screen Mode option from the flyout. Let's now learn about Full Screen Mode With Menu Bar.

Full Screen Mode With Menu Bar

Full Screen Mode With Menu Bar option is useful when you want to view an image on the entire window of Photoshop without the Title bar and the Scroll bar of the document. Whenever you use this mode, the document appears with all the interface elements of the Photoshop window, including the Menu bar. To view an image in Full Screen Mode With Menu Bar, click and hold the Change Screen Mode icon on the Tools panel. And then select the Full Screen Mode With Menu Bar option from the flyout. You will observe that the Title bar of the document appears, the Toolbar merges with the Menu bar, and the image now appears on the Full Screen Mode. Let's learn about Full Screen Mode.

Full Screen Mode

In Full Screen Mode, you can see the document set against a neutral black background. The Menu bar, Tools panel, and all the panels disappear. To view the Tools panel or panel group, simply move the mouse-pointer to their respective position. The Tools panel or panel groups appears temporarily on the screen and hides when you move the mouse-pointer away. To view an image in Full Screen Mode, click the Change Screen Mode icon and select Full Screen Mode from the flyout. You can also switch between these three screen mode options by pressing the F key repeatedly. Let's now learn to work with views.

Working with Photoshop Views

Photoshop gives you a variety of ways to view your images. Different views are ideal for performing different actions. For instance, you can view images in full screen mode, zoom in and out of the image, or rotate your canvas to view images at an angle. In the previous section, you have learned about the screen modes. In this section, you will learn about how to use Zoom Tool, Hand Tool, navigate in the image area, and use the Navigator panel.

Using Zoom Tool

It is essential to be able to zoom closely into your image while fixing imperfections, performing detailed cleanups, and drawing accurate selections. There are several ways to zoom in Photoshop. One way to zoom is to use Zoom Tool, which appears similar to a magnifying glass. You can click its icon in the Tools panel or simply press Z key on the keyboard to activate Zoom Tool. After selecting the tool, you can click and drag right to zoom in or drag left to zoom out. This method of zooming is possible when the Scrubby Zoom check box is selected in the Options bar.

Alternatively you can click on the image repeatedly with Zoom Tool to zoom in, and press the Alt key while clicking (Alt-click) the image to zoom out. You can also press the Ctrl and plus (+) keys simultaneously to zoom in; and Ctrl and minus (-) keys together to zoom out. Zoom Tool always magnifies or shrinks the image to the next predefined zoom percentage.

Keep in mind that when you select Zoom Tool, it appears with a plus (+) or minus (-) sign; however, when you reach the maximum zoom level that is 3200%, the magnifying glass appears empty. When Zoom Tool is active, following options are available in the Options bar:

- **Resize Window to fit:** Enables Photoshop to resize you Document window to accommodate the current magnification level.
- **Zoom All Windows:** Allows you to zoom in on all open windows by the same amount simultaneously. This setting is helpful if you have opened a duplicate of an image in order to compare the changes.
- **Scrubby Zoom:** Allows you to click and drag to zoom. You can drag left to zoom out or right to zoom in.
- **Actual Pixels:** Displays your image at 100 percent magnification. You can also press Ctrl+1 keys together, or double-click Zoom Tool in the Tools panel to display image at 100 percent.
- **Fit Screen:** Enables Photoshop resize the active image window to fit the available space on your screen and fit the image inside the Document window.
- **Fill Screen:** Fills the work area within the monitor screen.
- **Print Size:** Displays your image the size it will be when you print.

Keep in mind that your monitor's resolution settings can make print size sample look bigger or smaller, so consider this feature only as an approximation. In addition, you can type the zoom percentage in the text field in the Document window status bar to zoom to that level. Let's now learn about Hand Tool.

Using Hand Tool to Navigate the Image Area

Hand Tool is used to navigate from one part of the image to another. Typically, when you zoom in, the Document window is unable to display all the image area due to space constrains. Photoshop hides some portion of your document. In such cases, you can use Hand Tool to drag the hidden portion to the visible area of the Document window. You can simply select Hand Tool in the Tools panel and then click and drag to move the image.

You can temporarily activate Hand Tool by pressing the Spacebar key and keeping the Spacebar key pressed, you can pan your image while working with some other tool. When Hand Tool is active, following options are available in the Options bar:

- **Scroll All Windows:** Allows Photoshop to scroll all open windows simultaneously. This setting is helpful if you have opened a duplicate of an image in order to compare the changes.
- **Actual Pixels:** Displays your image at 100 percent magnification.
- **Fit Screen:** Enables Photoshop resize the active image window to fit the available space on your screen and fit the image inside the Document window.
- **Fill Screen:** Fills the monitor screen with the image.
- **Print Size:** Displays your image the size it will be when you print it.

Using Navigator Panel

The Navigator panel allows you to navigate in your image from a small window. It shows the exact portion of an image you are zoomed in. You can open the Navigator panel by selecting Window> Navigator from the Menu bar. The panel displays a smaller version of your image called a thumbnail and marks the area you are currently zoomed in with a red box called the proxy preview.

The Navigator panel shows the current zoom level in the zoom field, which appears at the bottom of the panel. You can also type a zoom percentage value in the zoom field and press the Enter key to move to that specific zoom level. In addition, you can click the zoom buttons or drag the slider to adjust the zoom level. You can also move the proxy preview to change your current viewing area in the Document window. The proxy preview box shrinks and expands as you zoom in and zoom out respectively in the Document window. Let's now learn about guides, grids, and rulers and their use in Photoshop.

Using Guides, Ruler, and Grid

When creating a design, placing all the elements of your design in right position is cumbersome. Photoshop offers guides, grids, and rulers to help accurately place your design elements. These are used as helping tools in Photoshop called as extras. You can access these helping tools under the View menu. For instance, using guides can help you align ensure specific design elements are precisely placed within the Document area. Let's briefly discuss these helping tools:

- **Guide:** Refers to non-printable lines that help to accurately place design elements. You can place a guide in your document by dragging them from the horizontal or vertical Ruler bars in the active document. In addition, you can create a guide in a specific position by selecting View> New Guide from the Menu bar. You can add multiple guides in a document. To remove a guide select View> Clear Guides from the Menu bar. The Lock Guides option under the View menu lets you lock the guides; in other words, you cannot move the guides when they are locked. You can also select a color and style of the guides using the Preferences dialog box. To create guides, you need to turn on Photoshop rulers.

- **Ruler:** Refers to the horizontal and vertical bar that appears when you select the Rulers option under the View menu. You can also press the Ctrl+R keys together to display the rulers. Rulers provide a reference to properly position elements on your canvas. Picture 1.7 shows the rulers and the use of guides in a Photoshop document:

Picture 1.7

In addition to guides, you can use smart guides to align objects on the Document window. Smart guides automatically appear when you move an object or layer and show the spatial relationship between them.

- **Grid:** Helps to align lots of different items. You can select View> Show> Grid from the Menu bar to turn on grids. You can adjust the gridline marks by changing the number in the Gridline Every field in the Preferences dialog box. Now, in the next section, let's learn how to use Adobe Mini Bridge.

Using Adobe Mini Bridge

Adobe Bridge is a visual manager that is included as an additional application in Photoshop. Adobe Bridge allows you to easily organize, browse, locate, and view your files. In addition to still images, you can also preview 3D files as well as video files. You can launch the Bridge application from the Photoshop CS6 window. The Mini Bridge is another feature introduced in Photoshop CS5. In Photoshop CS6, Mini Bridge appears below the Document window, (already shown in picture 1.1). You can click the tab to launch the Mini Bridge in a pop-up panel inside the main Photoshop window. Perform the following steps to open an existing image using Mini Bridge:

1. Click the **Mini Bridge** tab to launch the application in a panel. A message (Bridge must be running to browse files) appears on your screen.

2. Click the **Launch Bridge** button. After few seconds the application launches.

3. **Navigate** to the location in the left panel, where the image that you want to open is placed. The path appears at the top of the panel.

4. **Double-click** the image to open in the Photoshop Document window. Let's now learn how to exit from the Photoshop CS6 application.

Exiting Photoshop CS6

After finishing your session with Photoshop, you can close the document and exit from the application. If you have not saved the document you are currently working on, Photoshop offers you to save your document or discard the changes. If you save the changes, the content of the document remains unchanged until you open it again and make changes to it. You can exit from Photoshop in variety of ways. You can select File> Exit from the Menu bar or press the Ctrl and Q keys together to exit the application. Perform the following steps to close the document and exit Photoshop CS6:

1. Select **File**> **Close** from the Menu bar to close the active document.
Now you can notice the active Document window is closed. If there are multiple documents opened at the same time and you execute the command, it only closes the active document. To close multiple documents at a time, select File> Close All or press the Alt+Ctrl+W keys together. After closing the Document window, now you can close the Photoshop application.

2. Select **File**> **Exit** from the Menu bar to exit Photoshop CS6. With this, we come to the end of the lesson.

Lesson 2
Customizing Photoshop CS6

Photoshop is a powerful and memory intensive application. The way in which you customize your workflow decides the efficiency of the application. There are several ways by which you can customize the workflow to enhance the productivity of Photoshop. For instance, one of the ways is, you can define custom workspaces with the panels and menus that you use frequently. In addition, frequently used keyboard shortcuts and preferences can be configured with the custom workspace. Creating a new workspace for specific tasks lets you save time as you do not have to access those panels and menus multiple times. For instance, you might use the Style panel repeatedly to add special effects to layers; therefore, you can create a workspace including the Styles panel.

Photoshop CS6 provides several predefined shortcuts that you can use. You can also define your own keyboard shortcuts for any tool or command required for frequent usage. The Preferences dialog box contains all the settings needed to customize Photoshop including assigning keyboard shortcuts to a command. You can open the Preferences dialog box by selecting Edit> Preferences from the Menu bar; and then select an option from the submenu. In the Preferences dialog box, you can change the new dark gray color theme to another. You can also increase the size of the text labels in the Options bar and panels in the Preferences dialog box.

In this lesson, you will learn how to work with both default and custom workspaces, wherein you will learn to select, create, and delete workspaces. Next, you will learn to work with Photoshop panels, wherein you will learn to show or hide a panel, close a panel, add a panel to a panel group, and make a panel as a floating window. Further, you will learn to define a keyboard shortcut for the Open as Smart Object menu options. In the end, you will explore different categories of Photoshop CS6 preferences. Let's begin the chapter by learning about workspace.

Working with Workspace

A workspace is an arrangement of the interface elements, such as panels, bars, and windows, in the main Photoshop CS6 window. You create and manipulate your documents using these interface elements. The default workspace includes the Menu bar, the Options bar, the Tools panel, and three panel groups, such as Layers, Color, and Adjustments. This grouping of elements is made according to specific tasks and given a name, such as Painting and Motion that represents the task. By default, Essentials appears as the selected workspace when you launch Photoshop CS6 for the first time. The Essentials workspace contains the Menu bar, the Options bar, the Tools panel, and some important panel groups, such as Layers, Color, and Adjustments.

When you select a different workspace, the most frequently used panels and menus of the selected workspace appear in the main Photoshop window. For instance, if you select Photography as your current workspace, Photoshop displays various panels including Histogram, Adjustments, and Layers. These panels help you to work with digital photographs that you import from your digital camera. Some important workspaces present in Photoshop CS6 are discussed as follows:

- **Essentials:** Displays the basic menu options and essential panels. This is the default workspace and appears when you launch the Photoshop CS6 application for the first time. The Essentials workspace is used when you want to work with basic features of Photoshop.

- **New in CS6:** Displays panels that are new to Photoshop CS6 or includes enhanced options, such as Mini Bridge, Brush Presets, Properties, Paragraph Styles, and Character Styles. These panels are used when you want to use new options included in Photoshop CS6. In addition, the menu options that are new to Photoshop CS6 appear highlighted under different menus when this workspace is selected. For instance, the Find Layers and the New 3D Extrusion menu options appear highlighted indicating that they are new additions.
- **3D:** Displays the panels that are specific for viewing and editing 3D images. The panels that appear include Properties and 3D.
- **Motion:** Displays the panels that are specific for working with video and animation. When you select Motion as the workspace, the Timeline panel expands automatically. The other panels that appear include Histogram, Actions, Properties, Clone Source, and 3D.
- **Painting:** Displays the panels frequently used for painting and retouching work. The panels include Swatches, Brush Presets, Clone Source, and Tool Presets.
- **Photography:** Displays panels that are used while importing raw images from cameras or scanners. These panels include Histogram, Actions, Info, Properties, and Adjustments.
- **Typography:** Displays the panels that are frequently used while working with type. The panels that appear include Character, Paragraph Styles, Characters Styles, Styles, and Swatches. This is a new workspace introduced in Photoshop CS6 replacing the Design workspace that was present in Photoshop CS5. Let's now learn how to select a different workspace other than the default workspace.

Selecting a Different Workspace

Photoshop provides several ways for selecting a workspace. For instance, you can select a workspace using the Menu bar or the Options bar. You can select Window> Workspace from the Menu bar and then select the desired workspace, for instance, 3D from the submenu. In addition, you can select a workspace by clicking the workspace switcher in the Options bar and selecting a workspace from the dropdown list. Perform the following steps to select a workspace using the Options bar:

1. Click the **Workspace switcher** on the Options bar to open a dropdown list. The Workspace switcher is already shown in picture 1.1.

2. **Select** your desired workspace from the dropdown list. In our case, we select **Motion** workspace.

As a result, Photoshop rearranges panels and displays those panels that are specific to work with videos and animations. Similarly, you can select any desired workspace from the dropdown list. Let's now learn how to create a new workspace.

Creating a New Workspace

In the previous section, you learned how to work with several workspaces included in Photoshop CS6. However, if the available workspaces do not cater to your requirements, you can create your own workspace. To customize the active workspace, you can rearrange existing panels to your suitability, open more panels using the Window menu, and change menus and keyboard shortcuts. To retain the changes and make them available for future requirements, you must save the changes carried out in the workspace with a matching name. Perform the following steps on your computer to create a new workspace in Photoshop CS6:

1. **Ensure** the Essentials workspace is selected, which is the default workspace, as shown in picture 1.8 with the red arrow.

Picture 1.8

2. Click the **Swatches** tab in the Color panel group to make it the active panel, as shown in picture 1.8 with the second red arrow.

3. Click the **Styles** tab in the Adjustments panel group to make it the active panel, as shown in picture 1.8 with the third red arrow.

4. Choose **Window> Character** from the Menu bar to open the Character panel. After making the desired changes, you can save the arrangement as a new workspace.

5. Click the **Workspace switcher** in the Options bar to open its dropdown list. Then select the **New Workspace** option from the list. The New Workspace dialog box appears on your screen.

6. **Type** a name for the new workspace. In our case, we name it as **Text Editing**. Then click the **Save** button.

As a result, a new workspace is created and becomes the active workspace. In the New Workspace dialog box (which you saw before saving your workspace), the **Capture** group allows you to save keyboard shortcuts and menus with the workspace. The Panel locations are saved with the currently active workspace, by default. The other two options are optional, which are as follows:

- **Keyboard Shortcuts:** Saves the current set of keyboard shortcuts with the new workspace.
- **Menus:** Saves the current set of menus with the new workspace.

The next time you open Photoshop, it opens with the Text Editing workspace until you change to a different workspace. Similarly, you can create more than one workspace in Photoshop. Next, let's learn how to delete an existing workspace.

Deleting a Workspace

Over a period of time, you may create few workspaces while working in Photoshop. You can delete the workspace you no longer require for your workflow. Before deleting a workspace, you need to make it inactive, i.e. you can select another workspace because Photoshop CS6 does not allow you to delete an active workspace. Perform the following steps to delete a workspace:

1. **Select** a workspace other than the workspace you want to delete. In out case, we select the **Essentials** workspace.

2. Click the **workspace switcher** in the Options bar to open its dropdown list.

3. Click the **Delete Workspace** option in the dropdown list. It opens the Delete Workspace dialog box on your screen.

4. **Select** the workspace that you want to delete in the Workspace dropdown list. In our case, we select **Text Editing**.

5. Click the **Delete** button to delete the selected workspace. Then click the **Yes** button to confirm the deletion. Thus, the default workspace, Essentials replaces the deleted workspace.

Working with Panels

At times, you might need to rearrange and position the panels or panel groups on the screen to increase the workspace so that related panels are grouped together for improved accessibility. The optimization of the panels in relevant panel groups reduces the time taken to access a specific panel. You might also need to split an existing panel group to create multiple panel group or individual panels. For instance, you can make the Channels panel as a separate panel by splitting it from the Layers panel group. So in this section, you will learn to work with panels, wherein you will learn to show or hide panels, make a floating panel, and add a panel into an existing panel group. Let's learn how to show or hide a panel.

Showing and Hiding Panels

As you know, panels make the accessibility to many task-specific commands and operations easier. By default, the panels appear as panel groups along the right side of the Photoshop window. To increase available space for designing, hide the redundant panels or show the important panels necessary for the current task being performed. You can use the Window menu or click a panel tab within a panel group to display a panel. After displaying a panel, you can select options on the panel or choose panel-specific commands from the panel menu to perform actions. Perform the following steps on your computer to show and hide panels:

1. **Click** a panel tab to display that panel. In our case, we click the **Styles** tab to display it, as shown in picture 1.9.

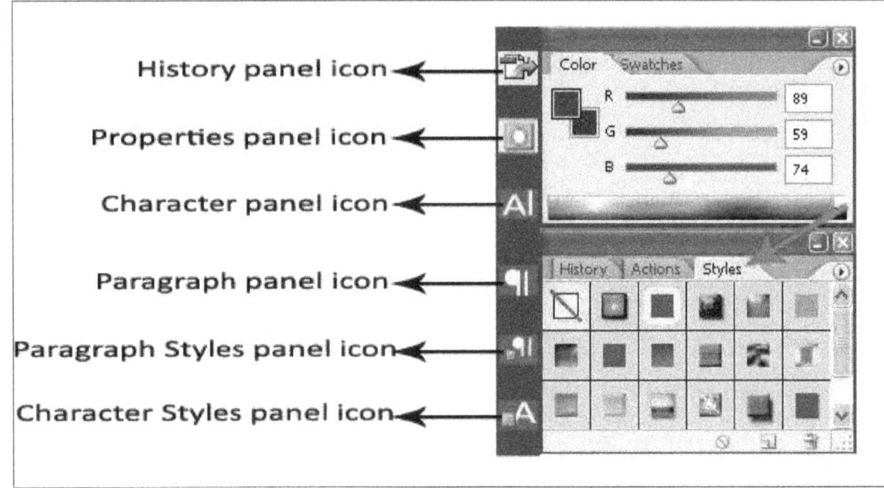

Picture 1.9

Keep in mind that alternatively, you can select Window> Styles from the Menu bar to show the Styles panel. If a panel name or icon does not appear in the active workspace, then you can select the name of the panel in the Window menu.

You can also click a panel icon to display the panel. You can place the mouse-pointer over a panel icon to display the name.

2. Click the **Paragraph** panel icon to display the Paragraph panel, as shown in picture 2.0.

To hide a panel, you can click a panel icon or a panel tab. For instance, if you click the Paragraph panel icon, when the panel is visible (picture 2.0), it hides or collapses to its icon form. On the other hand, if a panel is visible in a panel group; you can click another panel tab to hide the active panel. You can also hide a panel by closing it. Let's discuss the same in the next section.

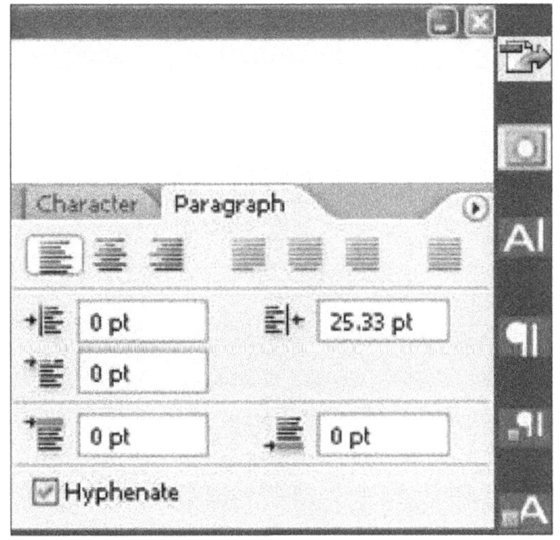

Picture 2.0

Closing a Panel or a Panel Group

When too many panels are open, it makes it difficult to manage and work in Photoshop window. In such cases, you must close a few panels that are not being used much. To save more space, you can either collapse a panel to its icon form or close it. Closing a panel makes the panel invisible; you can make this panel reappear by selecting the panel name in the Window menu. Photoshop CS6 offers different ways to close a panel or a panel group. You can close a panel or panel group by selecting the name in the Window menu. For instance, when you select the menu option Adjustments from the Window menu, the Adjustments panel group closes. Alternatively, you can use the panel menu of a panel or panel group to close a panel or the panel group.

Keep in mind that menu options with a tick mark indicate the panel or panel group is currently visible in the active workspace. Menu options without a tick mark indicate the currently hidden panels. Now perform the following steps to close a panel or panel group:

1. Ensure the **Essentials** workspace is active as in our case.

2. Choose **Window> Adjustments** from the Menu bar.

The Adjustments panel group disappears from the active workspace. Let's proceed to use the panel menu to close a panel or panel group.

3. **Click** the panel menu icon of the **Color panel** that you want to close. When you click, it opens its panel menu.

4. Select the **Close** option from the panel menu to close the Color panel or select the Close Tab Group option to close the Color panel group that is including Swatches panel.

By the way, you can also right-click a panel tab and select the Close and Close Tab Group options. And to re-open the closed panel, select the Window menu and click the name of the panel that you want to re-open. Let's now learn how to add and detach a panel to or from a panel group.

Making a Panel Float

A larger workspace is required to work on large images. To help manage and create more space, you can hide all the panels and make the most important panel as the floating panel. Floating panels are single standalone panels that are not docked to a panel group. You can drag a floating panel and place it wherever you want in the Photoshop window. Perform the following steps to make the Color panel as a floating panel:

1. **Click** and **drag** the panel tab of the panel that you want to make a floating panel. In our case, we drag the **Color panel** to a new location, as shown in picture 2.1.

Picture 2.1

2. **Release** the mouse button over the desired location. Now you can easily move the Color panel and place anywhere you want. In the next section, let's learn about adding a panel into a panel group.

Adding a Panel into a Panel Group

As mentioned earlier, panels are docked into the panel group by default. You can detach a panel from the panel group and place it anywhere in the Photoshop window as per your convenience. In case you want to re-dock the panel into the panel group, you can do this by dragging the panel tab back into the panel group. In addition, you can add a new panel to an existing panel group following the drag and drop method. Perform the following steps to add a panel into a panel group:

1. Choose **Window> Workspace> Reset Essentials** from the Menu bar to reset the workspace.

In the default Essentials workspace, the Color panel group includes the Swatches panel. In this section, you will learn to add another panel to the Color panel group.

2. **Select** a panel that you want to add to the Color panel group. In our case, we select **Window> Actions** from the Menu bar to show the Actions panel.

3. Drag the **Actions** panel tab over the Color panel group.

You will see on your screen that a blue border appears to assist you decide which panel group is highlighted. When you release the mouse button, the panel is added to the highlighted panel group. In our case, we add the Actions panel to the Color panel group.

Defining a Shortcut Key

Photoshop CS6 provides the flexibility of creating and modifying keyboard shortcuts and menu. Keyboard shortcuts can significantly reduce the amount of time you need to access a menu option or select tools. Photoshop CS6 has several built-in keyboard shortcuts and menus. You can also reassign keyboard shortcuts or define new ones. You can view the available keyboard shortcuts for the menus and commands in the Keyboard Shortcuts and Menus dialog box.

In this section, you will learn to define a new keyboard shortcut for the Open as Smart Object command that appear in the File menu. Perform the following steps to define a keyboard shortcut:

1. Choose **Edit> Keyboard Shortcuts** from the Menu bar to open the Keyboard Shortcuts and Menus dialog box, as shown in picture 2.2 below.

2. **Choose** the type of shortcuts you want to add or change from the **Shortcuts For** dropdown list. In our case, the default option (**Application Menus**) is selected.

3. Click the triangle before the **File** option to expand it, as shown in picture 2.2 with the red arrow numbered 3.

4. **Click** the empty space in the Shortcut field to display a text box. In our case, we click the empty space for **Open as Smart Object** menu option.

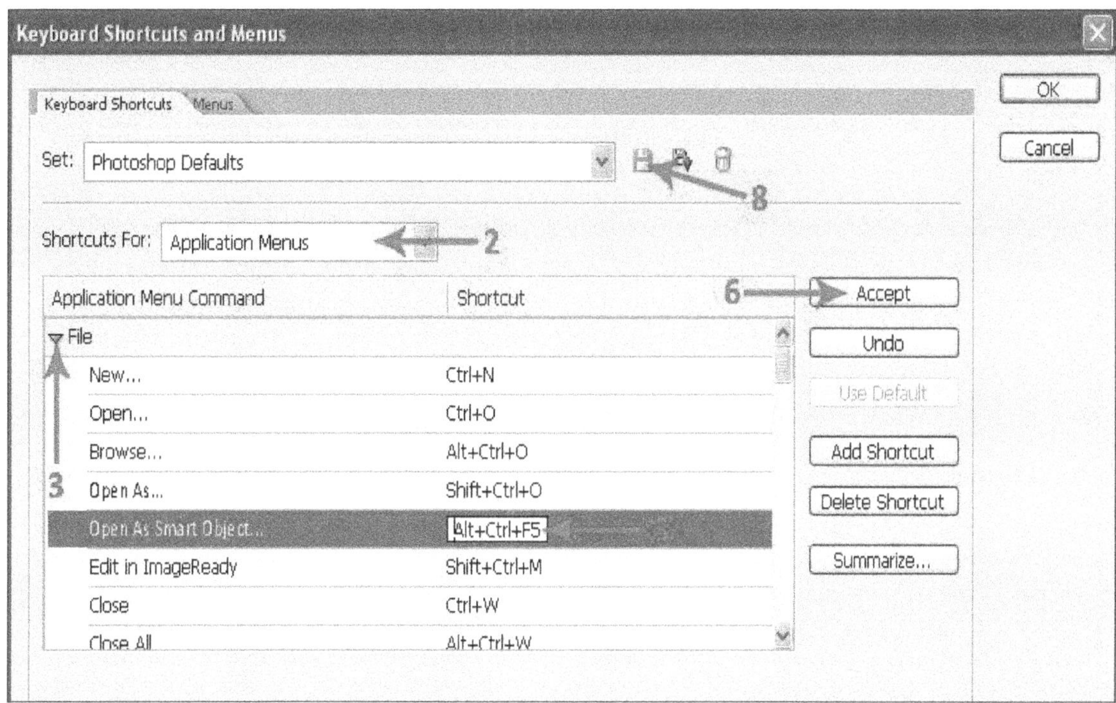

Picture 2.2

5. Press the **Alt**, **Ctrl**, and **F5** keys simultaneously to assign this key combination as the keyboard shortcut. The keyboard shortcut appears in the text box, as shown in picture 2.2 with the red arrow numbered 5.

6. Click the **Accept** button to accept the new keyboard shortcut.

7. Click the **OK** button to save the shortcut and close the dialog box.

Keep in mind that Photoshop displays a warning message if you type a shortcut key that is already in use. For instance, if you press Shift+P keys together, Photoshop shows a message "Shift+P is an invalid shortcut. Menu command must include Ctlr and/or and F-key in their shortcuts."

After assigning a shortcut for the Open as Smart Object command, you can press the Alt+Ctrl+F5 keys together to open the Open as Smart Object dialog box. You can also save your new shortcut to Photoshop's factory set of shortcuts.

8. **Click** the first hard-disk icon to the right of the Set dropdown list, as shown in picture 2.2 with the red arrow numbered 8.

9. Click the **Save** button in the Save dialog box with the default name and location. As a result, the shortcut assigned by you is saved.

You can also create a new set of shortcuts by clicking the second icon. Creating separate keyboard shortcut sets lets you quickly switch back to Photoshop's factory shortcuts, or switch between custom sets defined by you. Next, let's learn how to customize Photoshop preferences.

Customizing Photoshop's Preferences

In addition to workspace related settings, Photoshop CS6 contains numerous program-related settings. These program settings are known as preferences, which allow you to customize the way you work with Photoshop. You can set these preferences according to your requirements to enhance your productivity. Photoshop CS6 contains various options for general display, interface, file-handling, performance, cursors, and others. Preferences settings are saved with Photoshop, every time you close the Photoshop application. You can also modify the preference settings by using the Preferences dialog box. In the Preferences dialog box, click the required category of preferences on the left side panel to display the associated options. Then, edit the required settings. You can also switch between different categories of preferences by clicking the Next and Prev (Previous) buttons located on the right side of the dialog box. Now, let's discuss some of the important categories beginning with the General.

Exploring General Category

The General category in the Preferences dialog box lets you modify common Photoshop settings. This includes:

- Selecting a Color Picker option, such as Adobe or Windows, using the Shift key for tool switching
- Resizing the image window along with the image when you apply a zoom command
- Zooming in and out of an image by using the scroll wheel of the mouse

You can enable these options in the General category of the Preferences dialog box. All the changes made in the Preferences dialog box will be applied the next time you launch Photoshop. You can select the General category by selecting Edit> Preferences> General from the Menu bar or pressing the Ctrl+K keys on the keyboard together, as shown in picture 2.3.

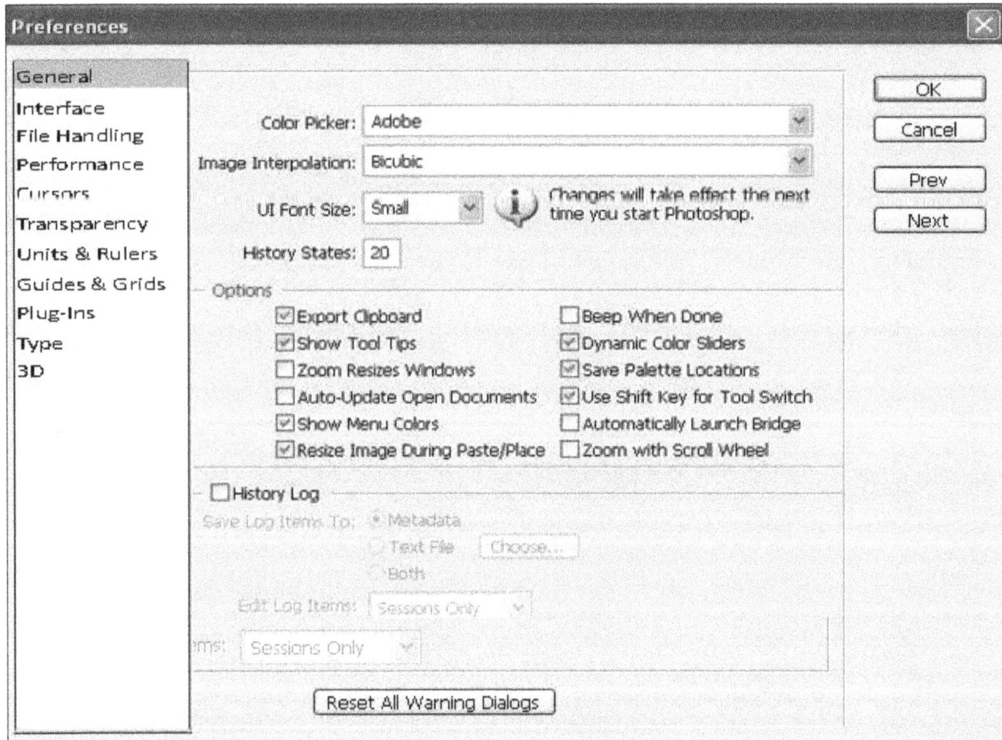

Picture 2.3

As you can see in this picture, the General category is active by default. The settings in this category are Color picker, Image Interpolation, and various other options in the Options group. Some options are selected by default, whereas the other options such as Auto-Update Open Documents, Beep When Done, or Zoom Resize Windows are not selected by default.

To change the preferences, select an option from the respective dropdown list. Alternatively, you can select or deselect the check boxes in the Preferences dialog box. The General category also includes the History Log settings. If you select the History Log checkbox, Photoshop keeps track of all the modification that happens to the images. Let's now learn about Interface category in the Preferences dialog box.

Exploring Interface Category

The Interface option is just below the General option in the Preferences dialog box. If you click this option, you will see that this category includes options that determine the appearance and behavior of the Photoshop interface. When clicked, on the right you will see three categories related to this option. The Interface preferences are categorized under the Appearance, Options, and Text groups. Now, we are going to discuss about these categories in detail:

- **Appearance Group:** In this group, the options determine the general appearance of the Photoshop interface, such as Color Theme and the appearance of the screen modes. Photoshop CS6 includes four different color themes that range from darker shades to lighter shades. For screen modes, you can specify color and border options from their respective dropdown list. For instance, you can specify whether to add drop shadow or a border in the Full Screen Mode, and specify a color for the canvas area. You can select a color from the available presets or customize a new color in the Color dropdown list.

  Keep in mind that you can cycle through Photoshop's color themes by pressing Shift+F1 and Shift+F2 keys in combination to go darker and lighter, respectively.

- **Options Group:** In this group, the auto-collapsing feature of panels can be enabled. With this, you can collapse an expanded panel docked in the panel group to an icon form on clicking anywhere in the Photoshop window. You can also specify whether to show channels in color, i.e. the appearance of the channels in the Channel panel, the appearance of the menu items, and whether to display the tooltips when the mouse-pointer is placed over a tool or option.

- **Text Group:** In this group, you can select a language for the Photoshop interface in the UI Language dropdown list. Besides this, you can also select a font size for the names of menus and panels, and tooltip in the UI Font Size dropdown list. Let's now learn about File Handling category.

Exploring File Handling Category

The File Handling category lets you control how Photoshop opens and saves files. The ability to save in the background is a new feature in Photoshop CS6. Various options are distributed into three groups namely – File Saving Options, File Compatibility, and Adobe Drive.

- **File Saving Options Group:** Allows you to add the preview of an image to the file and the type case in the File Extension option. You can also enable Photoshop to save in the background by selecting the Save in Background check box and set the time duration to automatically save recovery information. By default, the Automatically Save Recovery Information Every is set to 10 minutes.

- **File Compatibility Group:** Deals with the camera raw files, layered TIFF files, and file compatibility between the files created in different versions of Photoshop. You can also specify whether to compress Photoshop documents by selecting the Disable Compression of PSD and PSB Files check box. In addition, you can specify the number of files that appear when you select File> Open Recent.

- **Adobe Drive Group:** Lets you organize, track, and store files in a central location using the Enable Adobe Drive option. Other users working on the same project can access the file from the Adobe Drive. Let's now learn about Performance category.

Exploring Performance Category

The Performance category lets you control the performance of Preferences, i.e. the amount of memory used by the program directly affects the performance. The Performance category has four groups namely – Memory Usage, History & Cache, Scratch Disks, and Graphics Processor Settings.

- **Memory Usage Group:** Displays information, such as the available RAM and the ideal range for Photoshop to work efficiently. By default, Photoshop CS6 uses 60 percent of the available memory. If the RAM available in your system is not sufficient for Photoshop to perform an operation, Photoshop CS6 uses a drive with free memory as virtual memory, known as a scratch disk. You can enable any of the hard disk drives to be used as a scratch disk in the Scratch Disks group.

- **History & Cache group:** Allocates a number for history states, which control the undo levels, in the History States pop-up slider. The default setting for history states Is 20, which can be increased up to 1000. You can also set optimal cache levels and tile sizes by specifying the kind of document you require. You can select an option from Tall and Thin, Default, and Big and Flat. Cache levels controls the amount of image information that is temporarily stored in your computer's memory; whereas, the cache tile size is the amount of info Photoshop CS6 can store and process at one time. For instance, larger tile size can speed things up if you work with documents with really large pixel dimensions.

- **Graphics Processor Settings Group:** Specifies whether Photoshop uses the graphics processor in your computer. Let's now learn about Cursor category.

Exploring Cursor Category

The Cursor category lets you control the appearance of your cursors when using painting and other tools. The preferences are categorized into three groups namely – Painting Cursors, Other Cursors, and Brush Preview.

You can set the brush tip for painting cursors, such as Normal Brush Tip, Full Size Brush Tip, or Show Crosshair in Brush Tip. It has different styles that include Standard for brush tip, Precise for a cross-hair tip. Normal Brush Tip is the default setting. For Other Cursors, only two different styles are available, Standard and Precise.

When you choose different options, Photoshop CS6 shows you a preview of each cursor in the preview thumbnail. The Brush Preview group displays a color swatch that controls the color of the preview brush tip. To change the preview's color, click the color swatch and select a color. Let's learn about Transparency & Gamut category.

Transparency & Gamut Category

The Transparency & Gamut category has two groups namely – Transparency Settings and Gamut Warning.

- **Transparency Settings Group:** Let's you modify how a layer appears when part of it is transparent.
- **Gamut Warning Group:** Let's you set a highlight color. A highlight color shows the colors in your image that fall outside the safe range for the active color mode. Let's now learn about the Unit & Rulers category.

Exploring Units & Rulers Category

The Units & Rulers category lets you select the unit of measurement for Photoshop. The options are combined into four groups: Units, Column Size, New Document Preset Resolutions, and Point/Pica Size.

The Rulers controls the units displayed in your document's rulers and by default the unit is Centimeters. You can select Pixels, Inches, Centimeters, Millimeters, Points, Picas, and Percent option depending on the documents. If you want to print your document, then select Inches or Picas. If intend to use your image for the Web, select Pixels as the unit of measurement.

The Column Size settings are useful if you intend to send your graphics to a page-layout program, such as Adobe InDesign. New Document Preset Resolutions group allows you to specify Print Resolution and Screen Resolution settings. These settings will be used by Photoshop to automatically fill in the New dialog box when you create a new document. Let's learn about the Guides, Grids & Slices category.

Exploring Guides, Grids & Slices Category

The Guides, Grids & Slices category has four groups, namely – Guides, Smart Guides, Grid, and Slices. These groups let you choose the colors for your document guides, smart guides, grid, and slice lines. You can also set the grid's spacing by using the Gridline Every option. You can also set the number of subdivisions that appear between each major gridline by using the Subdivisions options.

In the Slices group, you can specify the color and whether to show slice numbers in your document. For Grid options, you can specify a custom color and style of the grid line. The grid line can be Lines, which is the default option, Dashed Lines, and Dots. Let's now learn about Plug-Ins category.

Exploring Plug-Ins Category

The Plug-Ins category lets you modify settings for Photoshop plug-ins, which are third-party programs. You can install plug-ins to perform additional operations that are rather difficult to perform in Photoshop. In this category, you can specify additional folder to store plug-ins other than your computer's Photoshop folder.

The Extension Panel group lets Photoshop CS6 connect to the Internet when a plug-in or panel needs information from a website. For instance, the Kuler panel lets you use color themes posted on the Web by folks in the Kuler community. If you deselect these checkboxes, Photoshop cannot connect to the Internet for color themes. Let's learn about the Type category.

Exploring Type Category

The Type category lets you toggle smart quotes on or off, as well as enable other languages. It has two groups: Type Options and Choose Text Engine Options. You can choose a language from East Asian or Middle Eastern. You need to ensure the Enable Missing Glyph Protection checkbox is also turned on. This avoids the weird symbols or boxes to appear when you use a letter or symbol not installed on your computer. You can now work with Middle Eastern languages, a new feature in Photoshop CS6. Let's now learn about the 3D category.

Exploring 3D Category

If you are using Photoshop CS6 Extended, you will notice the 3D category in the Preferences dialog box. You must enable the OpenGL feature under GPU Settings group of the Performance category of the Preferences. You can specify default selected colors for mesh, material, or light in 3D Overlays group.

Several other options for Interactive Rendering, Ground Plane, Ray Tracer, or 3D File Loading can also be set using the Preferences dialog box. The Description group under the dialog box describes each option when you place the mouse pointer over an option. Until now, you have learned about the Preferences dialog box of Photoshop CS6. Typically, you make changes to the preferences settings as per the requirements. In case you want to revert to the default settings, you can use the restore all preferences to default feature of Photoshop that you learn in the next section.

Restoring All Preferences to Default Settings

While working with Photoshop CS6 over a period of time, users tend to apply various preference settings as per their requirement and convenience. After some time, it is difficult to remember all the modifications made to the default settings. To help the user, Photoshop provides the facility to restore the preferences settings to its default. This feature also restores the panel locations, shortcuts, and menus to its default. Perform the following steps to restore all preferences to their default settings:

1. Select **Start> All Programs> Adobe Master Collection CS6> Adobe Photoshop CS6** from the Start menu, while holding down **Alt+Ctrl+Shift** keys together. Hold down Alt+Ctrl+Shift keys together until the Adobe Photoshop CS6 Extended message box appears prompting you to delete the current settings file.

2. Click the **Yes** button to restore default preferences. As a result, new preferences files are created the next time you start Photoshop CS6.

Lesson 3
Understanding Colors and Channels

Whether you take a photograph with a digital camera, use a scanner to import a photograph into Photoshop, or create an artwork in Photoshop, you actually digitize the photograph. This is called a digital image. In other words, your computer stores the information, such as the number of pixels and the color of each pixel, about the image in the form of digits or binary codes. Images in Photoshop CS6 are tiny square of color. These tiny squares of color are also referred to as picture elements or pixels, which are the most important and basic elements of any image.

Photoshop CS6 uses channels to store color information of an image. The Channels panel primarily holds the color information. Photoshop CS6 creates channels automatically depending on the color mode of the image. For instance, the RGB (red (R), green (G), and blue (B)) color mode has three channels, while the Grayscale color mode has one channel. The maximum number of channels an image can have is 56, while the minimum number is at least one channel. Channels are also used to store selections. You learn more about channels and color modes later in this chapter.

In this section, you first learn about color theories. Next, you will learn about different color modes in Photoshop. You will also learn to select a foreground and background colors using Color Picker, Eyedropper Tool, and the Color panel. In addition, you will learn how to fill a selection current foreground color. Further, you will learn to make color adjustments using Levels, Curves, Brightness/Contrast, Hue/Saturation, Variations, and Replace Color. Towards the end of this chapter, you will learn about channels. Let's begin the chapter by learning about color theories.

Understanding the Color Theory

Selecting the right color is important as colors represent a mood, evoke emotion, and capture attention. There are color theories, such as color schemes (or color palette), color wheels that are used to select the right color for your artwork. You can create a logical structure for color using color theories.

There are two categories of colors in an image: Dominant and Accent. The Dominant color always represents the majority of color in your painting; for instance, white in a snow field. On the other hand, the Accent color represents the focal point of your painting or image; for instance, a red house in the field of snow. The color schemes are described as follows:

Color scheme: Refers to the group of colors that you use in your project. For instance, any print advertisement, or a website page is made from a certain set of colors. These colors can usually range between three and five colors excluding white or black. The designer usually selects a color as the main color and then selects the other colors according to how they represent together as a group. Color schemes can be monochromatic (one color in varying intensities from light to dark) or analogous (two to six colors that are adjacent). These color combinations proven by color experts are known as color scheme harmonies. Picture 2.4 shows monochromatic and analogous color schemes:

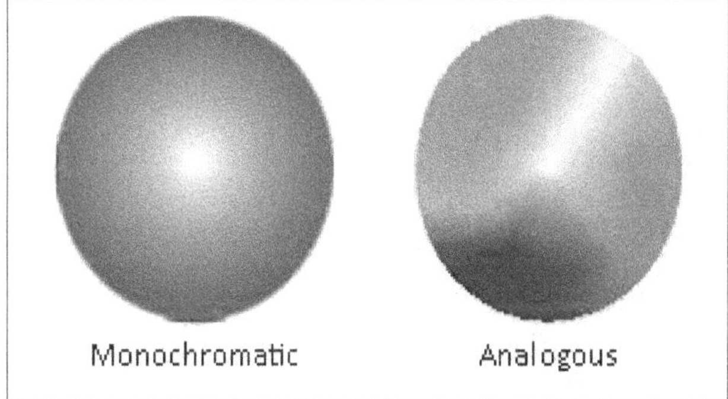

Picture 2.4

Color wheel: Refers to a tool that helps you select matching colors. The color wheel arranges logical colors on a round diagram according to their relationships. It is based on the three primary colors: red, blue, and yellow. By mixing equal amount of the primary colors, you define the secondary colors. Likewise, mixing equal parts of the secondary colors gives you a third set of colors called tertiary colors. Together, all these colors form the color wheel. The picture 2.5 shows the color wheel:

Keep in mind that primary colors are the three pigment colors and all other colors are derived from them.

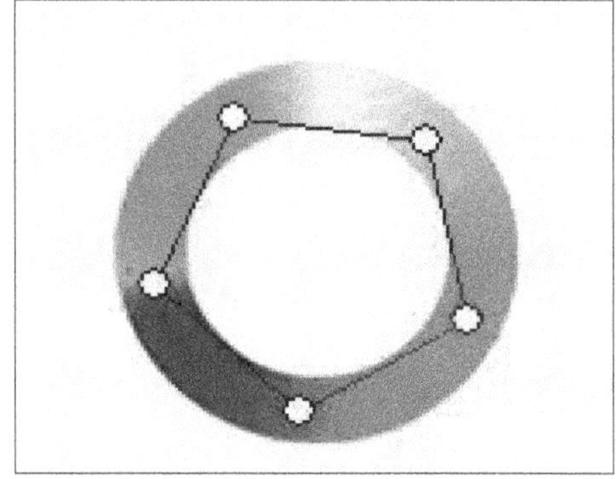

Picture 2.5

In addition, there are three different terms frequently used to describe color: hue, saturation, and brightness. They form all the colors the human eye can perceive:

- **Hue:** Represents colors in their purest form, measured in degrees.
- **Saturation:** Describes the strength or intensity of a color. For instance, zero saturation is equal to the gray color.
- **Brightness:** Controls the degree of lightness or darkness of a color. In other words, it determines how light or dark colors cab be. For instance, the value zero of brightness represents black. Next, you learn how to use a color wheel to select a color scheme based on color scheme harmonies.

Selecting a Color Scheme Using a Color Wheel

Unlike the conventional color wheel, the computer color wheel is comprised of red, green, blue, yellow, cyan, and magenta. You need to decide on a main color of your color scheme and then find it on the color wheel. Then, you can use one of the color scheme harmonies to help you select other colors that complement the main color. Perform the following steps to select a color scheme using a color wheel:

1. **Open** an image and **select** a main color.

2. **Select** or locate the main color in the color wheel.

3. **Locate** other colors that complement with the main color by using a color scheme harmony.

Selecting a Color Scheme Using Kuler

Kuler is an online community where you can share sets of colors and themes. You can browse thousands of tagged and themed color schemes on the Kuler community, and download or edit them in Photoshop using the Kuler panel. You can also use the Kuler panel to create and save color themes and share them with the Kuler community. The Kuler panel also offers certain built-in color themes. Only internet connection is required to access these available themes of the Kuler panel.

You can use the Kuler panel to load color themes into the Swatches panel. After you add the color theme into the Swatches panel, you can further include it in your Photoshop document. You can open the Kuler panel by selecting Window> Extensions> Kuler from the Menu bar.

In the Kuler panel, you can search for color schemes in the Browse tab, which is selected by default. You can also filter your search to Most Popular, Newest, or Random. If you want to modify a color scheme, select a color scheme and then click the Edit theme in Create panel button at the bottom of the Kuler panel. If you want to add a color scheme into the Swatches panel, click the Add selected theme to swatches button at the bottom of the Kuler panel. Next, let's learn about different color modes in Photoshop CS6.

Exploring Photoshop Color Modes

Color mode stands for the color model, where the color of each pixel of an image is a combination of the primary colors for the model in different proportions. For instance, if an image is in the RGB color mode, all the colors used in the image will be defined as combinations of red, green, and blue colors in different ratios.

Now what we need to understand that by default, every image has its own default color mode, which can be changed in Photoshop. Remember that a few editing commands do not work with some color modes. For instance, the Black & White, and Variations commands do not work on images that have the Indexed color mode.

All of us know the importance and relevance of colors in images and artworks. Every image opened in Photoshop CS6 has a color mode, such as Grayscale, RGB, or CMYk associated with it. In CMYK, C stands for cyan, M stands for magenta, Y stands for yellow, and K stands for black. You can select any one color mode, depending on the nature of your work and targeted output. For instance, if you plan to print your design, you can select the CMYK color mode, which is ideal for printing. Understanding the different color modes is a vital step to learn image editing in Photoshop CS6. For instance, it would be adverse to your efforts to compose an image for print using RGB color mode, as colors may not appear on paper as they do on screen. Photoshop provides eight different color modes. Let's discuss these color modes, starting with the RGB color mode.

RGB Color Mode

RGB color mode is one of the two color models you will work with most often, when preparing images for the Web. The other mode is Indexed color mode. RGB is derived from the initials of the three primary colors: red, green, and blue. In the RGB color mode, colors are created by adding visible lights. This color mode is dependent on the type of device. For instance, a given RGB value is reproduced differently by different devices. When you import images from scanner or digital camera, they are typically in RGB color mode. Scanners and digital cameras are called RGB input devices. Likewise, you can output RGB images to television, computer monitor, and mobile phones.

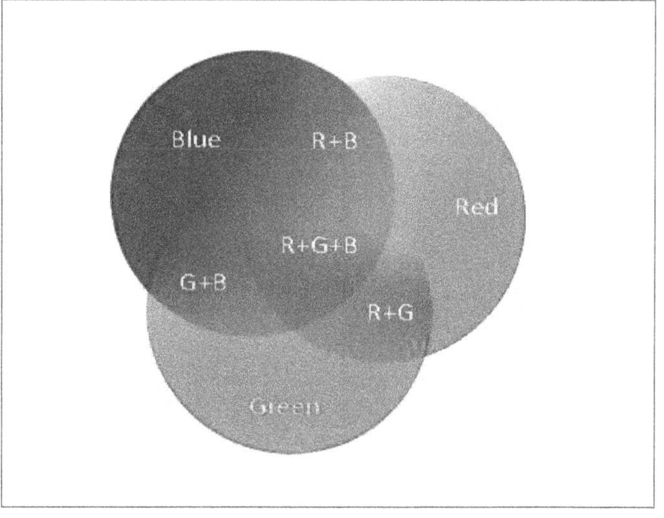

Picture 2.6

In the RGB color mode, each pixel is assigned an intensity value that ranges between: 0 (black) to 255 (white). When the values of all the three colors are equal, the resulting shade is neutral gray. Similarly, when the values of all the three colors are 255, the resultant color is pure white. However, when the values of all the three colors are 0, the color you get is pure black. Picture 2.6 above displays the primary and secondary colors.

As you can notice in picture 2.6, the primary colors are red (R), green (G), and blue (B), and the secondary colors are cyan, magenta, and yellow. The secondary colors are derived by adding primary colors or lights, which are depicted in the following equations:

Cyan   = Green (G) + Blue (B)
Magenta   = Red (R) + Blue (B)
Yellow   = Red (R) + Green (G)

The RGB images consist of three channels that are used to reproduce colors on a display screen. Hence, in an 8 bit per channel image, each pixel can contain 24 bit of color information. Display devices use the RGB color model to represent colors onscreen. If you are working on a color mode other than RGB, Photoshop interpolates the color that is suitable for onscreen display. Let's now learn about the CMYK color mode.

CMYK Color Mode

CMYK stands for cyan, magenta, yellow, and black. The color black is represented by the letter K, because certain printers refer to the black plate as the Key plate. You can mix these colors to create a gamut (range) of colors. For instance, mixing cyan and magenta creates blue; while, mixing yellow and magenta creates red. The colors in the CMYK color mode are also known as process colors and appear more accurate against a white background. This color mode is mainly used for color printing. It is considered as subtractive, because color subtracts brightness from white. You can create images in the CMYK color mode, if you intend to print using process colors. Picture 2.7 illustrates the CMYK color mode.

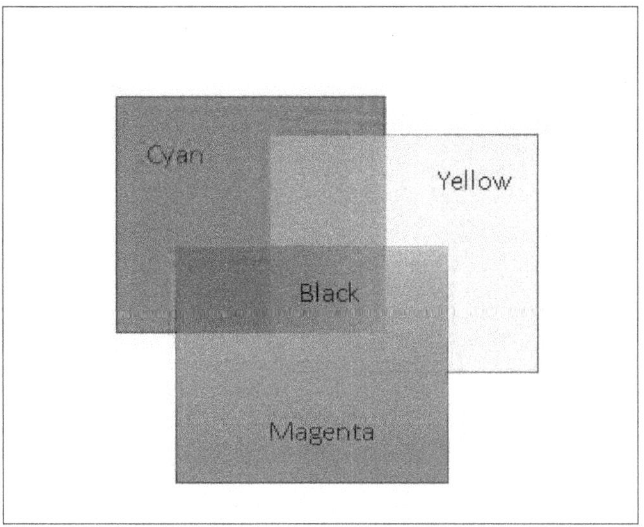

Picture 2.7

After an image is completely edited in Photoshop and is ready to be printed, it is always better to convert into the CMYK color mode because the CMYK color mode is printer-friendly. When an image is converted from the RGB color mode to the CMYK color mode, any color that is outside the CMYK gamut is adjusted by Photoshop CS6 to its nearest printable color. A gamut of a color mode can be described as the range of colors supported by that particular mode. If you print an image without converting it into the CMYK color mode, the colors outside the CMYK gamut are not printed properly, which may result in a low quality print. Photoshop also allows you to view the portions of an image that are outside the CMYK gamut.

You can select View> Gamut Warning from the Menu bar to show the color gamut in an image. The image appears with the colors supported by the CMYK color mode. The colors that are not supported by the CMYK color mode turn gray. Let's now learn about the Indexed color mode.

Indexed Color Mode

The Indexed color mode is used in images for multimedia and the Web. This color mode produces 8 bit images with up to 256 colors. When you convert an image into the Indexed color mode, Photoshop creates a color table. If a color in the original image is not in the table, Photoshop CS6 selects the closest matching color or makes a new color from the available colors. You can also use the Color Table dialog box to edit the colors in the Indexed color mode. Select Image> Mode> Color Table from the Menu bar in the Indexed color mode. Photoshop uses the color table to store and index colors in the image.

In the Color Table dialog box, click on the color cell to change the colors. However, if you change the colors, it creates irregular effects in the image. You can use the Indexed color mode for multimedia presentation and Web pages. The images in this color mode are smaller in file size. The Indexed color mode offers limited editing capabilities on an image. To address this drawback, you can convert your image temporarily to the RGB color mode for extensive editing capabilities. Indexed color files can be saved in Photoshop, BMP, Dicom, GIF, Photoshop EPS, PNG, or TIFF formats. Let's now learn about the Grayscale color mode.

Grayscale Color Mode

The Grayscale color mode represents image using shades of black. Hence, it is also referred as black and white color mode. In a grayscale image, each pixel can be displayed using 256 shades. The color shades range from pure black (0) to pure white (255). When you scan an image from black and white or grayscale scanner, the image is produced in the Grayscale color mode. Using the Grayscale color mode, you can also convert the color artwork to high quality black and white artwork. Let's now learn about the Duotone color mode.

Duotone Color Mode

The Duotone color mode defines an image in two colors. You can create different types of grayscale images, such as Monotone (one-color), Duotone (two-color), Tritone (three-color), and Quadtone (four-color) using custom inks. To convert an image into the Duotone color mode, you first have to convert it into the Grayscale color mode. You can select Image> Mode> Grayscale and then Image> Mode> Duotone from the Menu bar to convert your image into the Duotone color mode.

By default, the Monotone type is selected and you can select Duotone or Tritone from the Type dropdown list in the Duotone Options dialog box. You can also click the color swatches to select different colors from Color Picker that appears. Let's now learn about the Bitmap color mode.

Bitmap Color Mode

An image in Bitmap color mode is displayed in true black and white colors. Unlike, the Indexed color mode, the Bitmap color mode does not include shades of gray. Bitmap images sometimes can be used for the Web, as well as commercial print. You need to convert images to the Grayscale color mode before converting to the Bitmap color mode. You can select Image> Mode> Bitmap from the Menu bar to convert your image into the Bitmap color mode. Now, in the next section, we are going to learn about the Lab color mode.

Lab Color Mode

The Lab color mode closely resembles the human vision. It has three channels: Luminance, a, and b. It is the Luminance channel that matches how we perceive lightness in real-world. You cannot export an image in Lab color mode; hence, it is converted to either RGB or CMYK color modes before outputting. This mode has been prepared by an organization known as CIE (Commission Internationale de l'Eclairage). It provides a consistent color display. This color model includes the gamut of both the RGB and CMYK models.

The lab color mode is the preferred editing mode for color experts because it is device-independent that is, it appears consistent on various devices, such as computers, mobiles, and touch screen devices. The Lab color mode consists of a lightness channel; and two additional channels, a and b, in the Channels panel. The colors that range between green and red are in channel a and those that range between blue and yellow are in channel b. let's now learn about the Multichannel color mode.

Multichannel Color Mode

The Multichannel color mode is used for specialized color printing. It is ideally used in situations, such as creating logos. Images in the Multichannel color mode mainly comprised of 256 levels of gray. You can save images in Multichannel color mode in different file formats, such as PSD, PSB, or Photoshop Raw. You cannot convert Indexed color mode images to Multichannel color mode. Additionally, you cannot convert 32 bit per channel images to Multichannel color mode. When you save a layered image in Multichannel color mode, the layers are flattened and the color channels are converted to spot color channels. Let's now learn about an additional color mode in Photoshop, HSB (Hue, Saturation, and Brightness).

HSB Color Mode

The HSB color mode consists of three components: Hue, Saturation, and Brightness. This is an additional color model used in Photoshop. You can not convert an image to the HSB color mode. It is available in Color Picker. The following is a short description of these three components:

- **Hue:** Represents colors in their purest form, measured in degrees.
- **Saturation:** Refers to the purity of colors. For instance, zero saturation is equal to the gray color.
- **Brightness:** Refers to the degree of lightness or darkness of a color. For instance, the value zero for brightness represents the black color.

Changing Color Mode of an Image

As discussed earlier, Photoshop allows you to switch between color modes. You can select a color mode based on the end use of the image. Some color modes need to be saved in a specific file format. For instance, an image in the CMYK color mode cannot be saved in the GIF file format. On the other hand, if you plan to use an image for the Internet, you must use the RGB or the Indexed color mode. And if you plan to take a grayscale printout of the image, you must first convert the image into the Grayscale color mode. Perform the following simple steps on your computer to convert an image from one color mode to another:

1. **Open** an image in Photoshop. In our case, the image opens in the **RGB** color mode.

2. Choose **Image> Mode> Grayscale** from the Menu bar to select the Grayscale color mode. It opens a message box on your screen.

3. Click the **Discard** button in the message box to discard the color information in the image. Now, the image on your screen appears in the Grayscale color mode.

Remember that while converting an image from one color mode to another, a message box is displayed depending on the mode you are converting the image into. For instance, when converting from the CMYK color mode to the RGB color mode, there is no message box displayed.

Setting Foreground and Background Colors

The most important and basic element in Photoshop is the color. The foreground and background colors are the two types of color that you come across while working in Photoshop. In the Photoshop CS6, the foreground color is used to draw, paint, spray, or type. It also fills and strokes the selection. The background color is used to make gradient fills and to fill the erased areas of an image. Both foreground and background colors are also used by filters to create special effects.

You can select the foreground and background colors in the Tools panel, as shown in picture 2.8.

As shown in this picture, the two color boxes in the Tools panel (indicated in the blue rectangular box), indicates the current foreground and background colors. The default foreground and background colors are black and white, respectively. You can select two colors at the same time for different purposes.

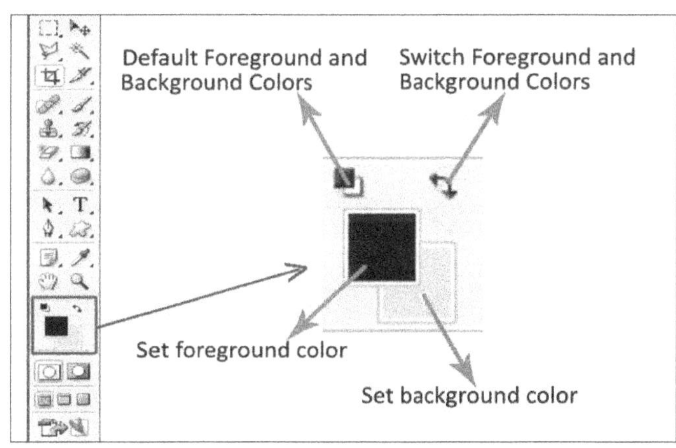

Picture 2.8

In Photoshop, you can set the foreground and background colors of an image in many different ways using Color Picker, the Swatches panel, Eyedropper Tool, and Color Sample Tool. When you click on any of the color boxes in the Tools panel, Color Picker appears. You can select and design a new color as the current foreground or background color using Color Picker. As mentioned earlier, you can set the current foreground or background color of a Photoshop document in any of the following ways, and we will discuss about the same in the next section:

- Using Color Picker
- Using Eyedropper Tool
- Using the Color panel

Using Color Picker

Color Picker is the most frequently used way of assigning a color in Photoshop CS6. It contains a color mixture box, different color modes, and a color slider from where you can select and apply the foreground or background color to full or part of an image. You can display Color Picker on the screen by clicking the foreground or background color box in the Tools panel. Perform the following steps to set the foreground color using Color Picker:

1. **Create** a new Photoshop document or **open** an existing document in which you want to set the foreground color.

2. Click the **Set foreground color** box in the Tools panel. It opens the Color Picker (Foreground Color) dialog box, as shown in picture 2.9.

3. **Click** the color that you want to select in the color field. A circle surrounds the clicked area and the clicked color appears in the new color box.

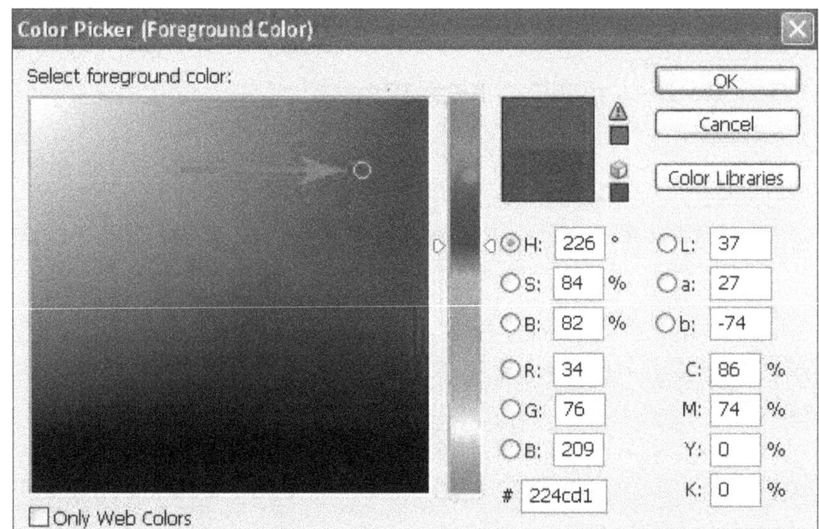

Picture 2.9

You can also move the color slider upward and downward until you select the desired color. In our case, we select blue color as the foreground color.

4. Click the **OK** button in the dialog box. As a result, the foreground color is set to blue in the Tools panel.

Keep in mind that Photoshop retains the last selected foreground and background colors. Pressing the D key on the keyboard set the foreground and background color to their default color. Now, let's discuss about the components of Color Picker.

- **Color Slider:** Displays different colors from which you can make a selection. The two small triangular-shaped handles attached to the slider are used to select a color from the slider. Drag the handles up or down to select a color.
- **Color field:** Displays the various shades of the color you have selected in the color slider.
- **Current Color Box:** Displays the original color before the color selection is made; also displays a small color box inside the color slider.
- **Adjusted color:** Displays the color after modifications have been made to it (by moving the sliders in the color slider up and down) and the color has been selected. The Adjusted Color Box is displayed in a small color box beside the color slider.
- **Out-of-gamut alert icon:** Appears beside the new or current color box if the selected color is not print-safe. Therefore, if you open an image in Photoshop that has complex colors and send it for printing, the final output will not be satisfactory. There is also a possibility that the colors that appear on the screen might not appear in the printout.

- **Not a web safe color alert icon:** Appears when you select a color that is not Web-safe. This means the color will not appear if it is saved in a World Wide Web-friendly file extension, such as JPEG, GIF, or BMP, and viewed on the Internet through a Web browser.
- **Only Web Colors check box:** Displays Web-safe colors only if this checkbox is selected.

In this section, you learned to set the foreground color. Likewise, you can set the background color. Now, let's learn to set foreground or background color using Eyedropper Tool.

Using Eyedropper Tool

Eyedropper Tool is used to pick colors for the foreground or background color from an image. Suppose you want to select a color from an image and use the selected color in another image. In such cases, you can use Eyedropper Tool to pick a sample of the color. This is an easy and convenient method for adding and selecting colors not originally found or difficult to find in Color Picker.

To pick a color from an image, select Eyedropper Tool from the Tools panel and click the image area from which you want to pick a color. Depending on the active color box, Photoshop selects the color. Perform the following steps to set foreground color using Eyedropper Tool:

1. **Open** an image from which you want to pick a color, as shown in picture 3.0.

2. Select **Eyedropper Tool** in the Tools panel, as shown in picture 3.0 with the green arrow numbered 2.

3. **Click** the image area to pick the color for the foreground color (green arrow numbered 3).

In our case, the picked color appears as the foreground color, as shown in picture 3.0 with the green arrow numbered 4.

Likewise, you can select the background color using Eyedropper Tool in Photoshop. If the foreground color box is active, you can simply hold the Alt key down while clicking the color to set the background color.

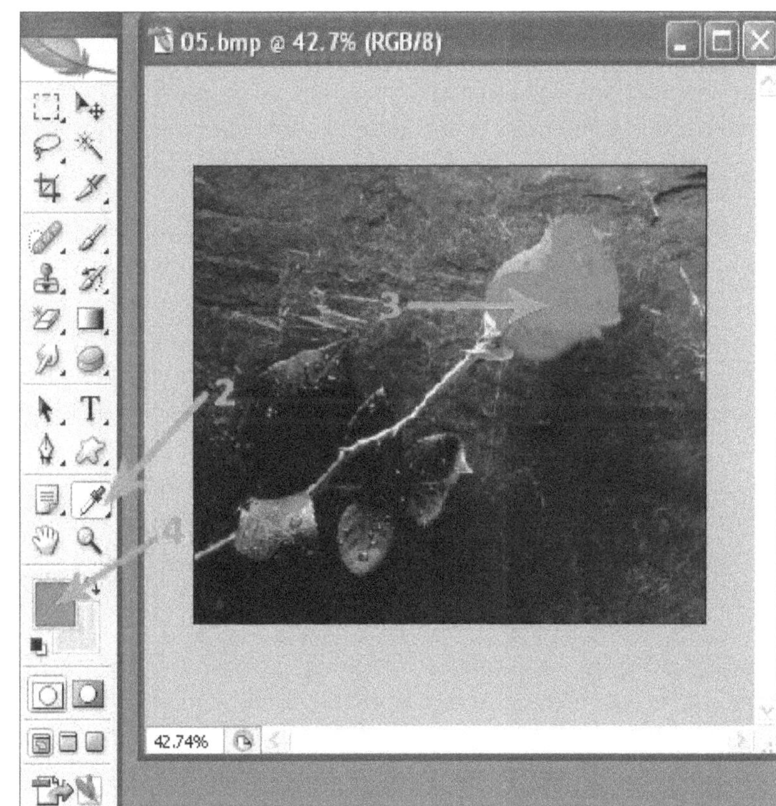

Picture 3.0

When setting foreground and background color, you can toggle/switch the foreground and background colors using the Switch Foreground and Background Colors icon. Alternatively, you can press the X key on the keyboard to toggle between the foreground and background colors. Let's now learn to set foreground or background color using the Color panel.

Using the Color Panel

One of the easiest ways to set the foreground and background colors is using the Color panel. The Color panel contains several sliders representing individual colors of the selected color mode; you can drag the sliders to set foreground or background colors. A color spectrum appears at the bottom of the panel, which helps to select random colors. By default, the RGB Sliders and CMYK Spectrum are selected. You can click the panel menu icon and select another sliders or color spectrum from the panel menu. By default, the Color panel appears in the default workspace. If you cannot find the Color panel in your workspace, you can display it by selecting Window> Color from the Menu bar or by pressing the F6 key on the keyboard.

As you move the mouse-pointer over the spectrum, the mouse-pointer converts into Eyedropper Tool. Now, click the spectrum to select a color. You can see that the sliders are automatically adjusted. And the values corresponding to the selected color appear in the related text boxes. If the values for a particular color are known, you can type the values in their respective text boxes to select the color. Next, we discuss how to enhance the quality of an image by making adjustments to its color.

Making Color Adjustment

The overall tonal quality of an image is what grabs the attention of the viewers. Therefore, an old photograph, or even a new one taken with a digital camera, or scanned documents need some color and tonal corrections to enhance their overall quality. Photoshop offers a wide variety of tools and commands to make color adjustment in an image, often referred as color correction.

You can color-correct an image by using the settings available in the Levels and Curves dialog boxes or Levels or Curves adjustments. In addition, you can even enhance selected colors of the image or control the brightness and contrast of the image, and more. The process of color corrections using the tools and methods are known as color adjustments. Photoshop introduced the Adjustments panel to access all the commands and dialog boxes related to color corrections from a single window.

The Adjustment panel is active by default, when you launch Photoshop for the first time. In case, the Adjustment panel is not displayed in the Photoshop window, click Window> Adjustments from the Menu bar to access it. Picture 3.1 shows Adjustments panel:

To apply an adjustment, click the respective icon in the Adjustment panel. For instance, to apply Levels adjustment, click the Create a new Levels adjustment layer icon in the Adjustment panel. This operation opens the Properties panel with all the settings related to the Levels adjustments and a new adjustment layer is created in the Layer panel.

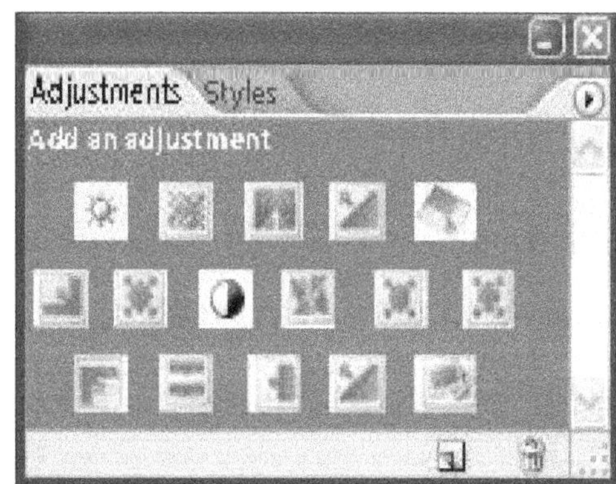

Picture 3.1

In the Properties panel, presets are available for Levels, Curves, Exposure, Hue/Saturation, Black & White, Channel Mixer, and Selective Color adjustment layers. Photoshop CS6 adds an extra layer over the original pixels known as adjustment layer. Adjustment layers let you make successive tonal adjustments without discarding or permanently modifying data of the image. You can also save your adjustment settings as preset and add it to the presets list.

If you want to modify the original image, you can use the Levels command by selecting Image> Adjustments> Levels from the Menu bar or by pressing the Ctrl+L keys together. Both the Levels dialog box and Levels Adjustments in the adjustments panel have the same options. The only difference is Level's adjustment automatically creates an adjustment layer in the Layers panel.

The powerful tools and commands in Photoshop CS6 can enhance, repair, and correct the color and tonality (that is, lightness, darkness, and contrast) in an image. You need to consider following points before making color and tonal adjustments:

- Use adjustment layer to adjust the tonal range and color balance of your image.
- Create adjustment layers automatically by accessing the color and tonal commands in the Adjustments panel.
- Apply adjustments directly to an image layer using the Levels dialog box, if you do not want to use adjustment layers.
- Use 16-bit image rather than 8-bit image for high level of color and tonal adjustments.
- Duplicate or make a copy of the image layer to preserve the original image.
- Correct the image by removing dust spots, blemishes, and scratches.
- Confine adjustments to part of the image through selections and masks.

After understanding these points for making color and tonal adjustments, we are going to discuss the different ways to make color and tonal corrections, starting with Levels.

Levels Adjustment

Photoshop CS6 uses Levels adjustment to correct the tonal range (that is, the light and dark pixels) and color balance of an image by adjusting intensity levels of image shadows, midtones, and highlights. The Levels adjustment in the Adjustments panel appears with two different levels: Input Levels and Output Levels, along with a histogram. Histogram is a graphical representation of the tonal range (brightness value) in a digital image. It shows the amount of pure black, pure white, and between black and white. Input levels allow you to change the specific values for highlights, shadows, and midtones in an image. The attributes of an image are:

- Highlights are the highlighted or lightened areas of an image
- Shadows are the darkened areas of the image
- Midtones define the middle range of color tones of the image

Let's discuss several elements and options in the Levels adjustment. Picture 3.2 below shows important options and elements of the Levels adjustment.

Move the black slider for the Input Levels to the left or right direction to decrease or increase the level of shadow in an image, respectively.

Use the gray and white sliders to increase or decrease the levels of midtones and highlights in the image respectively. The Input slider at the middle is used to adjust the gamma value in the image. This changes the intensity values of the middle range of gray tones without affecting the highlights and shadows in the image.

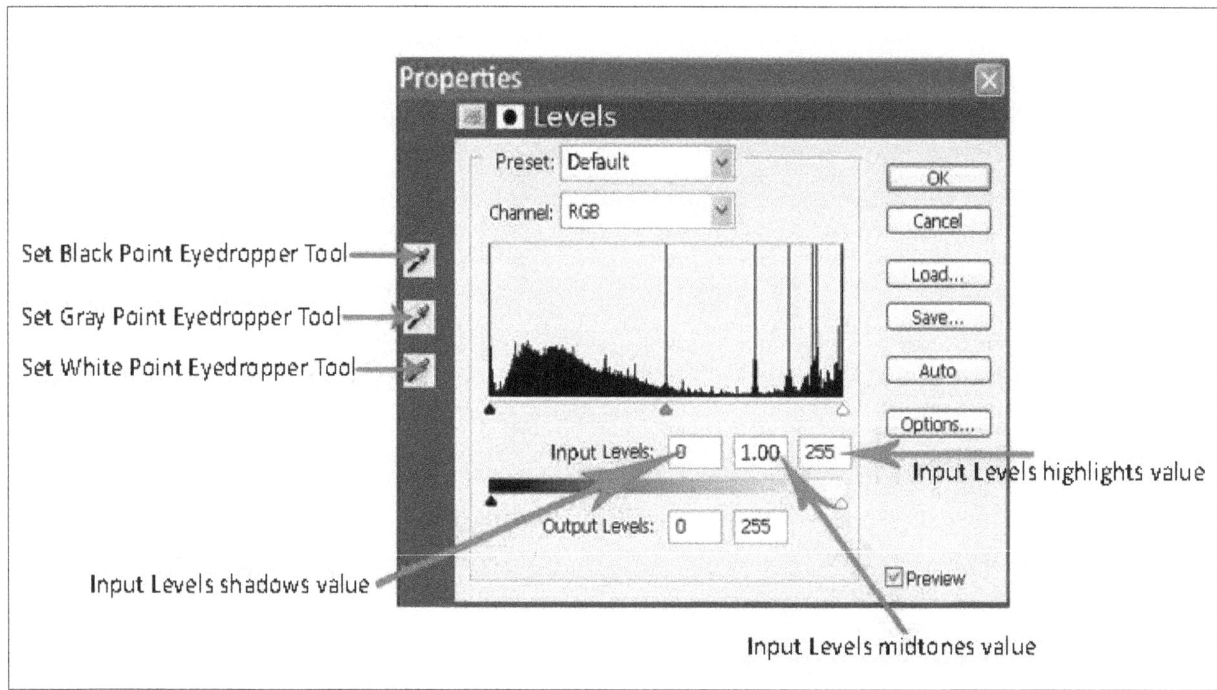

Picture 3.2

Use the black and white sliders of the Output Levels to limit the darkest and lightest pixels of the image. The default Output sliders are at level 0 and 255, where the pixels are black and white respectively. You can move the black and white input sliders to map the pixels value to 0 and 255 levels when the Output sliders are set to their defaults. The Output Levels is not used unless you are using an outdated method of printing.

In the Adjustments panel, you can click the Set Gray Point Eyedropper Tool. Then click on a part of the image that is neutral gray to neutralize a color cast. In general, assign equal color component values to achieve a neutral. For instance, you can produce a neutral gray by assigning equal values of Red, Green, and Blue.

After exploring several elements of the Levels adjustment in the Adjustments panel, let's now use the Levels adjustment to correct the tonal range and the color balance of an image. Perform the following steps to correct the tonal range of an image:

1. **Open** the image for tonal correction using Level adjustment.

2. Click the **Create a new Levels adjustment layer** icon in the Adjustments panel (picture 3.1) to create a Levels adjustment layer and open the Properties panel with all the settings.

As you can notice, the above image has higher level of shadows and lower level of highlights as depicted by the histogram. You can also notice an adjustment layer named Levels 1 is created in the Layers panel.

3. **Type** a value in the **Adjust shadow input level** text box to increase the shadows in the image. In our case, we type **17**.

4. **Type** a value in the **Adjust highlight input level** text box to decrease the highlights. In our case, we type **146**.

As a result, the color-corrected image appears on your screen. You can type the values in the respective text boxes for Input Levels. You can also click the Auto button in the Levels adjustment to allow Photoshop color-correct the image automatically. You can save Levels adjustment settings as presets. Let's now learn about Curves adjustments.

Curves Adjustment

The Curves adjustment used to adjust the tonal range of an image. The Curves adjustments are also used to adjust individual color channels of an image. Likewise Levels adjustments, you can use Curves adjustments directly on image layers or using adjustment layers. You can use built-in preset settings. In addition, Curves adjustment settings can also be saved as presets.

Curves adjustment is a useful tool in Photoshop CS6, since it offers 16 different points throughout an image. From these points, you can adjust the tonal range of the image. You can create the tonal points on the diagonal line appearing between the two gradients called Output and Input. You can also move these points up or down to make a specific area of the image darker of lighter. You can also improve the color contrast of an image by using the Curves dialog box. You can access the Curves dialog box by choosing Image> Adjustments> Curves from the Menu bar.

You can add a Curves adjustment layer by clicking the Create a new Curves adjustment layer icon in the Adjustments panel. An adjustment layer named Curves 1 is created in the Layers panel. The settings appear in the Properties panel, as shown in picture 3.3.

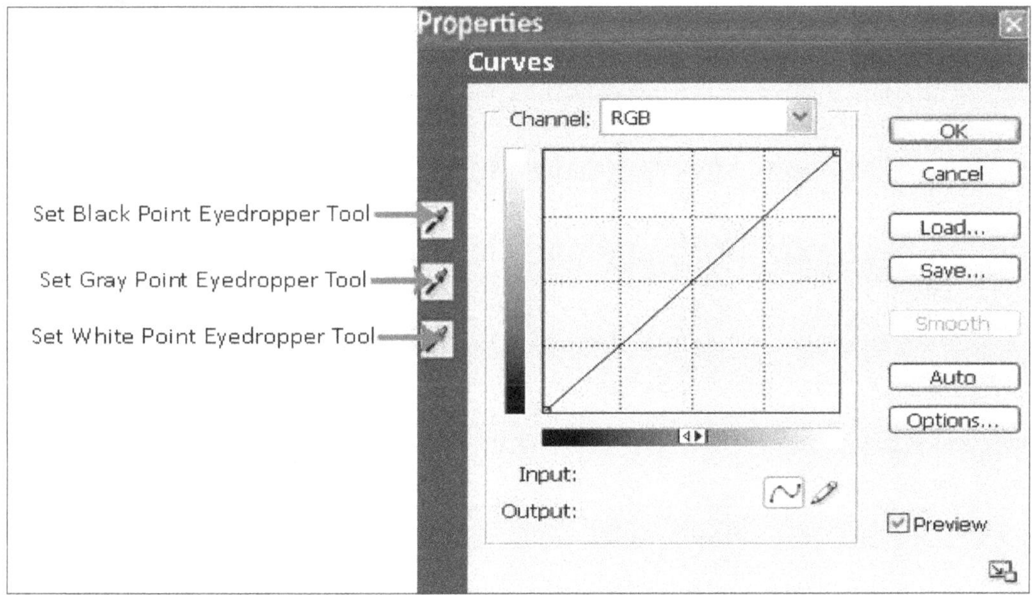

Picture 3.3

Unlike Levels adjustment, the Curves adjustment has a histogram graph with a diagonal line instead. The histogram is represented with faded opacity in the background of the graph. The horizontal axis of the graph represents the input levels; the vertical axis represents the output levels. Perform the following steps to color-correct an image using the Curves adjustment:

1. **Open** an image to use the Curves adjustment.

2. Click the **Create a new Curves adjustment layer** icon in the Adjustments panel. The Properties panel appears with the Curves settings, as shown in picture 3.3.

3. Select **Set Black Point Eyedropper Tool** and **click** the darkest area in your image.

4. Select **Set Gray Point Eyedropper Tool** and **click** the gray area in your image.

5. Select **Set White Point Eyedropper Tool** and **click** the brightest area.

As a result, your image updates with the new values simultaneously. Now, you can see on your screen that the image appears with more contrast. You can check the difference by clicking the Toggle layer visibility button at the bottom of the Adjustments panel. Let's now learn about Brightness/Contrast adjustment in the next section.

Brightness/Contrast Adjustment

The Brightness/Contrast adjustment is useful for making color adjustment to the tonal range of an image. When you click the Create a new Brightness/Contrast adjustment layer icon, the settings appear in the Properties panel. The Brightness slider increases or decreases the tonal values of the image; and the Contrast slider expands or shrinks the overall range of tonal values of the image.

When you click the Brightness/Contrast icon in the Adjustments panel, both the Brightness and Contrast sliders appear with the default value 0 in the Properties panel, as shown in picture 3.4.

Moving the Brightness slider to the right increases the tonal range of the image, and as a result, the image appears brighter; while moving the slider to the left decreases the tonal range and increases the shadow range of the image. The Brightness slider has a maximum limit of +150 to the right and -150 to the left; while the corresponding limits of the Contrast slider is +100 to the right and -50 to the left. You can also type the values in the respective text field to change the values. The Brightness/Contrast adjustment applies proportionate (nonlinear) adjustments to image pixels, similar to the adjustments made in the Levels and Curves adjustments.

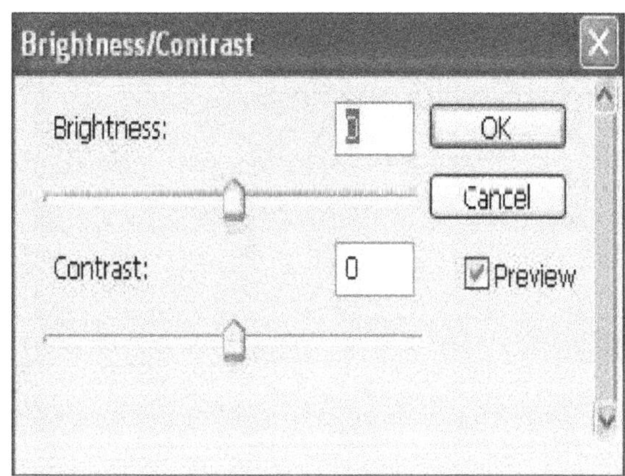

Picture 3.4

When the Use Legacy check box is selected in the Brightness/Contrast adjustment options, the brightness and contrast levels for all the pixels are taken. However, using the Brightness/Contrast adjustment in the legacy mode is not recommended for high end output, as it can cause clipping or loss of image detail in the highlighted or shadow areas.

After learning about Brightness/Contrast adjustment, let's now discuss how to use the Hue/Saturation adjustment for color correction.

Hue/Saturation Adjustment

The Hue/Saturation adjustment helps you to make color changes in the image. The Hue/Saturation adjustment settings in the Properties panel appear with three sliders: Hue, Saturation, and Lightness, as shown in picture 3.5.

You can change the complete color theme of an image by moving the Hue slider, which works similar to Photoshop's Color Picker. The Saturation slider is used to adjust the saturation level of an image. For instance, you can use this slider to change the color of a shirt from bright green to dull green.

The Lightness slider lightens the image when moved to the right and darkens it when moved to the left. You can also apply the Hue/Saturation adjustment in a selected area of an image. Let's now learn about the Replace Color command.

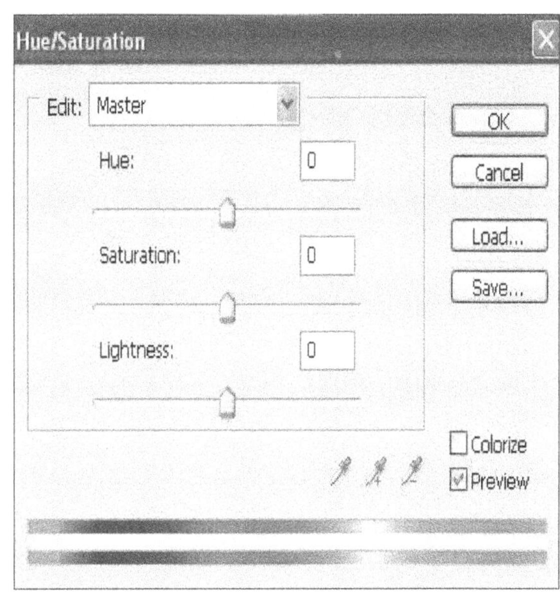

Picture 3.5

The Replace Color Command

The Replace Color command lets you create a selection based on image color. After making a selection, you can replace the selected color selection with any other color. For instance, you can replace the red color of an image with blue color. You can select the Replace Color command by selecting Image> Adjustments> Replace Color from the Menu bar. The Replace Color dialog box is shown in picture 3.6.

In the Selection section of the Replace Color dialog box, you need to select the color that you want to replace. The Replacement section in the above dialog box provides three components of color: Hue, Saturation, and Lightness. These components let you select the replacement color for the color selected in the Selection section.

Hue lets you change the image's actual color, Saturation lets you control the amount of color in your image, and Lightness lets you determine how bright the color is based on its Hue and Saturation values. Let's now learn about channels in the next section.

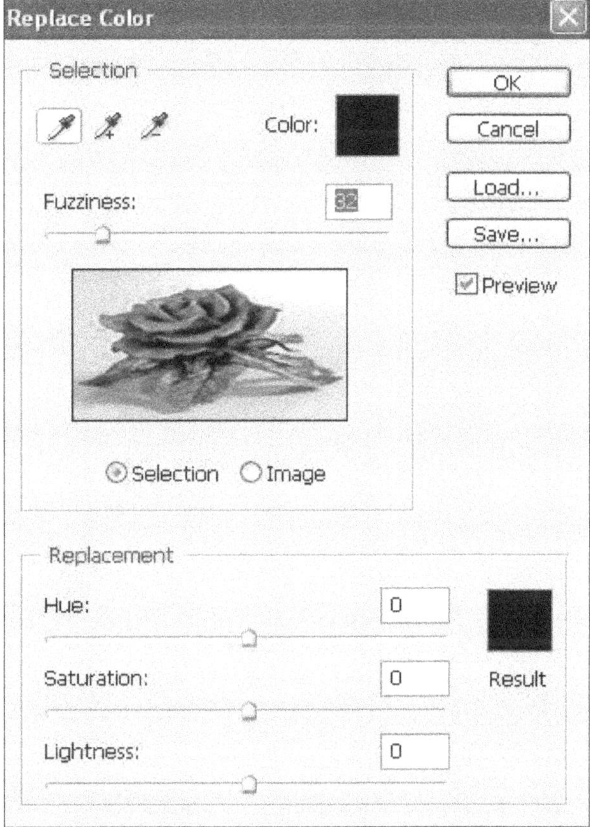

Picture 3.6

Understanding Channels

Photoshop CS6's channels are originally grayscale images that stores different types of information, such as color and selections. Channels have the same dimensions and number of pixels as the original image. When you open an image, Photoshop CS6 automatically creates channels that contain color information. The number of channels created depends upon the color mode of the image. For instance, a CMYK image has a channel for each color (cyan, magenta, yellow, and black).

In addition, a composite channel also appears in the Channels panel that is used for editing the image. The Channels panel appears in the Layers panel group by default. You can click the Channels panel tab to show the panel. The Channels panel is shown in picture 3.7.

As you can notice in the picture 3.7, channels appear as layer. The first channel is the composite channel. You can click the individual channel to see and compare the color information of each channel in an image. You can also modify two channels together by selecting them. If you want to select two or more channels, you need to hold the Shift key down and click the channels to select them.

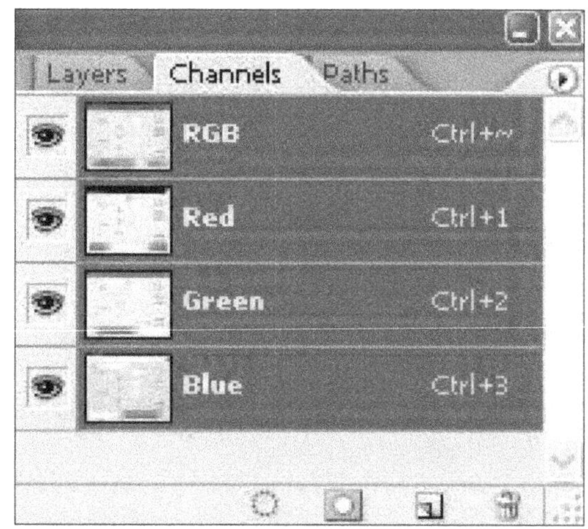

Picture 3.7

The Channels panel can also contain alpha channels that store selections as grayscale images. You can create an alpha channel by clicking the Create new channel button at the bottom of the Channels panel. You can also create spot color channels using the Channels panel menu. Spot color channels provide additional inks for printing.

Lesson 4
Working with Images

An image replaces a thousand words, especially when it comes to depicting visual perception. It can represent a real-life scenario as well as an imaginary scenario. When images are displayed digitally using display services, such as computer screen, they are referred as digital images. These images are represented numerically using binary code. Nowadays, digital images have become popular compared to the analog images, as they offer more color and better contrast. In Photoshop CS6, images are amalgamation of tiny squares where each tiny square represents a distinct color. These tiny squares of colors, also referred to as pixels, are the basic building blocks of an image.

There are two basic types of digital images: raster (or bitmap) and vector. Raster images are defined in terms of fixed rows and columns of individual pixels. They are pixel-dependent as the numbers of pixels are fixed. On the other hand, vector images are defined in terms of lines (both straight and curved). Vector images are pixel-independent as they are mathematically defined functions and can be scaled to any size without the loss of quality.

Photoshop CS6, which is primarily a raster image-editing application, has addressed some of the most sought after features, such as the ability to edit vectors the same way as you would in latest edition of the Illustrator. You can open both raster and vector images in Photoshop CS6 and modify them using various tools and commands. For instance, you can rotate, crop, or change the resolution of an image. The term resolution refers to the total number of pixels in an image. You can also create vector images with the help of some drawing tools, such as Pen Tool and Shape Tool available in the Tool panel Photoshop.

In this section, you will first learn to differentiate raster and vector images. Next, you will learn about resolution and how it affects images. Further, you will learn to edit images, wherein you will learn to rotate, straighten, and crop images. In addition, you will learn to create and modify smart objects. Next, you will learn about vector images and use various drawing tools. Towards the end, you will learn to use Pen Tool to create and edit paths, save a path as selection. Let's begin the lesson by learning about raster and vector images.

Comparing Raster and Vector Images

Raster images are made up of pixels that lie in a horizontal grid. Pixel is the unit for measuring the quality of the image. Higher number of pixels means higher quality images. Using scanner, you can digitize images to a collection of pixels. Scanned images and photographs from digital cameras are the most common source of raster images.

A vector image can be described by using mathematical definitions. Let's understand the difference between raster and vector images by considering an example of drawing a line. You can draw the line by joining a number of linearly placed tiny squares. Alternatively, you can define two points, for instance, A and B, and then join these two points with a line. A is the start point where B is the end point in the coordinates of the line. The line drawn by using the former approach is a raster image and that drawn by using the later approach is a vector image, as shown in picture 3.8.

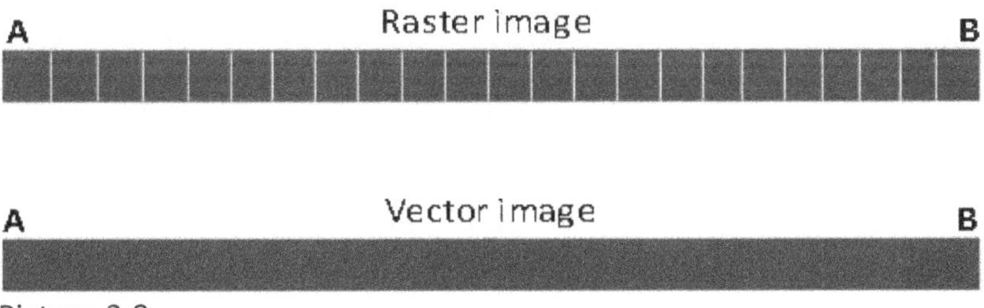

Picture 3.8

Raster images are resolution-dependent because the pixels that describe the image are fixed to a particular size and number. Therefore, enlarging a raster image redistributes the fixed number of pixels in the large area, often making the edges of the image appear jagged. Hence, raster images are not ideal choice for photo-realistic images with complex color variations. You can modify a raster image by editing one or more pixels; unlike a vector image where you modify a mathematical shape. In other words, vector images are resolution independent. You can scale vector images up to any size without creating jagged or pixilated images.

Vectors are mathematically defined shapes that are object-oriented. Each vector is made up of lines and curves, known as segments. The segments are connected using anchor points, which are the most basic elements of any vector image. You can modify a vector image by modifying the anchor points. Picture 3.9 below illustrates the difference between bitmap and vector image, when magnified:

As you can notice in picture 3.9, the vector image when magnified retains its quality; but in case of raster image, the quality is lost and jagged edges are created. At times, you may notice a jagged vector image, which is because the monitor can display images only on grid, so vector images are also displayed onscreen as pixels. The recommended resolution for displaying images onscreen can range between 72 ppi and 96 ppi. This is because monitors display images in this pixel range. Let's now learn about images resolution in the next section.

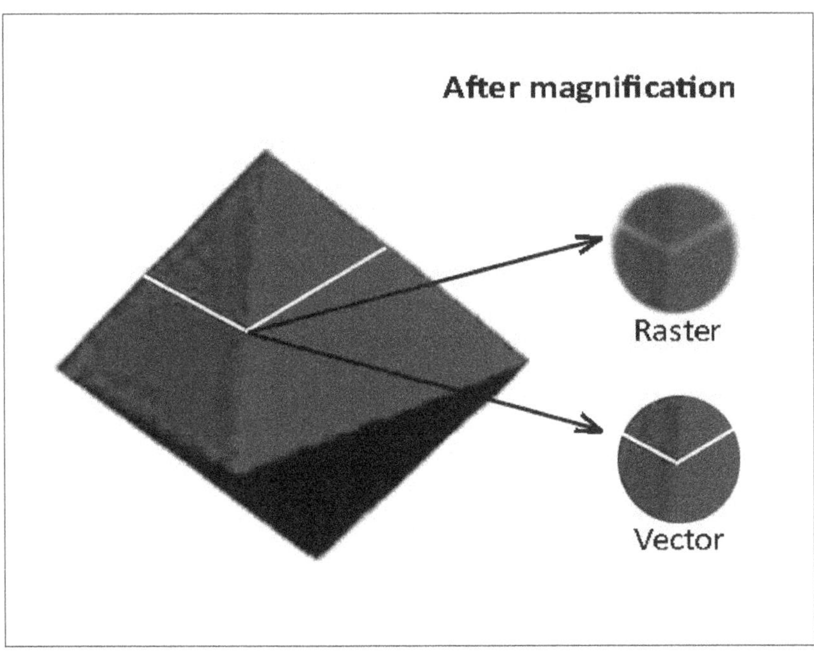

Picture 3.9

Understanding Image Resolution

Image resolution or simply resolution can be defined as the number of pixels per unit length; for instance, in a square inch of an image. Resolution is measured in pixels per inch (ppi), which is the measurement that defines the size of an image for printing. For instance, if you print an image with a resolution of 900 x 1200 pixels at 300 dpi; the print size will be 3 x 4 inches. However, if you print the image with a resolution of 900 x 1200 pixels but decreased resolution, for instance 150 ppi, the print size will increase to 6 x 8 inches. Hence, typically you get better quality print if the resolution is high. Consequently, a higher resolution means greater number of pixels per square inch of an image and a lower resolution means fewer numbers of pixels per square inch of the image. 300 dpi (dots per inch) is generally considered the optimum resolution for printing digital images using the Inkjet printers. Increasing the resolution to greater than 300 ppi, does not affect image quality; however, increases the file size. This is why increasing the resolution beyond 300 ppi is not recommended.

With respect to printing, the term dpi is used instead of ppi. Dpi is often used interchangeably with the term ppi. It defines the number of dots of ink placed on the page while printing. Note that dpi refers to the resolution of a printing device, not the resolution of the image. If you are creating an image to be displayed on the Internet or display devices, the resolution of the image can be set to 72 ppi at 100% of its intended viewing size. As you know, the resolution of an image is pixel-dependent. You can understand this better after you become familiar with the term pixel, discussed in the next section.

Understanding Pixel

Picture elements or pixels are the basic building blocks that make up raster images. Every digital image that you open in Photoshop CS6 is made up of thousands or even millions of tiny square elements known as pixels. These tiny squares are not visible at 100% zoom level. You can zoom in on a raster image to make the pixels visible. Digital images are made up of binary numbers: 0s and 1s, which represent the color of a single pixel. One of advantages of the raster image is that each pixel's value can be arbitrarily different to the next, which suits it perfectly to create photo-realistic artwork that needs continuous tone of colors.

Pixel dimension refers to the total number of pixels along the width (horizontally) and height (vertically). For instance, with a pixel dimension of 300 x 300, an image has a total of 90,000 pixels. Likewise, with a pixel dimension of 600 x 600, the image has a total of 360,000 pixels. Typically, the larger the total number of pixels, the more details an image will produce.

To understand the concept of pixel logic, open an image in the Photoshop Document window and view the image at two different resolutions. In our case, an image is shown in two different resolutions: 72 ppi and 18 ppi, as shown in picture 4.0.

Picture 4.0

As you notice in picture 4.0, the lower resolution of the image appears pixelated or blurred as compared to the higher resolution version. As discussed earlier, the total number of pixels of an image can be increased or decreased. You can enhance the clarity of an image by making modifications to its resolution, pixel dimension, and document size (height and width). We discuss all these topics in the following sections.

Changing the Resolution of an Image
As you know, raster images are resolution-dependent, so it is not feasible to increase or decrease their dimension without losing a certain degree of image quality. When you decrease the size of a raster image using the resample option of Photoshop CS6, you lose pixels. When you increase the size of a raster image using the resample option, Photoshop CS6 creates new pixels to accommodate the extra image area that is added. Photoshop creates the new pixels based on the color value of the surrounding pixels. This process is called interpolation.

The Image Size command displays vital information about the image, such as pixel dimensions, the resulting file (the size of the file after making changes, such as increasing or decreasing the height or width of the image), the current document size, and the resolution of the image. The file size is measured in kilobyte or megabyte.

The pixel dimensions of a file can be changed by modifying the resolution or document size of the image in the Image Size dialog box. If you want to maintain the same output dimensions, but enhance the quality of the image, you can do so by changing the resolution of the image by changing the Bit Depth or Color Depth values. Each pixel represents certain number of colors also referred to as Bit Depth. In a 24-bit RGB image, a pixel can represent 256 levels of red, green, and blue or over 16 million colors. On the other hand, in an 8-bit indexed or grayscale image, a pixel can represent 256 colors. Perform the following steps to change the resolution of an image:

1. **Open** an image in Photoshop. In our case, we have used the Open command to open an existing image (picture 4.1). Let's now check the current resolution of the image.

Picture 4.1

2. **Click** the right arrow in the Status bar of the Document window, as shown in picture 4.1 with the blue arrow. A dropdown list appears. You can also note that the current zoom level is 100%.

3. Select the **Document Dimensions** option from the dropdown list (shown with blue arrow).

Now you can see the information box displays the image size and resolution with their default units in the Status bar of the Document window, as shown in picture 4.2.

Picture 4.2

As you can see, the size is 22.58 cm x 16.93 cm and the resolution is 72 ppi. You can go ahead and change the default unit for Photoshop in the Preference dialog box. In the Units & Rulers category of the Preferences dialog box, we select the **Pixels** option in the Rulers dropdown list. In our case, the current document dimension in pixels (640 pixels x 480 pixels) is shown in picture 4.3.

Picture 4.3

4. Choose **Image> Image Size** from the Menu bar. It opens the Image Size dialog box on your screen in which the <u>Resolution</u> is set to 72 ppi, by default.

5. Type a new value in the **Resolution** text box in the Document Size section. In our case, we type **150**.

In the <u>Image Size dialog box</u> on your screen, note that the values in Width and Height text boxes in the Pixel Dimensions section simultaneously change when you change the resolution value. Moreover, note that with the increase in pixel resolution, the document size also changes. In our case, the document size has changed from 22.58 cm to 30.44 cm, showing in Image Size dialog box. You need to ensure the **Constrain Proportions** check box in the Image Size dialog box is selected. This option maintains the proportion of width and height during resizing.

6. Click **OK** button in the Image Size dialog box. In Photoshop's Document window, the document size increases. Picture 4.4 shows the preview image with the new resolution at the same zoom level (100%).

Picture 4.4

You can also notice that the information box displays the increased document dimensions for the image. In addition, note that when you change the image resolution, Photoshop CS6 automatically changes the image dimension to a pre-defined dimension. If you want specific dimension for the image, you can make changes in the Width and Height text boxes separately in the Pixel Dimensions section. Let's now learn how to change the document size of an image in the next section.

Changing the Document Size of an Image

Document size is defined as the height and width of an image. The height and width of an image can be measured in different measurement units, such as percentage, inches, centimeters, millimeters, points, and picas. The height and width can be increased or decreased in a constrained proportion, that is, if you increase the width of the file, the height increases automatically in the same proportion. This can be done by selecting the Constrain Proportions check box in the Image Size dialog box. Perform the following steps to change the document size of an image:

1. **Open** an image in Photoshop, and select **Image**> **Image Size** from the Menu bar.

2. **Type** a new value in the **Width** text box in the Document Size section. In our case, we type **40**.

Notice that the value in the Height text box also changes simultaneously to a predefined value depending on the selection of the Constrain Proportions check box. The values under Pixel Dimensions section also changes with the change in the Width value.

3. Click the **OK** button to close the Image Size dialog box. As a result, the document size of the image increases in the Photoshop window at the same zoom level on your screen.

In the Image Size dialog box, you can notice three options: Scale Styles, Constrain Proportions, and Resample Image. Following list briefly explains the three options:

- **Scale Style:** Allows you to scale Layer Style, such as Bevel, Stroke, and Emboss along with the layers. While this can be quite useful for creating buttons, banners, and other Web graphics, it has no relevance when you resize an image that does not use Layer Styles.

- **Constrain Proportions:** Changes the height of the image in the same proportion of the change in the width, automatically. This option links the width and height of the image together. It helps preserve the proportions of the image and is enabled by default. When this option is unselected, you can change the width and height of the image independently of each other.

- **Resample Image:** Changes the actual number of pixel when selected. Resampling is the process by which Photoshop either adds or subtracts pixels when you change its size. This option is selected by default. Let's now learn more about the difference between resizing and resampling.

Resizing vs Resampling an Image

There are two ways to change the size of an image in Photoshop: resize or resample. Resizing and resampling are often misinterpreted, and assumed to be identical in their meanings; however, there is an important difference between the two. The difference is whether or not the total number of pixels in the image is changing. The two ways to change the size of an image are described as follows:

- **Resizing:** Modifies the image size without altering the total number of pixels.
- **Resampling:** Modifies the image size as well as alters the actual number of pixels.

You can select the Resample Image check box to resample the image. If you want to increase or decrease the resolution of the image without altering the pixel dimension, clear the Resample Image check box in the Image Size dialog box. When resizing, Photoshop adjusts the document size to accommodate the pixels without altering the total number of pixels. In the next section, let's learn how to modify images in Photoshop.

Modifying Images

In Photoshop, there are several ways to modify/edit an image. The way you choose depends on the kind and extent of editing required in the image. In the subsequent sections, you learn how to perform some of the commonly used editing tasks including rotating, straightening, cropping images. In addition, you learn how to adjust the size of the canvas. Let's begin with rotating an image.

Rotating an Image

In Photoshop CS6, you can rotate an image at a predefined angle or at an angle of your choice. You can also flip the image vertically or horizontally. You can rotate or flip an entire image using the Image Rotation commands that are available under the Image> Image Rotation submenu. However, these commands do not work on individual layers, paths, or selections. Perform the following simple steps to rotate an image using the Image Rotation command:

1. **Open** an image you want to rotate in Photoshop. Then choose **Image> Image Rotation> Arbitrary** from the Menu bar. It opens the Rotate Canvas dialog box.

2. **Type** a rotation value in the Angle text box. In our case, we type **150** as the degree of rotation.

By default, the Clock Wise (CW) radio button is selected, which rotates the image in the clockwise direction. The Counter Clock Wise (CCW) option rotates the image in anti-clockwise direction.

3. Click the **OK** button in the Rotate Canvas dialog box. As a result, the image in you Document window rotates 150 degree in the clockwise direction.

Photoshop adjusts the original canvas size to accommodate the image and fills it with the current background color. In case you want to rotate the image to a predefined angle, such as 180^0, 90^0 CW, or 90^0 CCW, you can select the respective option from the Image> Image Rotation submenus. In addition, you can also flip the image vertically or horizontally using the Flip Canvas Horizontal and Flip Canvas Vertical options in the submenus. Let's learn how to straighten an image in the next section.

Straightening an Image

While shooting pictures using digital camera, the image usually gets tilted or distorted due to the little movement of the camera that occurs. The technique of straightening an image using Ruler Tool can help you save lots of time required for re-shooting those pictures. To decide the magnitude of rotation required for straightening the image, you can use Ruler Tool. It helps you to correct imperfections in the image, such as straightening a tilted image, by allowing you to calculate the distance and angle between two points in an image. Perform the following simple steps on your computer to use Ruler Tool to straighten a distorted image:

1. **Open** an image you want to straighten in Photoshop. In our case, we take a tilted image.

2. **Click** and **hold** Eyedropper Tool in the Tools panel to open a flyout. Then select **Ruler Tool** from the flyout. The default pointer changes to a ruler icon with a plus (+) sign.

3. **Drag** the mouse pointer on your image to manually define the degree of rotation.

Photoshop uses this line as a reference for measuring the angle at which the image needs to be rotated in order to straighten it. Deciding where to place the line is the trickiest part of using Ruler Tool. If you want to straighten the image horizontally, you have to find a straight area.

4. Click the **Straighten Layer** button in the Options bar. As a result you see on your screen that Photoshop straightens your image.

The Straighten Layer button is an improved feature in Photoshop CS6, which replaced the Straighten button of Photoshop CS5. By the way, the Clear button on the Options bar clears the line drawn using Ruler Tool. Now, you can crop the image to remove the unwanted area.

Cropping an Image Using Crop Tool

While working with raw images, most of the times you need to crop the image to remove the extra area that is added intentionally or unintentionally to the image during the shoot. Raw images are the images imported to Photoshop from devices like a digital camera or a scanner.

Cropping is the process of removing unwanted portions from an image to focus on important portion of the image. It also reduces the size of the document. In Photoshop, you can crop an image by using Crop Tool, the Crop command, and the Trim command. Each of these cropping methods works in different ways. Note that when you crop an image, Photoshop CS6 deletes the portion in the shielded area permanently, unless you uncheck the Delete Cropped Pixels checkbox in the Options bar. Perform the following simple steps to crop an image by using Crop Tool:

1. **Open** the image that you want to crop in Photoshop. In our case, we want to remove the transparent area in the image.

2. Select **Crop Tool** in the Tools panel or press the **C key** on the keyboard to select it. A crop box automatically appears surrounding your image.

The crop box has multiple handles that you can use to resize and rotate it. You can also move and reposition the crop box to precisely crop your image. You can also simply click and drag to define a new crop area, which was the way it is used to crop in previous versions of Photoshop.

3. **Drag** different handles to resize the crop box. In our case, we resized the crop box to remove the transparent area using multiple handles.

As you can see, the remaining part of the image is covered with a black transparent shield. You need to remember a few points while refining using the bounding box:

- To move the bounding box to another position, place the mouse-pointer inside the bounding box and then drag.
- To scale the bounding box, drag a handle.
- To constrain the proportions, hold down Shift key as you drag a corner handle.
- To rotate the bounding box, position the pointer outside the bounding box (the pointer turns into a curved arrow), and drag.
- To move the center point around which the bounding box rotates, drag the circle at the center of the bounding box.
- In Photoshop CS6, a useful information overlay appears near the cursor. When you drag a handle to resize the crop box, the overlay includes information about the size of the box.

Similarly, when you reposition the crop box, the information indicates how much the crop box has moved, and when you rotate the crop box, the information displays angle of rotation. Let's now learn how to crop perspective image in Photoshop CS6.

Cropping an Image Using Perspective Crop Tool

Photoshop CS6 introduced a new cropping tool, named Perspective Crop Tool. It is placed in Crop Tool flyout in the Tools panel. Perspective Crop Tool is a very useful tool that you can use to straighten the image which was earlier shot at an angle. It allows you to crop the image and simultaneously change its perspective. To use Perspective Crop Tool, click the four corners of the area you want to straighten and crop. Photoshop creates a grid overlay over the area. You can also drag the square corner handles to adjust according to the area you want to crop. Perform the following simple steps to crop an image using Perspective Crop Tool:

1. **Open** an image in Photoshop, and select **Perspective Crop Tool** by clicking and holding the Crop Tool.

2. **Click** the four corners one by one covering the area you want to select. A grid appears over the selected area.

If necessary, you can adjust the grid using the square corner handles according to the area you want to crop.

3. Press the **Enter** key on the keyboard to execute the crop operation. As a result, Photoshop CS6 crops the image and then straightens the image.

In addition to Crop Tool and Perspective Crop Tool, Photoshop CS6 provides the Crop and Trim commands to perform crop operations. The Crop command crops an image based on the selection. For instance, to perform the crop operation, you make a selection and then select Image> Crop from the Menu bar.

You can use any of the selection tools to select the area that you want to retain. The Trim command in Photoshop is slightly different from Crop Tool. It allows you to trim your image based on the surrounding transparent pixels or background pixels of the color you specify. When your image has a solid-colored or transparent background, you can quickly remove the area by using the Trim command. Unlike the Crop command, the Trim command does not allow you to adjust the crop-area. To trim an image with solid or transparent backgrounds, select the image and then choose Image> Trim from the Menu bar. Let's now learn to adjust canvas size of a Photoshop document.

Adjusting Canvas Size

Canvas is the complete area of an image that can be edited and printed. Using the Canvas Size command, you can increase or decrease the size of the canvas. Increasing canvas size adds space around an existing image, while decreasing the canvas size crops into the image. When you increase canvas size, Photoshop fills the extra area with the current background fill color. If the image does not have a transparent background, the added canvas automatically fills with the currently selected background color, and if the size of the canvas is reduced to a size that is less than its current size, the image is cropped. Perform the following steps to change the size of the canvas:

1. **Open** the document whose canvas size you want to change.

2. Choose **Image> Canvas Size** from the Menu bar or press **Alt+Ctrl+C** keys together.

The Canvas Size dialog box appears, as shown in picture 4.5. It displays the current canvas and file size in the Current Size selection. The Canvas Size dialog box also displays the new canvas and the file size in the New Size section and the Canvas extension color option.

3. **Type** the new value for **Width** and **Height** in their respective text boxes. In our case, Width value is **1200 px** and the Height value is **800 px**.

As shown in picture 4.5, the new file size changes to 2.75 megabytes from 1.38 megabytes as the result of increase in the width and the height. In our case, the unit is Pixels. You can change the unit to another within the Canvas Size dialog box or you can change it in the Preferences dialog box globally.

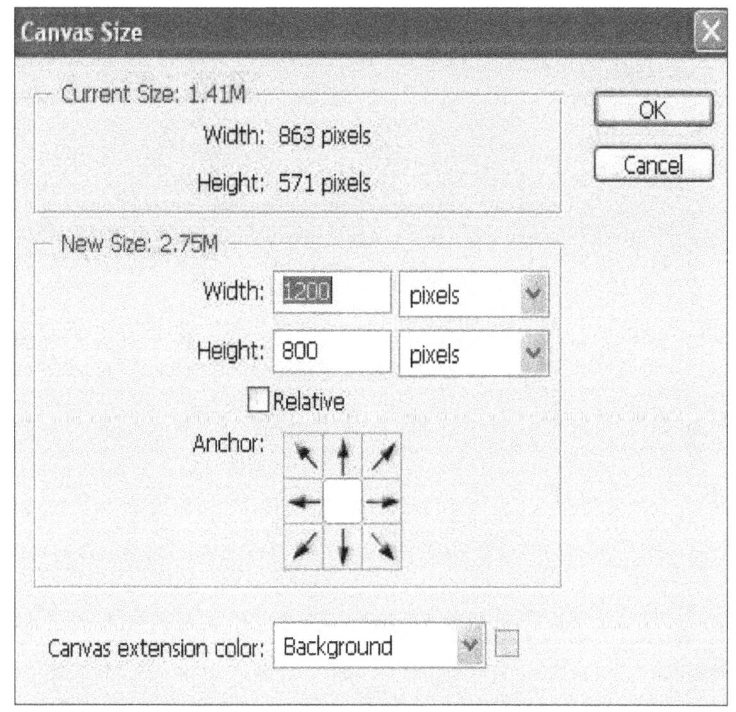

Picture 4.5

Alternatively, you can select Relative check box, and type the values you want to add or subtract from the image's current canvas size. You can enter positive values to extend the canvas size, and negative values subtract from the current canvas size. You can select a color for the extended canvas area in the Canvas extension color dropdown list. For Anchor option, click the square with arrow indicating directions, to indicate the position of the existing image on the new canvas. In our case, the default options are being used.

4. Click the **OK** button to apply the new canvas size settings and close the dialog box. The image with extended canvas (white area) appears on your screen.

If the new canvas size is smaller than the current canvas size, a message box appears on the screen warning you about clipping the canvas to the new canvas size. You need to click the Proceed button on the message box to carry on with the operation. The image appears with some part of it clipped in the new canvas size. Now, let's discuss another interesting and important feature of Photoshop, known as smart object.

Working with Smart Objects

In Photoshop, smart objects are layers that act as containers in which you can embed raster or vector image data from another Photoshop or Adobe Illustrator file. The advantage of using smart objects is that they preserve original characteristics of the source content. You can transform (scale, rotate, and distort) a smart object nondestructively that is without losing the original quality and data of your image.

Smart objects can also embed a complex set of layers. You can duplicate a smart object many times within the Photoshop document. When you edit one of the smart objects, Photoshop updates all its instances in the document. You can apply filters to a smart object non-destructively, that is you can remove the filters later if you do not need. Now, let's learn to create a smart object.

Creating a Smart Object

In Photoshop, there are different ways to create smart objects. You can create smart objects by converting existing layers, pasting Illustrator data from clipboard, importing images using the Place command, or opening images into Photoshop using the Open As Smart Object command. The difference between the Place and Open As Smart Object commands is that, the Place command lets you import into an existing document. While the Open As Smart Object command allows you to create new document with smart objects. You can also convert both vector or raster layers into smart objects. Perform the following steps to import an Illustrator file as a smart object:

1. **Open** the Photoshop CS6 application, and click **File> Open As Smart Object** from the Menu bar. It opens a dialog box.

2. **Browse** and **select** the file you want to open as smart object. In our case, we select an Illustrator file named **Guitar**.

3. Click the **Open** button. The Open As Smart Object dialog box appears again.

4. Click the **OK** button with the default settings. As a result, the file opens in Photoshop as a document and smart object icon appears in the layer thumbnail in the Layers panel.

You can also use the Place command under the File menu to import a file as a smart object into an open Photoshop CS6 document. If you use the Place command to import a smart object, use the bounding box to modify the image to the shape you desire. Then press Enter key to convert the image to a smart object. Now, let's learn to edit the content of a smart object.

Editing Smart Objects

After importing a file as a smart object into Photoshop, you can still edit the original content of the smart object. A smart object lets you work on the representation as it uses original object to store source data. For instance, when an Illustrator smart object is double-clicked in the Layers panel, Photoshop CS6 launches the Illustrator application and opens a working copy of the artwork. You can make changes in Illustrator and then save the file; Photoshop automatically updates and re-rasterizes the file. You can make a copy of the smart object by dragging the smart object layer to the Create a new layer button in the Layers panel. You can also use painting and retouching tools on the smart object layer after converting it to a normal layer. You can also convert a 3D layer to a smart object. Perform the following steps to edit the content of a smart object:

1. **Select** the smart object in the Layers panel, and double-click the **Guitar** layer thumbnail. The Adobe Photoshop CS6 Extended message box appears on your screen.

2. Click the **OK** button to accept and close the dialog box. Adobe Illustrator application launches and the PDF Modification Detected message box appears.

3. Click **OK** button with the default option. The smart object content appears in the Illustrator window, where you can edit as per your requirement. In our case, we rotate and scale down the guitar object.

4. Choose **File> Save**, and then choose **File> Exit** from the Menu bar to close the Illustrator application. As a result, the smart object content in the Photoshop window updates automatically.

Until now, you have learnt how to create and edit smart objects. Now, let's learn to work with shape tools to create vector shapes in Photoshop.

Working with Shape Tools

In raster-based programs, such as Photoshop, the shape and type tools are used to create vector graphics. While Photoshop is not really considered a vector graphic editor, such as Illustrator, the latest edition of Photoshop, possesses several enhanced features that will help to work with vector objects. Photoshop provides a collection of drawing tools for drawing basic geometric and custom shapes.

In addition, you can use Pen Tool to create or edit vector shapes. Besides Pen Tool, there are few predefined vector-based shapes in Photoshop, all of which can be easily added to your design composition. There are six different types of shape tools listed as follows:

- **Rectangle Tool:** Creates a rectangle or square shape. Holding the Shift key down while dragging creates a square shape.
- **Rounded Rectangle Tool:** Creates a rectangle or square with rounded corners. The roundness of the corner can be controlled by setting the radius value in the Options bar.
- **Ellipse Tool:** Creates an ellipse or a circle. Holding the Shift key down while dragging creates a circular shape.
- **Polygon Tool:** Creates a polygon shape with a specified number of sides as you have specified in the Options bar.
- **Line Tool:** Creates straight or diagonal lines.
- **Custom Shape Tool:** Allows you to use predefined shapes or define new custom shapes.

To create a shape in an image, simply select a shape tool you want to use from the Tools panel, adjust the settings for that tool in the Options bar. Then, drag the shape in the active image area as you drag when creating a selection with one of the selection tools. Perform the following steps to create a vector shape in Photoshop:

1. **Open** a document in Photoshop in which you want to create a vector shape.

2. **Click** and **hold** Rectangle Tool to open its flyout. Then select **Ellipse Tool** from the flyout.

3. **Drag** in your document while holding the **Shift** key down to create a circle of the desired size and location. Likewise, you can create other shapes to enhance your design.

When you are creating new shapes in Photoshop, make sure the Shape option from the Pick tool mode setting is selected on the Options bar. If the Shape option is not selected, you create raster shapes or paths on the current layer. When the Shape option is selected, each time you create a new shape, a new corresponding shape layer is created in the Layers panel.

In Photoshop, working with Shapes provides several advantages over raster-based shapes, which are shapes created using the selection tools. Some advantages of using shapes are as follows:

- **Shapes are object-oriented:** Allows you to select, resize, and move a shape. You can also edit a shape's outline (path) and attributes (stroke, fill color, and style). You can use shapes to make selections and create libraries of custom shapes with the Preset Manager dialog box.
- **Shapes are resolution-independent:** Allows you to resize without creating jagged edges.

When you select a shape tool, the Options bar displays options related to the selected tool. Photoshop CS6 includes several new options, Pick tool mode, Path operation, Path alignment, and Path arrangement for the shape tools.

When you draw using any of the shape or pen tools, Photoshop allows you to draw using any one of the tool modes discussed in the following list:

- **Shape:** Draws a vector shape on a separate layer. For instance, if you draw a rectangle by selecting the Shape layers option, you'll see that the rectangle is drawn on a separate layer. You can draw multiple shapes on a layer. A shape layer consists of a fill layer and a linked Vector Mask. Fill layer defines the shape color, while the Vector Mask defines the shape outline. The outline of a shape is a path, which appears in the Paths panel. The rectangle can be edited, moved, and deleted independently without making any changes to the other layers and image as a whole.
- **Path:** Draws a work path (a path used to select portions of an image) in the current active layer. For instance, when you draw a circle by selecting the Paths option, a circular path is created instead of a circle; that is, a circular selection is made on the image, and this selection remains available when you close and reopen the image. You can access and load the selection from the Paths panel.
- **Pixels:** Draws a raster shape on the current layer of the image. Such figures cannot be edited, moved, or deleted independently. Only the shape tools work in this mode. You learn more about text (type) later in this book. Let's now learn to work with Pen Tool.

Working with Pen Tool

Pen Tool is the most advanced shape tool and frequently used to trace part of the image. It offers a great degree of editing capabilities and helps you create complex shapes, such as curved shapes, which are otherwise difficult to create. You can use Pen Tool to create straight lines as well as smooth flowing curved paths. A path is an anchor-based selection around an image or artwork, which can be edited after they are created. Anchor points are connecting points in a path that help you to edit, expand, and contract a path. You can use Add Anchor Point Tool and Delete Anchor Point Tool to add and delete the paths. Paths can also be edited by Convert Point Tool. These tools can be accessed from Pen Tool flyout.

In the subsequent sections, you learn how to create a path by using Pen Tool; add and delete anchor points; select a path and anchor points; save a path and convert a path into a selection.

Creating a Path Using Pen Tool

You can use the Pen Tool to create simple shapes, such as square and circle and more complex shapes, such as the shape of a car. You create complex shapes by tracing an object of an image. Perform the following steps to create a path using Pen Tool:

1. **Open** an image to trace an object using Pen Tool. Then select **Pen Tool** from the Tools panel, as shown in picture 4.6 with the red arrow numbered 1.

You can also press the **P** key as a shortcut of this tool.

2. Click the **Settings** button in the Options bar and select the **Rubber Band** checkbox to preview the path segments as you draw the path (red arrow 2 in picture 4.6)

Picture 4.6

3. **Select** (click) the **Path** button in the Options bar, as shown picture 4.6 above with the red arrow numbered 3.

4. **Click** the desired location in the image, where you want to place the first anchor point. The first anchor point appears as a small solid box.

5. **Click** and **drag** the mouse-pointer to place a curve segment for the second anchor point, as shown in picture 4.7.

6. **Click** the mouse-pointer to place a segment for the third and fourth (and so on) anchor points.

7. **Click** the first anchor point to close the path by positioning the pen-pointer over it. A small loop sign appears next to the tip of Pen Tool. In our case, we have created the path with both curved and straight segments, as shown in picture 4.8.

Picture 4.7

Keep in mind that to create an open path, keep the **Ctrl** key pressed and click outside the path or press the **Esc** key on the keyboard.

Note that while placing anchor points, you can adjust the curvature of the segments. In case, you do not want the segments in curvaceous form, you can simply click to place the anchor point instead clicking and dragging. You can click as many times to add more and more anchor points to complete the desired shape. Now, let's learn how to add and delete anchor points to the existing shape.

Picture 4.8

Adding and Deleting Anchor Points

While creating a path, you may need to add more anchor points or you may need to remove some of the unnecessary anchor points according to your requirements. You can add anchor points to the path by using Add Anchor Point Tool. Similarly, you can remove anchor points using Delete Anchor Point Tool. When adding anchor points to the path, you can make intricate curves and corners to the path. Perform the following steps to add and delete anchor points to a path:

1. Click and hold **Pen Tool** in the Tools panel and select **Add Anchor Point Tool** from the flyout.

A plus (+) sign appears below Pen Tool, when you move the mouse-pointer above an existing path. However, outside the path, Add Anchor Point Tool appears as Direct Selection Tool.

2. **Click** the path to add an anchor point.

Likewise, to delete anchor points, select Delete Anchor Point Tool from the Pen Tool flyout. A minus (-) sign appears below Pen Tool.

3. **Move** the mouse-pointer over the anchor point you want to delete. In our case, we want to delete a corner anchor point.

4. **Click** the existing anchor point to delete it. As a result, the anchor point is now deleted from the path. Let's learn how to select paths and anchor points in the next section.

Selecting Paths and Anchor Points

Paths are outlines that can be stored, which you can turn into selections later. You can also convert the path into fill and stroke with color. You can easily change the shape of a path by editing its anchor points. After creating a path, you can edit it in various ways. In addition to adding and deleting anchor points, you can move a complete path by selecting the path by using Path Selection Tool or a single anchor point by using Direct Selection Tool. If you want to move the entire path, select the path with the help of Path Selection Tool and drag the path to a new location in the Document window.

On the other hand, if you want to move an anchor point to a new position in the Document window, then select an anchor point with the help of Direct Selection Tool and drag the anchor point. The position of anchor point changes, as a result, the path expands or contracts, according to how the mouse-pointer is moved.

Selecting a path segment with Path Selection Tool displays all the anchor points on a path. The anchor points appear as filled squares. However, when you select an anchor point with Direct Selection Tool, the unselected anchor points appear hollow squares. Let's learn about Convert Point Tool in the next section.

Exploring Convert Point Tool

A path consists of one or more straight or curved segments. A path segment ends at the anchor points. Each selected anchor point displays one or two direction lines on a curved segment. Picture 4.9 displays the various components of a path:

The position of direction lines and points determine the size and shape of a curved segment.

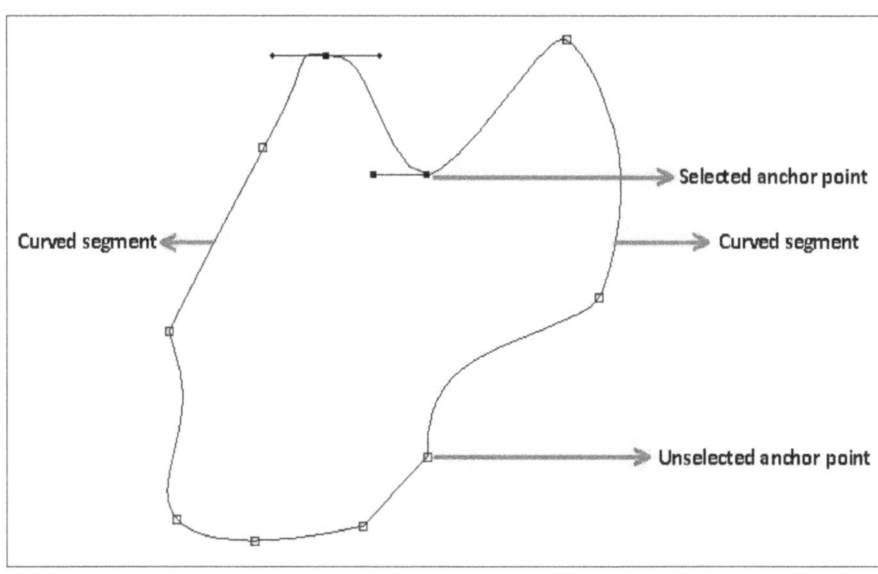

Picture 4.9

Moving either the direction line or the direction point reshapes the curves in a path. You can also reposition anchor points to make the path smooth and curved by selecting Convert Point Tool to change the direction of a selected point's curve on an existing path. The position of the direction lines and points determine the size and shape of the path. You can click an existing anchor point to reset the curve, or click and drag the anchor point to change the curve. To temporarily access Convert Point Tool while working with Pen Tool, place the mouse-pointer on any anchor point between two segments and press the Alt key. The mouse-pointer changes to Convert Point Tool.

Converting a Path into a Selection

One of the benefits of using paths is that you can convert them into selections at any time. This eliminates the need for creating a new selection from scratch every time when required. Paths are accurate selections. You can still edit paths that are saved any time using Convert Point Tool and Direct Selection Tool. Perform the following steps to convert a path into a selection:

1. **Click** the path you want to convert into a selection.

2. Click the **Paths** tab in the <u>Layers</u> panel group to show the Paths panel.

3. Click the **Load path as a selection** button at the bottom of the Paths panel. As a result, the existing path turns into a selection marquee.

You can also press the Ctrl+Enter keys simultaneously to convert a selected path into a selection. Alternatively, you can select the Make Selection option from the Paths panel menu. You can also convert a path into a selection by clicking path thumbnail in the Paths panel, while keeping the Ctrl key pressed.

After the path is converted into a selection, you can save it and use it with other images by loading the selection. If you have made a selection by using any selection tools, such as Ellipse Tool or Quick Selection Tool, you can convert the selection into a path. Doing this allows you to transform or edit the converted selection with more flexibility by adding, deleting or repositioning the anchor points. To make a path from an existing selection, click the Make work path from selection button or select Make Work Path from the Panel menu. Until now, you have learned to create and edit a path. Next, you learn to save the path.

Saving a Path

When you draw a path with Pen Tool, Photoshop creates a work path that appears in the Paths panel. A work path defines the outline of a shape. It appears temporarily in the Paths panel. In Photoshop CS6, you can also save paths and apply them on different images. The paths can be saved with a specified name given by you. Perform the following steps to save a path:

1. **Open** a Photoshop document and **create** a path that you want to save.

2. Select the **Save Path** option from the <u>Paths</u> panel menu. It opens the Save Path dialog box.

3. **Type** a name in the <u>Name</u> text box. In our case, we type **New Path**. Then click the **OK** button to save the work path. As a result the path is saved.

Lesson 5
Making Photoshop Selections

Photoshop CS6 is primarily an image editing software and uses pixels to represent an image. When you edit an image, Photoshop CS6 actually modifies the underlying pixels, which are the basic components of any image. You can either edit all the pixels in the image or select the pixels in a specific portion to edit. Selection of the pixels is the most significant stage while editing an image in Photoshop. It helps you isolate the portion of the image you want to edit from the portion that you do not want to edit. The unselected portion is not affected when you perform an operation, such as applying effects and filters or moving a selection. After you make a selection, you can fill it with color or pixels from the image's background, add an outline, resize or transform it, or use it as mask.

In Photoshop CS6, you make selections using one of the selection tools, such as Rectangular Marquee Tool, Lasso Tool, and Quick Selection Tool. You can also make selections based on size, shape, and color. For instance, you can create any shape using shape tools and later convert the shape into a selection; or use a command, such as Color Range to make selections based on colors. In addition, you can copy, paste, and move selections from one image to another. Moreover, you can also save a selection as an alpha channel, which stores selections as grayscale images. These types of selections are called masks. A mask hides the unselected image area and does not allow you to edit the masked area. You can also use the alpha channel to load the mask as a selection.

In this chapter, you will learn about making selection in different ways by using various selection tools, such as Elliptical Marquee Tool, Magnetic Lasso Tool, Quick Selection Tool, and Magic Wand Tool; and commands, such as Color Range available in Photoshop. You will also learn to create a path using Pen Tool and convert the path into a selection. Then, you will learn to modify selections by expanding, refining, or inversing selections. Further, you will learn to fill a selection, scale a selection, warp a selection, and reshape a selection using the Puppet Warp command. In the end, you will learn how to save a selection for further use and load a saved selection. Let's begin the chapter by learning how to make selections using selection tools.

Making a Selection with Selection Tools

Making a selection is a two-step process. First, you select one of the selection tools in the Tools panel. Second, you drag or click on the image to select specific portion of the image. You can also refine your selection by adding to or subtracting from the selection using several options in the Options bar. Photoshop CS6 provides three broad ways of making selections: Shape-based selection, tolerance-based selection, and color-based selection. There are different types of tools for each type of selection. For instance, to make shape-based selection, you can use selection tools or shape tools. Photoshop CS6 provides a number of selection tools, such as marquee tools, lasso tools, Quick Selection Tool, and Magic Wand Tool, which are used in different ways to make selections of different shapes and sizes. Let's discuss how to make selections using various selection tools, starting with the marquee tools.

Using Marquee Tools

Marquee selection tools help you select desired areas of an image in geometrical shapes. You can select portions of an image in rectangular, square, elliptical, or a single row or column shaped selection by using various marquee tools. When you use marquee tools to select an image area, the selected area of the image is surrounded by a marquee selection also known as marching ants.

When you click and hold Rectangular Marquee Tool in the Tools panel, which is selected by default, a flyout appears that includes other marquee selection tools. You can release the mouse-pointer over any of the tool in the flyout to select it. The marquee tool flyout contains the following tools:

- **Rectangular Marquee Tool:** Selects portions of an image in the shape of a rectangle of square. It creates a square marquee selection if you hold the Shift key down while making the selection.
- **Elliptical Marquee Tool:** Selects portions of an image in an elliptical or circular shape. It creates a circular marquee selection if you hold the Shift key down while making the selection.
- **Single Row Marquee Tool:** Selects a single row of pixels of an image.
- **Single Column Marquee Tool:** Selects a single column of pixels of an image.

After knowing about the functions of the marquee tool, perform the following simple steps on your computer to make a selection using a marquee selection tool:

1. **Open** an image in Photoshop in which you want to make selection.

2. **Select** a marquee selection tool in the Tools panel. In our case, we select **Rectangular Marquee Tool**, as shown in picture 5.0 with the arrow numbered 2.

Now you can see on your screen that when you select a marquee tool, the mouse pointer changes to plus sign.

Picture 5.0

3. **Drag** the mouse-pointer over the area you want to select. In our case, the marquee selection border appears, as shown in picture 5.0 with the arrow numbered 3.

In our case, we have created a rectangular marquee selection. However, you can also create a square marquee selection by holding down the Shift key while making a selection. Likewise, you can drag a circular or elliptical marquee selection using Elliptical Marquee Tool. You can also reposition the selection marquee in the image by pressing and holding the Spacebar key, while making the selection.

Notice a pop-up information box appearing when you make a selection. This provides information about the width and height of the selection. Photoshop CS6's new feature, the pop-up information box provides you the basic information, such as dimensions and degree of rotation when you make, move, and transform a selection or shape.

You can also reposition the selection after you create it. In this case, place the selection tool's mouse-pointer inside the selection. Then click and drag the selection to a new location. In addition, you can press the Shift key to constrain the movement to a straight line. All the other marquee tools follow the same approach as Rectangular Marquee Tool. When you select a marquee tool, the Options bar displays the settings related to the selected tool, as shown in picture 5.1. Below the picture, we discuss various options in the Options bar for Rectangular Marquee Tool:

Picture 5.1

- **Tool Preset picker:** Provides presets that you can use to make selection.
- **New selection:** Creates a new selection if selected. By default, this option is selected. The previous selection, if any, is discarded when you select this option.
- **Add to selection:** Adds new areas to the existing selection. The new selection is added to the existing selection and both selections are treated as a single selection. If the new selection is dragged overlapping the existing selection, then Photoshop merges the selection.
- **Subtract from selection:** Subtracts the overlapping portion from an existing selection. To subtract, the new selection must overlap the previous selection. When this option is selected, the overlapping portion gets deselected.
- **Intersect with selection:** Selects only the overlapping portion of two selections. In case, the new selection does not overlap the existing selection, no changes made to the selection.
- **Feather:** Creates soft edges around the selection so that it blends into the background or another image. This process is known as feathering. You must enter a value in pixels in the Feather field before you create the selection, as it applies to the next selection you make.
- **Anti-alias:** Creates a blurred, softer-edged selection. This option is enabled only when Elliptical Marquee Tool is active. You must specify Anti-alias option before using the selection tools. You cannot add anti-aliasing to a selection that is already made.
- **Style:** Provides a number of styles with which you can make a selection. When you click down-arrow beside the Style option, a dropdown list appears with the following options:
      Normal: Creates a default normal (unconstrained) selection.
      Fixed Ratio: Creates proportional selections where height and width are in proportion. This option enables the Width and Height options in the Options bar.
      Fixed Size: Creates selections of specific dimensions. This option enables the Width and Height options in the Options bar. You have to specify the height and width values for a selection area in the Height and Width text boxes respectively.
- **Refine Edge:** Lets you refine the edges of a selection. When you click this button on the Options bar, the Refine Edge dialog box appears that enables you view the current selection against different backgrounds for easy editing. By default, the Refine Edge button is enabled only when there is a selection. The Refine Edge feature is discussed in detail later in this chapter. In the next section, let's learn to make a selection using lasso tools.

Using Lasso Tools

Marquee tools let you make selections in a pre-defined shape, such as rectangular, square, elliptical, and circular. However, the lasso tools let you make freeform selection that is you can select any kind of irregular shapes. Lasso tools are used when you want to make precise selection without using conventional marquee tools. Photoshop CS6 provides different types of lasso tools, such as Lasso Tool,

Polygon Lasso Tool, and Magnetic Lasso Tool to make selection. You can click and hold Lasso Tool in the Tools panel to access the various lasso tools present in the Lasso Tool flyout. You can click to select any of the tools in the flyout. The Lasso Tool flyout contains the following three tools:

- **Lasso Tool:** Makes freeform selection in an image. To make a selection, click and drag around the area you want to select.
- **Polygonal Lasso Tool:** Makes freeform straight-edged selections in an image. To make a selection, click multiple times surrounding the area you want to select. This tool is ideal to select objects with straight edges, such as buildings.
- **Magnetic Lasso Tool:** Makes selections by snapping to the distinct edges in the image. To make a selection using Magnetic Lasso Tool, click once to set a starting point, and then move the mouse-pointer closer to the area you want to select. You do not need to hold the mouse button down while moving it. Magnetic Lasso Tool makes quick selections based on the pixels below your cursor. This tool is ideal to make selections where there are distinct edges.

To complete the selection, simply return to the starting point and release your mouse button. In case of Polygon Lasso Tool and Magnetic Lasso Tool, click the starting point to complete the selection. You can also release the mouse button anywhere while making the selection. Photoshop automatically closes the selection by drawing a straight line between the start and end points. Now, perform the following steps to make a selection using a lasso tool:

1. **Open** an image in Photoshop, and **select** a lasso tool in the Tools panel. In our case, we select **Magnetic Lasso Tool**.

2. **Click** a point where you want to start. Then, **move** around the border of the object you want to select, as shown in picture 5.2.

3. **Click** the starting point to complete the selection. A small circle appears attached to Magnetic Lasso Tool when you place the cursor over the start point. The think black line changes to a marquee selection.

Along with the options discussed in the previous section, few additional options appear in the Options bar when Magnetic Lasso Tool is selected. Let's discuss these options briefly

Picture 5.2

- **Width:** Allows you to specify the distance from within which the tool detects edges. For instance, if you enter 10 in the Width textbox, the tool selects pixels that are within a distance of 10 pixels from the cursor.
- **Contrast:** Specifies how precisely Magnetic Lasso Tool makes a selection in and around an image. The higher the value of this option, the greater is the contrast between the edges and the background. The value is measured in percentage and can range from 1% to 100%.

- **Frequency:** Allows you to specify the rate at which the tool sets anchor points. The value for this option can range from 0 to 100.
- **Pen Width:** Changes the edges width of your pen tablet using pen pressure. When this option is selected, the edges width decreases.

Keep in mind that you need to keep the cursor close to the edge to make a precise selection using Magnetic Lasso Tool. The anchor points appear automatically, as you keep moving the mouse-pointer. Anchor points, also known as fastening points, are editable points that appear around the border of an image. Anchor points help you to edit selection by expanding or contracting them. You can press the Backspace key to delete or undo the placement of anchor points during the selection.

You are now familiar with the various shape-based selection tools in Photoshop which will help you in editing the images. In addition to these tools, Photoshop CS6 has the tolerance-based selection tools, such as Magic Wand Tool and Quick Selection Tool. In the next section, let's learn about Quick Selection Tool.

Using Quick Selection Tool

Quick Selection Tool provides an easy way to make selection by painting over the desired area in an image. To make selections, simply click and drag the mouse-pointer over the area that you want to select. Its cursor appears as a brush-tip with a plus sign inside it. The size of its brush-tip can be increased or decreased.

In the Options bar, click the down arrow beside the Brush picker. A dropdown list appears with the Size, Hardness, and Spacing options. You can also change the Angle and Roundness options. The options for Quick Selection Tool, such as New Selection, Add to selection, and Subtract from selection, appear in the Options bar. You can click a respective button to turn on/off an option. You can also toggle between the Add to selection by keeping the Shift key pressed; and the Subtract from selection option by keeping Alt key pressed. Perform the following simple steps on your computer to make a selection using Quick Selection Tool:

1. **Open** an image in Photoshop, and click **Quick Selection Tool** in the Tools panel. The mouse pointer changes to a rounded brush with a cross-hair (plus sign) inside.

2. **Click** and **drag** the mouse-pointer over the area to start selection. As you drag, the marquee selection expands outwards and automatically snaps to the distinct edge in the image. You need to continue dragging the mouse-pointer until you select the area.

When making selection using Quick Selection Tool, start from the center and gradually move towards the edge for better result. You can also use smaller brush size to select finer details. To increase the brush tip size, press the right bracket (]) key and press the left ([) bracket key to decrease the brush tip size.

If you happen to over select an area in the image, then you can deselect it by clicking the Subtract from selection (Quick Selection Tool with a minus sign) button in the Options bar or hold down the Alt key and drag over the area that you wish to deselect. So, after learning about Quick Selection Tool, let's now learn to make selections using Magic Wand Tool.

Using Magic Wand Tool

Magic Wand Tool is used to select contiguous or detached areas of the same color. The selection depends on a value referred to as the tolerance setting. If you specify higher tolerance value, a wider range of pixels is selected. You can change the tolerance value using the Tolerance option in the Options bar. In Photoshop, Magic Wand Tool is present in Quick Selection Tool flyout. When you click Magic Wand Tool, the Options bar displays the options for Magic Wand Tool. The additional options available for Magic Wand Tool in the Options bar are:

- **Tolerance:** Determines the similarity of the pixels that will be selected. Enter a value ranging from 0 to 255. The default Tolerance value is 32. A low value selects few colors that are very similar to the pixel you click. A higher value selects a broader range of colors. Tolerance setting determines the range of luminosity values that are also selected.
- **Contiguous:** Selects only adjacent areas of the clicked or selected colors. If you wish to select similar color but in non-adjacent areas, then uncheck this option.
- **Sample All Layers:** Selects colors using data from all the visible layers. By default, Magic Wand Tool selects colors from the active layer only. Perform the following steps to make a selection using Magic Wand Tool:

1. **Open** an image, and click **Magic Wand Tool** from the Quick Selection Tool flyout.

2. **Click** the blue color (in our case) in the image, as shown in picture 5.3.

Depending on the color shade you clicked, the selection appears. In our case, the selection with default Tolerance value (32) appears.

3. **Type** 160 and press **Enter** key in the Tolerance text box in the **Options bar**.

4. Choose **Select> Deselect** from the Menu bar or press Ctrl+D keys together to deselect the existing selection.

Picture 5.3

5. **Click** the same blue color (in our case) in the image that you clicked in step 2. This time with a higher tolerance value, the selection appears to cover more area.

As with other selection tools, you can add more area to the selection by holding down the Shift key, while holding the Alt key lets you subtract areas from the selection. Next, let's learn to make color-based selection using the Color Range command.

Using the Color Range Command

The Color Range command selects areas of your image based on a single color or range of colors. You can specify the sample color or color range using the Color Range dialog box. Open the Color Range dialog box by selecting Select> Color Range from the Menu bar. However, you cannot apply the Color

Range command on 32-bits per channel images. Unlike, Magic Wand Tool that tends to select solid pixels, the Color Range command tends to select more transparent pixels than solid pixels. This results softer edge selections. Now you can perform the following steps to use the Color Range command to make a selection:

1. **Open** an image to make a selection using the Color Range command. In our case, we want to select the green color of the image shown in picture 5.4.

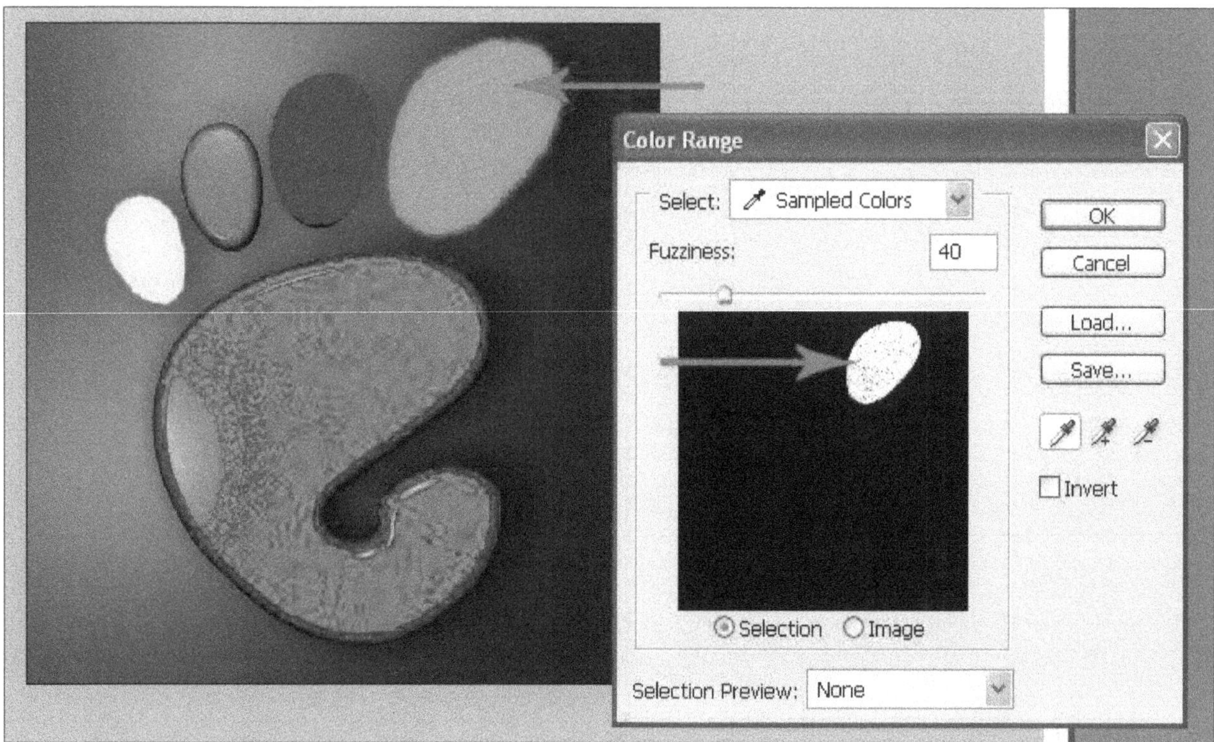

Picture 5.4

2. Choose **Select> Color Range** from the Menu bar to open the Color Range dialog box. You can see the Selection Preview box. There are two options for the thumbnail preview which are as follows:

- **Selection:** Previews the selection that will result from the colors you sample in the image. By default, white areas are selected pixels, black areas are unselected, and gray areas are partially selected.
- **Image:** Previews the entire image. For instance, you might want to sample from a part of the image that is not visible.

3. **Move** the mouse-pointer over the image, the pointer appears as an eyedropper and then **click** in the image to select a color.

If you look at your Photoshop window, you can also notice that the Selection Preview box in the Color Range dialog box highlights the range of colors that will be selected if you click the OK button. Now you can see limited color is selected when a single sample color is picked. You can add more color shades by adding more samples to the existing color. The Add to Sample icon in the Color Range dialog box allows you to add more samples.

4. Click the **Add to Sample** icon (icon with a + sign) in the <u>Color Range</u> dialog box.

5. **Click** another shade of color to add to the selection. Repeat this step multiple times to add all the shades of colors to the selection.

If you add colors that you do not want to include in the selection, select the Subtract from Sample icon and then click the color you want to remove.

6. **Adjust** the range of colors using the Fuzziness slider or by entering a value in the text box. Then click the OK button in the Color Range dialog box.

The Select dropdown list at the top of the Color Range dialog box allows you to select specific colors that you want to include in the selection. This option is automatically set to Sampled Colors, which lets you select a color from the image. You can also select a specific color from the Select dropdown list and click the OK button to select that color only.

The Out of Gamut option in the Select dropdown list works only on RGB and Lab color mode images. If you are selecting multiple color ranges or adjacent pixels in the image, select Localized Color Clusters option to build a more accurate selection. When this option is selected, the Range slider becomes active. Keep in mind that an out of gamut color is the color that a color system or printer cannot display or print.

Making a Selection Using Pen Tool

In Photoshop CS6, Pen Tool is frequently used to create variety of shapes by tracing part of an image. You can create precise selection based on paths using Pen Tool. One of benefits of using paths is that you can convert them into selections at any time. This eliminates the need for creating a new selection from scratch every time when required. Perform the following steps to make a selection using Pen Tool:

1. **Open** an image in Photoshop, and select **Pen Tool** in Tools panel.

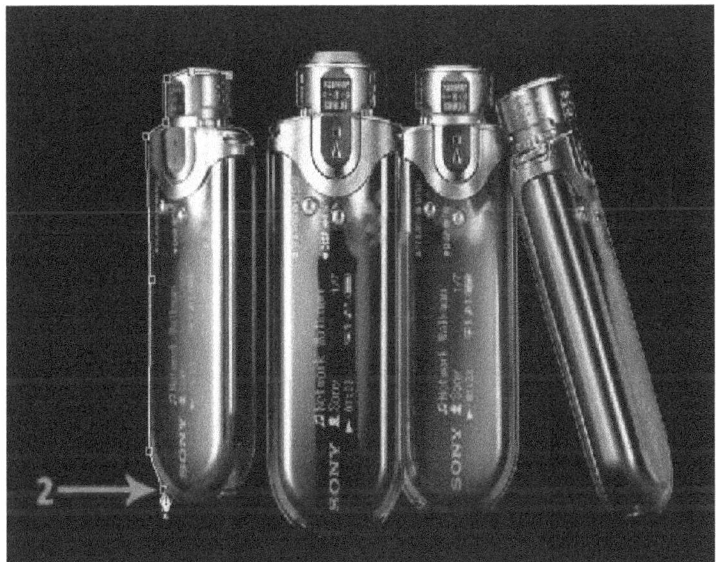

Picture 5.5

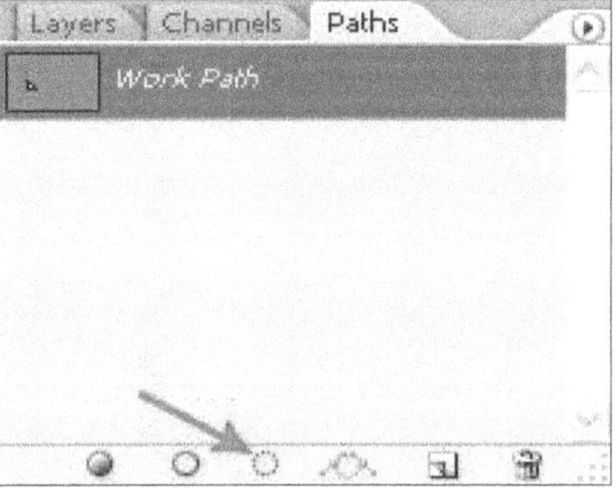

Picture 5.6

2. **Make** a path using <u>Pen Tool</u> surrounding the edge of your image, as shown in picture 5.5 with the red arrow numbered 2.

3. **Click** the starting anchor point to close the path. Then click the **Load path as a selection** button in the <u>Paths</u> panel, as shown in picture 5.6.

The selection marquee appears in the image. You can also use the Make Selection option from the Panel menu of the Paths panel to make a selection from a path.

Modifying a Selection

In most cases, while making selection, you need to modify the selection to improve or refine the selection. A selection can be modified in a number of ways in Photoshop CS6. For instance, a selection made by Lasso Tool or any other selection tools or commands can be modified by expanding or contracting.

You can copy and paste a selection in Photoshop; you can also add area to the current selection or remove area from a selection. In this section, you will learn about – Expanding a selection, Refining a selection, and Making an inverse selection. Let's first learn to add to or subtract from a selection.

Expanding a Selection

Adding and subtracting pixels from an existing selection is the most common modification made to refine the selection. When you make a selection by using a selection tool or command, it is likely that you may miss an area you want to select. In such a case, press and hold the Shift key along with the selection tool, and then select the area you want to add to the selection. The new selection will be added to the perspective one. Similarly, if you wish to subtract or remove an area from the original selection, press and hold the Alt key with the selection tool and reselect the area you want to remove from the selection.

These commands are similar to the Add to selection and Subtract from selection buttons present in the Options bar when a selection tool is active. Perform the following steps on your computer to add or subtract from a selection:

1. **Open** an image and make a selection using a selection tool. In our case, we make the selection using **Elliptical Marquee Tool**.

2. Press and hold the **Shift** key down on your keyboard and **drag** over the area you want to include in the selection.

Another way to add to a selection is by using the Expand commands. As the names suggests, the Expand command is used to expand the area of an existing selection. You can also use the Contract command to contract or reduce the area of an existing selection by a specific value. You can perform the following steps to use the <u>Expand</u> command to add to the selection:

1. **Make** a selection that you want to expand to a specific value. Then choose Select> Modify> Expand from the Menu bar. It opens the <u>Expand Selection</u> dialog box.

2. **Type** the new value in the Expand By text box as per the requirement. In our case, the value is set to **100** pixels.

3. Click the **OK** button in the dialog box. As a result, the selection in the image expands by 100 pixels. Similarly, you can use the Contract command in Photoshop to contract or reduce the selection by the specified value.

Refining Selection Outline

Although you can refine a selection using various options available under the Modify command, Photoshop CS6 offers a special command for refining selection outlines, called Refine Edge. Refine Edge enables you to enhance your selection by setting the selection against different backgrounds. This is an advanced tool for cleaning up those unwanted selection that do not give you precise selection results. The Refine Edge feature is available as a command or as an option for most of the selection tools. To use the Refine Edge dialog box, click the Refine Edge button in the Options bar when a selection tool is active, or choose Select> Refine Edge from the Menu bar. Perform the following steps to refine a selection outline in Photoshop:

1. **Open** an image and **make** a selection that you want to refine. Then click the **Refine Edge** button on the Options bar.

The Refine Edge dialog box appears as well as the unselected portion of the image fills with white color by default.

2. **Press** the Ctrl and + keys together to zoom in the image so that you can see the change. In our case, we change the Smooth and Contrast values.

3. **Drag** the slider handle for the Smooth option set its value to **30**. Then **drag** the slider handle for Contrast option to set its value to **70**.

4. Click the **OK** button to apply the changes. The result of the modification appears simultaneously on your screen.

You can set the selection against different backgrounds using the View Mode option as per your requirement. Let's discuss the options available in the Refine Edge dialog box:

View Mode: Allows you to choose a display mode for the selection from the dropdown list. The default is On White (W). You can cycle through these modes by pressing the F key. The Show Original option displays the original selection for comparison; while the Show Radius option displays the selection border where edge refinement occurs when selected.

Refine Radius Tool: Enables you to precisely adjust the border area in which edge refinement occurs using a brush. You can adjust the brush size by pressing the bracket keys.

Smart Radius: Adjusts the radius for hard and soft edges of the selection. Clear the checkbox, if the border is uniformly hard or soft edged, or if you want to control the Radius setting and refinement brushes more precisely.

Radius: Specifies the size of the selection border in which edge refinement occurs. You can use a small radius for sharp edges, and a large radius for softer edges.

Smooth: Reduces irregular areas in the selection and creates a smooth outline.

Feather: Adds a soft-edged transition between the edges of a selection and the surrounding pixels by blurring the transition. Using large values in this option creates soft transitions.

Contrast: Improves the crispness of soft edges, and removes fuzzy edges of a selection. This option also removes the effects created because of a high Radius value.

Shift Edge: Moves selection outline inward with negative values or outward with positive ones.

Decontaminate Colors: Replaces color fringes with the color of fully selected pixels nearby. The strength of color replacement is proportionate to the softness of selection edges.

Amount: Changes the level of decontamination and fringe replacement.

Output To: Determines whether the refined selection becomes a selection or mask on the current layer, or produces a new layer or document.

In this section, you have learnt about the powerful Refine Edge feature of Photoshop. Next, let's learn how to inverse a selection in Photoshop.

Making Inverse Selection

The Inverse command helps you to select the unselected area. You can use this command to change a part of the selection area by selecting the simple or smaller part and then inverting the selection. You can make the selection using any of the selection tools. In most cases it is used to separate an object from its background in an image. Perform the following simple steps to invert a selection using the Inverse command:

1. **Open** an image and make a selection. In our case, we want to change the background of the image.

2. Choose **Select> Inverse** from the Menu bar. As a result, the current selection inverses and selects the background.

After selecting the background, you can fill it with a different color. In the next section, you will learn to fill the selection with current foreground color. You will also learn to scale and warp a selection. In addition, you will learn how to use the Puppet Warp command.

Working with Selection

A selection can be transformed by using transformation options available in Photoshop CS6, such as scaling and rotating. Photoshop provides the facility to change the orientation and scale of a selection. A selection can be easily rotated, skewed, scaled, or distorted to form a different selection outline. You can apply transformations to a selection, an entire layer, multiple layers, or a layer mask. You can also apply transformations to a path, a vector shape, a vector mask, a selection border, or an alpha channel. Note that transforming affects the overall quality of the image. Keep in mind that you can use smart objects to apply non-destructive transformations to raster images. Let's first learn how to fill a selection with current foreground and background color.

Filling a Selection with a Color

Most of your work in Photoshop begins with a selection that is made using different ways, and many times, you need to fill the selection with a desired color. In Photoshop, you can fill the selection with the current foreground or background colors. You can also fill your selection with a pattern. You learn more about pattern later in this book. Perform the following simple steps on your computer to fill a selection with a color:

1. **Make** a selection that you want to fill with a color.

2. Select **Edit> Fill** from the Menu bar or press the **Shift+F5** keys to open the Fill dialog box.

3. Select the **Foreground Color** option from the Use dropdown list. Then click the **OK** button to fill the selection with the foreground color.

You can also use the Use dropdown list to fill a selection with the current background color, a user-defined color, a pattern, a history, etc. The options in the Use dropdown list are described as follows:

Foreground Color: Fills the selection with the current Foreground color.
Background Color: Fills the selection with the current Background color.
Color: Enables you to select a new color from the Color Picker dialog box.
Content-Aware: Fills the selection seamlessly with the similar pixel surrounding the selection.
Pattern: Fills the selection with the selected pattern. The Custom pattern option activates and enables you to select from the list of available patterns.
History: Restores the selected area to the source state or snapshot set in the HISTORY panel.
Black: Fills the selection with black.
50% Gray: Fills the selection with 50% gray.
White: Fills the selection with white.

Alternatively, you can press the Alt and the Backspace keys simultaneously to fill the selection with the current foreground color and press the Ctrl and the Backspace keys together to fill the selection with the current background color. Now, let's learn about scaling a selection outline in the next section.

Scaling Selection Outline

Scaling refers to changing the size of a selection outline. You can enlarge or reduce a selection outline relative to its reference point, which is located at the center by default. You can scale horizontally, vertically, or both horizontally and vertically. In Photoshop CS6, you can use the Transform Selection option to scale your selection outline. You can right-click your selection and select the Transform Selection command from the context menu or choose Select Transform Selection from the Menu bar.

The Transform Selection commands let you scale, rotate, skew, distort, apply perspective, and warp your selection outline in different ways. The important point to note is that this command only transforms the selection outline. In other words, it rotates or scales the selection outline, not the actual pixels inside selection perform the following steps to scale a selection:

1. **Open** an image and **make** a selection.

2. **Right-click** inside the selection marquee and select the **Transform Selection** option from the context menu. A bounding box appears surrounding the selection. The bounding box has eight handles, which are represented by small boxes and a reference point in the center of the selection.

3. **Right-click** inside the bounding box and select the **Scale** option from the context menu.

4. **Drag** the top-right handle upward to enlarge the selection. Then press the **Enter** key or double-click inside the bounding box to exit the transformation mode. The selection marquee appears replacing the bounding box.

5. Press the **Ctrl+Backspace** keys together to fill the selection with current background color.

Similarly, you can transform a selection outline using the other options available in the context menu. The remaining options available in the context menu are:

Rotate: Rotates the selection with random degree of rotation. The information box shows the exact rotation degree.
Skew: Slants a selection vertically and horizontally. Drag the transformation handles to skew.
Distort: Stretches a selection in all directions.
Perspective: Adds perspective to the selection.
Warp: Manipulates the shape of a selection, shape, or path.
Rotate 180, Rotate 90 CW, and Rotate 90 CCW: Rotates the selection by the specified number of degrees, either clockwise or counterclockwise. Use the negative value to rotate counterclockwise.
Flip: Flips the selection vertically or horizontally.

In this section, you have learnt to transform a selection outline using the Transform Selection command. Next, let's learn how to transform the actual pixels inside the selection in Photoshop.

Scaling Actual Pixels

As discussed earlier, the Transform Selection command only transforms the selection outline. The pixels inside the selection outline remain unaffected. If you wish to transform the actual pixels inside the selection, you need to use the Transform command under the Edit menu. The Transform command offers all those commands that are available under Transform Selection command. Although you can achieve some special effects using this command, the disadvantage is that the pixels lose their sharpness when distorted and are pixelated when scaled. Perform the following steps to scale a selection in an image using the Transform command:

1. **Open** an image and select an area by using a selection tool. In our case, we make a selection using Rectangular Marquee Tool.

2. Choose **Edit> Transform> Scale** from the Menu bar. The marquee selection is converted into a bounding box, which indicates that you are in the transformation mode.

3. **Drag** the top-right handle in the bounding box upward to scale the selection. The actual pixels enlarge.

4. Press the **Enter** key on the keyboard to exit the transformation mode.

As a result, the selection appears enlarged. Next, let's learn to warp a selection using the Transform command.

Warping a Selection using the Transform command

The Warp transformation allows you to drag control points that manipulate the pixels inside a selection. The Warp transformation is quite different compared to the other transformations, such as scaling and rotating. When you select the Warp option, a mesh appears over your object, which you can adjust by dragging control points, lines, or any other area inside the mesh. Additionally, you can apply a preset warp from the options bar. Warping distorts and stretches pixels inside the selection. Perform the following steps to warp a selection in an image using the Transform command:

1. **Open** an image and **select** an area by using a selection tool.

2. Select **Edit> Transform> Warp** from the Menu bar. A mesh surrounding the marquee selection appears. The mesh has control points that you can move to adjust warp. By default, the control points are aligned to the external boundaries.

3. **Move** the control points as per the shape you wish to convert. The shape of the mesh changes according.

4. Press the **Enter** key to exit the transformation mode. Then **deselect** the marquee selection by pressing the **Ctrl+D** keys together.

Using Puppet Warp

The Puppet Warp command was introduced in Photoshop CS5. It provides a visual mesh that lets you radically distort/reshape specific image areas, while leaving other areas intact. You can achieve various effects ranging from shaping hair to realistically transforming arms and legs. For instance, you can reposition a hand in a photograph that is awkwardly positioned in the initial image. You can apply the Puppet Warp command to shape, text layers, smart objects, or layer and vector masks in addition to image area. You add number of pins to the mesh, when you move a pin in the mesh; adjoining pins keep the nearby area intact. Perform the following steps to use the Puppet Warp command:

1. **Open** an image to use the Puppet Warp command.

2. Double-click the **Background layer** in the Layers panel and click the **OK** button in the New Layer dialog box to convert it to a normal layer. The Puppet Warp command does not work on the locked Background layer.

3. **Select** the image area that you want to reshape. Then choose Edit> Puppet Warp from the Menu bar. A puppet mesh appears over the selected image area.

You can see several options for the Puppet Warp command in the Options bar. The available options in the Options bar are:

Mode: Determines the elasticity of the puppet mesh. Distort option in the Mode dropdown list stretches the puppet mesh maximum; while the Rigid option stretches the minimum. By default, Mode option is set to Normal.

Density: Determines the spacing of the puppet mesh. The Fewer Points option in the Density dropdown list creates fewer meshes and the More Points option creates more and smaller meshes.

Expansion: Expands or contracts the outer edge of the puppet mesh. The default value is 2.

Show Mesh: Displays the mesh when selected. Deselect to display only the pins, and hide the mesh.

Pin Depth: Changes the stacking order of the pins, where a Puppet Warp distortion results in elements or pins overlapping each other.

Rotate: Sets the pin rotation. Fixed option in the Rotate dropdown list rotates the pin with the value mentioned in the text box beside the Rotate dropdown list.

4. **Add** pins by clicking the points in the puppet mesh that you want to remain intact. You can notice that the selected pin appears with a black dot inside. You can also click and drag these pins to move the mesh.

5. **Add** more pins in the area you want to move in the puppet mesh. In our case, we add extra pins in the hands and legs to reshape our image.

Keep in mind that you can select a pin and press the Delete key to delete the pin. You can select and move multiple pins simultaneously. To select multiple pins, hold-down the Shift key and click pins that you want to select.

6. **Click** and **drag** the pins to reshape the mesh. Similarly, you can adjust other pins to get the desired result.

7. Press **Enter** key or click the **Commit Puppet Warp** button on the Options bar to apply the transformation.

8. Press the **Ctrl+D** keys together to deselect. As a result, the reshaped image appears on your screen.

Until now, you have learnt about the different methods to transform a selection. In the next section, you will learn how to save a selection and reuse it by loading into the same image or into a different image.

Saving and Loading a Selection

Saving a selection saves lots of time. When you save a selection, it is saved with the Photoshop document. Photoshop CS6's native format (PSD) supports the saving of a selection. In Photoshop CS6, you can save your selections and reload them anytime as per the requirement. This is especially useful when making detailed selections that you might want to reuse. The Save Selection command works with the Channels panel. When you save a selection, a new channel is created in the Channels panel with the name you provide while saving the selection. Perform the following steps to first save a selection and then load the selection:

1. **Open** an image and **make** a selection with a selection tool. Then choose **Select> Save Selection** from the Menu bar.

As you can notice, the Load Selection is not active by default. It becomes enabled when you save a selection.

The **Save Selection** dialog box appears. This dialog box has two groups: **Destination** and **Operation**. The file name of the current image appears in the Document dropdown list of the Destination group. The

Destination group also contains the Channel dropdown list and Name text boxes. The Operation group provides several radio buttons to specify how the new selection is saved. All these options are active if there is a saved selection.

2. **Select** an option from the Document dropdown list if you want to save a selection other than the current document. In our case, the default name is selected, which is the name of the current document.

3. **Type** the name for the selection in the Name text box. Then click the **OK** button to save the selection as new channel.

By default, the New Channel radio button is selected. If there is a selection saved before, you can add, subtract, or intersect the new selection with the saved selection using other radio button present in the Operation group. After you have saved the selection, you can reload it anytime, even after you reopen the file. When you open your file again, notice that the new channel that is created is still there in the Channels panel. The selection is saved with the assigned name, in the Channels panel.

The new channel created is known as alpha channel. Where the white portion defines the selected area and the black portion defines the unselected area. You can perform the following steps to load the selection:

4. **Deselect** the earlier selection by pressing the **Ctrl+D** keys together.

5. Choose **Select> Load Selection** from the Menu bar. The Load Selection dialog box appears on your screen.

6. Click the **OK** button to load the selection with the default settings as displayed. Alternatively, you can click the thumbnail of the new channel created in the Channels panel, while holding down the Ctrl key to load the selection.

Lesson 6
Working with Layers and Masks

Photoshop allows you to modify images in two ways: destructively, and nondestructively. In destructive editing, you modify the original pixels of an image. You cannot retrieve the original pixels once you exceed the history limit or Undo level. By default, the Undo level is set to 20, which can be set up to 1000 in Photoshop. In nondestructive editing, you do not change the original pixels rather you use layers or mart objects to edit the image. In Photoshop, layers are stacks of individual images that are placed on top of one another; and play an integral part in nondestructive editing.

Layers give you the ability to separate individual elements of your design, and then modify those elements separately. You can also group layers together to help organize and manage your design. A layer can contain both transparent and opaque areas. You can see through the transparent areas of a layer to the layer below, while the opaque areas hide the underneath layer. In addition, you can reposition a part of layer by selecting it, and can also change the opacity of a layer to make its content partially visible. Using layers you can composite multiple images or add text and vector shapes. In addition, you can add special effects, such as drop shadows or bevel using layer styles.

A mask stores information about selection or layer visibility in the Channels panel. When you save a selection as a mask, it is referred as an alpha channel. Masks create transparent areas in the image. They help you remove elements of an image without physically erasing them. You can add masks to a layer by clicking the Add layer mask button at the bottom of the Layers panel. The Layers panel allows you to work with layers and masks.

In this chapter, you will first learn about the Layers panel. Next, you will learn how to create a new layer, create a new layer from selection, create layer group, merge layers, and delete a layer. You will also learn to apply blending modes and change layer opacity. In addition, you will learn to work with layer styles. Moreover, you will learn about masks including layer mask, vector mask, and channel mask; and use them for precise selections. In the end, you will learn to work in Quick Mask Mode of Photoshop. Let's begin the chapter by exploring the improved Layers panel in Photoshop CS6.

Exploring Layers Panel

The Layers panel is a panel that contains all the layers, layer groups, and layer effects in a Photoshop document. Using the Layers panel, you can create, delete, show, and hide layers. You can also create layer sets (layer groups), link two or more layers, and merge multiple layers using the Layers panel. You can access additional commands and options from the Layers panel menu. Photoshop CS6 has added a new layer filter feature in the Layers panel, which allows you to manage layers efficiently.

Before working on a layer, click to select a layer in the Layers panel. If you double-click a layer besides the layer name, the Layer Style dialog box opens. However, if you double-click the layer name, Photoshop allows you to rename the layer. The selected layer or layers appear highlighted.

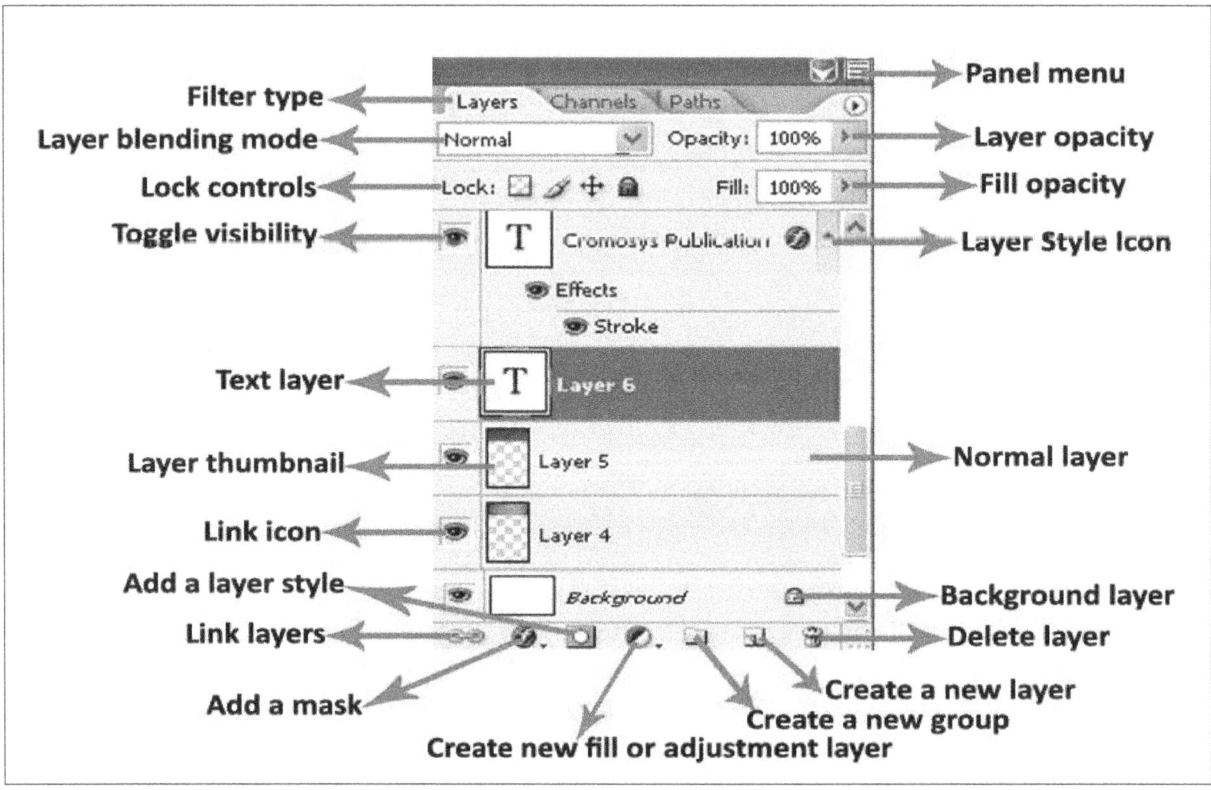

Picture 5.7

Photoshop's Layers panel can contain different layer types, including the Background layer, normal layers, type layers, and adjustment layers. The default workspace (Essentials) includes the Layers panel. In case the Layers panel is not visible on the screen, select Window> Layers from the Menu bar or alternatively, press the F7 key to display it. By default, the Layers panel is grouped with Channels and Paths panel, as shown above in picture 5.7.

In the Layers panel, as shown in the picture above, a layer thumbnail appears in each layer showing a small preview of the actual content of that layer. When you first open an image, it opens as a Background layer, which is by default locked and non-editable. The Background layer always appears at the bottom. To edit a Background layer, you need to convert it to a normal layer. To convert a Background layer to a normal layer, double-click the Background layer and then type a new layer name in the New Layer dialog box. By default, Photoshop names new layers with suffixing numerical, for instance Layer 0 and Layer 1.

At the top of the Layers panel, you can see several options in two rows. The options in the first row are the new additions to the Layers panel in Photoshop CS6. You click on an option to perform respective functions, as described below:

- **Filter type:** Lets you organize and manage layers. You can filter layers based on different categories: Name, Effect, Mode, and Color. For instance, if you filter the Effect category, all the layers that contain effects are displayed. You can also search a layer based on its name. Besides the filter type dropdown list, there are several icons that let you filter your pixel layers, adjustment layers, type layers, shape layers, and smart objects.
- **Blend Mode:** Determines how the pixels in a layer are blended with underlying pixels on the layers below. Using Blend Modes, you can create a wide variety of effects in Photoshop. You can select a Blend Mode from the dropdown list.
- **Layer opacity:** Adjusts the transparency of each layer. Click the down arrow of the Opacity pop-up slider; a slider bar appears. Drag the slider to increase or decrease the opacity of the selected layer. Zero (0%) is completely transparent, and 100% is completely opaque.
- **Lock transparent pixels:** Locks only the transparent areas of the layer and restricts any modification to the transparency.
- **Lock image pixels:** Locks the entire layer, including the transparent areas, and restricts any modification.
- **Lock position:** Prevents any kind of movement of the layer content, but you can make changes in the content.
- **Lock all:** Disables any kind of editing on the layer, similar to the Background layer that you have learnt about in the previous lesson.

At the bottom of the Layers panel, you can also see several buttons. You can click on these buttons to perform their respective functions, as described below:

- **Link layers:** Links two or more layers or groups. You can move and apply transformations on linked layers simultaneously. You can also create clipping masks from linked layers.
- **Add a layer style:** Adds style to the layer. Styles add visual effects, such as drop shadow, glow, bevel, and emboss to a layer; and thereby improves the appearance of the image. The list of the available styles appear as a dropdown list when you click the small black arrow present at the bottom right hand side corner of the Add a layer Style button.

- **Add layer mask:** Creates a mask layer, which is an extra layer above the original layer, and can be edited without damaging the original image.
- **Create new fill or adjustment layer:** Creates a new fill or adjustment layer. These layers allow non-destructive (can be undone anytime, even after closing the document) adjustment of colors to a layer.
- **Create a new group:** Creates a layer group from the selected layers and allows you to organize layers into folders.
- **Create new layer:** Creates a new normal blank layer. You can also drag an existing layer thumbnail to create a duplicate layer.
- **Delete layer:** Deletes the selected layer or layer group. You can either drag the thumbnail to the button or select the layer and click on the trash can (or Delete layer button).

In addition to all the commands mentioned above, the Layers panel has a panel menu. You can click the button at the top-right corner of the Layers panel to access the Layers panel menu. You can use the Layers panel menu to perform several tasks, such as create, delete, merge, and flatten layers. In addition, you can use the Layers panel menu to create layer groups, convert a layer into a smart object, and create clipping mask. You learn more about these options as you proceed with this chapter. Let's now learn how to work with layers in Photoshop CS6.

Working with Layers

As discussed earlier, layers can be referred to as sheets of pixels placed on top of one another. A layer can be opaque, transparent, or both. An opaque layer contains pixels that you can alter using various tools and commands in Photoshop. Picture 5.8 illustrates the layers in Photoshop.

Layers help you to extend your creative capabilities in many ways; whether by applying effects to the layer or blending different layers to create special effects. You can manipulate images endlessly and more efficiently in Photoshop CS6 with the help of layers. Photoshop offers the ability to control each and every pixel of single or multiple layered images. In next sections, you will learn how to work with layers:

Picture 5.8

1. Create a new layer 2. Create a new layer from a selection 3. Create a layer group 4. Hide or show layers 5. Merge layers 6. Align and distribute layers 7. Delete layers.

After knowing about layers, now we need to learn these things practically. So, let's proceed to learn how to create a new layer in Photoshop.

Creating a New Layer

A new layer is created to add a sheet of pixels to an image, where you can copy, paste, or create shapes, object, or image and edit them separately. You can create a new layer from the Layers panel as well as the Layer menu. In the Layers panel, you can click the Create a new layer button. Clicking the Create a new layer button does not open the New Layer dialog box; it directly creates the new layer.

Likewise, you can select the New Layer option from the Layers panel menu. In addition, you can make a selection, and then create a new layer from the selection. Perform the following steps to create a new layer in Photoshop:

1. In Photoshop CS6 program, **open** an image or **create** a new document in which you want to create a new layer.

2. Click **Layer> New> Layer** from the Menu bar or press the **Shift+Ctrl+N** keys together. It opens the New Layer dialog box.

3. **Type** a new name in the Name text box. In our case, we type **First Layer**. Then, **select** a color for the new layer from the Color dropdown list. In our case, we select **Red**, as shown in picture 5.9.

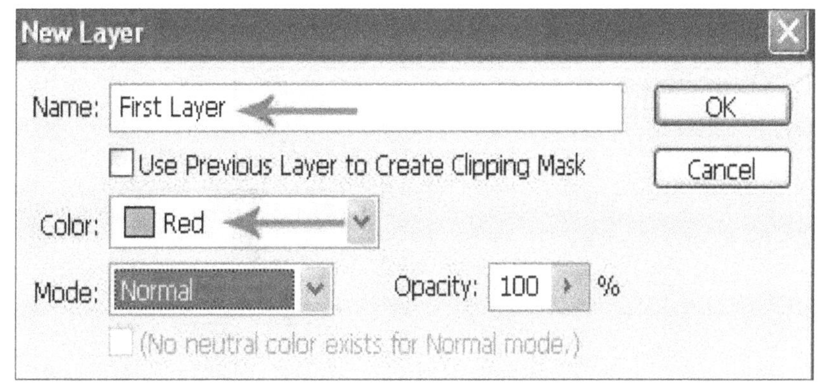

Picture 5.9

You can use the New Layer dialog box to assign a name and color to the layer, so that the layer can be easily indentified in the Layers panel. The default name always appears as Layer 1. You can also set the blending mode and opacity level for the layer in the New Layer dialog box. The default blending mode is set to Normal and the Opacity value is set to 100%.

4. Click the **OK** button with remaining options to their default. A blank layer colored red appears above the selected layer in the Layers panel.

When you create a new layer, it appears above the active layer by default. If you want to create the new layer below an active layer, hold down the Ctrl key and click the Create a new layer button at the bottom of the Layers panel. However, if there is no layer selected, the new layer always appears at the top of the layer stack. You can copy the Background layer by dragging it onto the Create a new layer button and work on the copied layer instead of converting it to a normal layer. Now, let's learn to create a new layer from a selection.

Creating a New Layer from a Selection

In Photoshop, you can create a layer in variety of ways. You can either create a new layer from scratch or from an existing layer by selecting a portion of it. Photoshop's Layer Via Copy and Layer Via Cut commands in the Layer menu allow you to create new layers. The Layer Via Copy command copies the selected pixels (selection) to a new layer while the Layer Via Cut command moves the selected pixels to a new layer. Moving pixels to a new layer creates a transparent area in the current layer. You can copy the selected pixels to a new layer in the currently open Photoshop document or to another Photoshop document. Perform the following steps to create a new layer from a selection:

1. **Open** an image and **make** a marquee selection. In our case, we use Polygonal Lasso Tool to make the selection.

2. Select **Layer> New> Layer Via Copy** from the Menu bar. A new layer with the name Layer 1 is created with the selected pixels.

The selected pixels are automatically copied from the Background layer (or the layer from which the selection is copied). The new created layer is displayed in Layers panel. Alternatively, you can press Ctrl+J keys together to create a layer via copy or press Ctrl+Shift+J to create a layer via cut.

Creating a Layer Group

In Photoshop CS6, managing complex designs that include hundreds of layers has always been challenging. Photoshop provides several features that help to optimize workflow while working with multiple layers. For instance, you can group color related layers or group multiple layers. Grouping allows you to gather layers into folders called layer groups. You can make a layer group from similar or related layers. You can also expand and collapse layer groups like the folders on your monitor screen. Perform the following steps to create a layer group in Photoshop:

1. **Open** a document that has multiple layers or **create** multiple layers in a new document.

2. **Select** the layers that you want to include in the layer group. Hold the **Shift** key down to select multiple layers.

3. Choose **Layer> New> Group from Layers** from the Menu bar. The New Group from Layers dialog box appears.

4. **Type** a name in the Name text box. In our case, we type **Transparency**. Then select a **color** from the color dropdown list. In our case, we select **Green**.

5. Click the **OK** button. As a result, a new layer group appears in the Layers panel.

By default, the new layer group appears in the collapsed form. You can click the right-arrow icon to expand the layer group. Layer groups not only help you save space in your Layers panel, but they also let you apply masks to all the layers in the group simultaneously. In Photoshop CS6, a handy new feature is the ability to collapse or expand all layer groups at the same time by clicking the right-arrow icon while holding the Ctrl key down.

Hiding and Showing Layers

When you hide a layer, its corresponding pixels no longer appear in the image. Therefore, you can hide pixels without deleting them. You can compare the appearance of the image with or without the content of a layer by showing or hiding layers respectively. When you hide a layer, the contents of that particular layer are removed from the screen, that is, they become hidden. Likewise, when you show the layer it reappears in your document. You can hide and show the layers of an image using the Layer menu or the Layers panel. Now, to understand this practically, perform the following simple steps to hide and show a layer:

1. **Open** a Photoshop document with multiple layers. In our case, all the layers are currently visible.

2. **Click** the eye icons for the layers that you want to hide. You can notice on your screen that the content of the layer is hidden in the Document window.

Similarly, you can click the eye icons again to show the hidden layers. Alternatively, you can select Layer> Hide Layers or Layer> Show Layers from the Menu bar to hide and show layers, respectively. To hide all layers except one, Alt+click on the eye icon for the layer you want to remain visible. You can Alt+click on the eye icon of the visible layer to reveal all hidden layers.

Merging Layers
In Photoshop, you can merge or flatten two or more layers or groups and convert them into single layer. When you complete editing the content of all the layers, you can merge them to reduce the size of the file, since the file size increases with the number of layers in a file. When you merge layers, the data on the top layers replaces any data overlapping with the lower layers. All the transparent areas in the merged layers remain transparent, if there are no pixels to overlap. Layers are merged permanently. You can only Undo to restore the merged layers. However, if you save a document with merged layers, you cannot revert back to the individual layers state.

When you merge layers, the layer at the top serves as the target layer. You cannot use an adjustment or fill layer as the target layer for a merge. You can also select the Merge Layers command from the Layers panel menu or press the Ctrl+E keys together to merge selected layers. Perform the following steps to merge layers into a single layer:

1. **Select** the layers you want to merge. In our case, we select three layers. As you know, to select more than one layer, click the layers while holding the **Ctrl key** down.

2. Choose **Layer> Merge Layers** from the Menu bar. As a result, Photoshop merges all the selected layers into the target layer. There are three commands available for merging layers in Photoshop, as follows:

- **Merge Layers:** Merges the selected layer and the layer below it or merges multiple layers.
- **Merge Down:** Merges the selected layer with the layer below it.
- **Merge Visible:** Merges all the visible layers into a single layer and ignores the hidden layers.
- **Flatten Image:** Merges all the visible layers into a single layer and converts the single layer into a Background layer.

Flattening is the process of merging all the visible layers and discarding the hidden layers, if any. You can flatten layers prior to exporting the image to a different file format or printing the image. Unlike Merge Layers and Merge Visible commands, the Flatten Image command fills any transparent areas with white. Let's now learn to align and distribute layers in Photoshop.

Aligning and Distributing Layers

In Photoshop, the Align commands automatically align or arrange layers either to each other or to selection edges; and Distribute commands evenly space selected layers. For instance, you can align the left edge of several shapes contained in a single layer or distribute several components in a work path along with their horizontal centers. You can align layers, selection outlines, shapes, paths, or mask. The Distribute commands evenly space the layers between the first and the last elements either horizontally or vertically. Perform the following steps to first align and then distribute selected layers in Photoshop:

1. **Open** a document having multiple layers. Then **select** all the layers in the Layers panel that you want to align.

In our case, the contents of all the layers are scattered all over the Photoshop window. We proceed and use the align command to arrange all the layers to the horizontal center of the document.

2. Choose **Layer> Align> Vertical Centers** from the Menu bar to align layers to the vertical centers. As a result, the layers on your screen now appear aligned.

You can also access these alignment and distribution commands from the Options bar. These commands are only available when Move Tool is active in the Tools panel. You can place the mouse-pointer above an icon to display the name of each alignment types in a tooltip.

Depending on the alignment type you choose, Photoshop aligns the layer element that is the farthest to the top, bottom, left, or right. If you align to the center, Photoshop splits the difference among the various layer elements.

3. Click the **Distribute horizontal centers** button in the distribution group of the Options bar.

The elements of the selected layers on your screen are now spaced evenly, that is the distance between two adjacent layers is equal. Now, let's learn how to delete a layer from the Layers panel.

Deleting Layers

Sometimes a document may contain layers that are no longer required. Such layers cause difficulty in the tracking and organization of layers and increase the file size. Therefore, to avoid clustering of layers in the Layers panel and reduce the file size, you can delete unwanted layers. You can delete a layer either from the Layer menu or from the Layers panel. You can also simply press the Delete key to delete the selected layer or layers. Perform the following steps to delete a layer:

1. **Select** a layer that you want to delete. Then choose **Layer> Delete> Layers** from the Menu bar. The Adobe Photoshop CS6 Extended message box appears.

2. Click the **Yes** button to confirm the deletion of the selected layers. As a result, the layers are deleted with its content in the Document window as well as disappear from the Layers panel.

You can also drag both the layers over the Delete layer button, present at the bottom of the Layers panel to quickly delete them. This method saves time and can be performed from the Layers panel. Now, let's learn about the layer opacity and blending modes in Photoshop.

Working with Opacity and Blend Modes

In Photoshop CS6, the layer opacity and blending modes are used to create sophisticated images by ghosting one image over another. Ghosting involves placing one image over another and conflating them by changing the opacity or blend modes. With Photoshop, you can adjust the opacity or fill of multiple layers simultaneously by selecting the layers and moving the Opacity slider. You can change the fill opacity in addition to the Opacity option, which affects the layer content as well as layer style (if any) applied to a layer. The Fill option only affects the interior opacity for the layer. Let's start by learning how to change the opacity using the Opacity option.

Changing the Layer Opacity

The Opacity option in the Layers panel affects the layer content and the layer styles. You can adjust the opacity in two ways; by selecting the desired layers in the Layers panel, and then either accessing the slider by clicking the right arrow, entering a percentage value in the Opacity text box, or simply scrubbing over the word Opacity in the Layers panel. Note that you cannot change the opacity for the Background layer. Perform the following steps to change the opacity and fill opacity of a layer:

1. **Open** a document with multiple layers. Then **select** the layers to change the opacity. In our case, we select multiple layers.

Picture 6.0

2. **Drag** the Opacity text slider in the Layers panel. In our case, we set the opacity value to **50%**, as shown in picture 6.0 with the black arrow.

The opacity changes to 50% for the selected layers while unselected layers remain unaffected. Similarly, you can change the fill opacity of a layer using the Fill option, which changes the interior content of the layer and does not affect the layer styles. You can also change the Opacity value by using keyboard shortcuts. With any active tool, except the painting or editing tools, press a numeric key. For instance, press the 6 key once to change opacity to 60% and press 2 and 5 keys quickly to change the opacity value to 25%. To change to the default opacity value (100%), press the 0 key once. In the next section, let's learn to apply blending modes on a layer.

Applying Blending Modes

Blending modes determines the interaction of colors in different layers. Blending modes also help produce a multitude of interesting and unusual effects. You can easily apply, change, or distract blend modes with no permanent damage to your layers. The default blending mode for a layer is Normal. If you change a layer's blending mode, it affects only the layers below the active layer, and not the layers above it. The target layer must have pixels to apply the blending mode. Perform the following steps to apply a blending mode to a layer:

1. **Open** a new document in Photoshop, and create a background color using <u>Gradient Tool</u> which is under Paint Bucket Tool in Tools panel.

2. Select the **Text Tool** and **click** on your document to place the cursor for typing.

3. **Type** a text in your page. In our case, we type **Cromosys** in <u>green</u> color, as shown in picture 6.1.

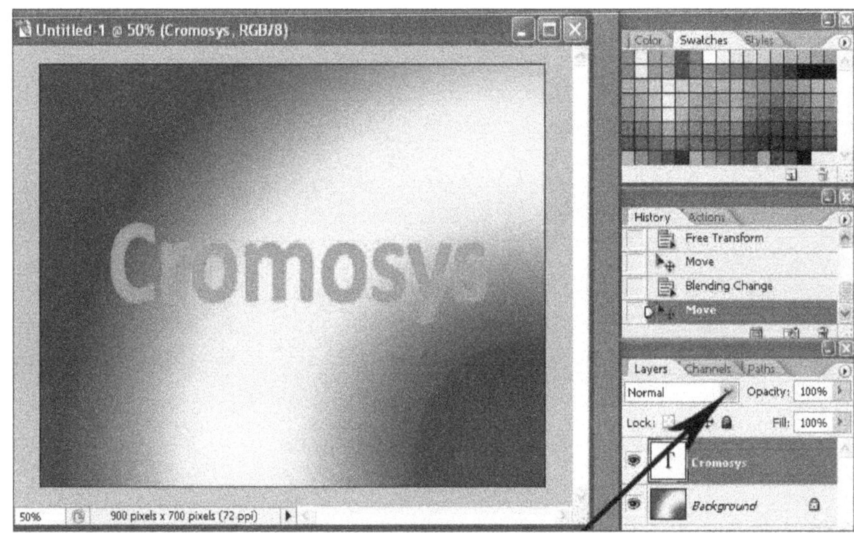

Picture 6.1

4. Click the **Set the blending mode for the layer** dropdown list which is shown in picture 6.1 with the black arrow. Then choose **Difference** Blend Mode from the dropdown list.

Picture 6.2

As a result, the Difference blending mode is applied to the text, as shown in picture 6.2. You can see in this picture that after applying the Difference blending mode, the color of the text is changed automatically. It makes the design amazing. And if you move the text using Move Tool in the page, the text will automatically change the color.

Similarly, you can select other blending mode as per the effect you want to create in your design. You will notice other blending modes affect layers differently. Now we will move ahead, and explore various blending modes available in Photoshop CS6.

Exploring Types of Blending Modes

Photoshop provides 27 different blending modes, which are available in the Layers panel. You can apply any of these blending modes according to your requirement. Let's briefly learn about these blending modes:

- **Normal:** Allows each pixel to appear in its original state. The colors of the selected layer do not blend with that of the layer beneath it at 100% opacity. This is the default blending mode.
- **Dissolve:** Works with a layer that has an Opacity setting of less than 100%. The effect of Dissolve blending mode appears best when a layer has a lower opacity value. It creates grainy effect as anti-aliasing is used. Dissolve blending mode uses random pixels from both target and the layer-below.
- **Darken:** Converts lighter pixels to transparent and retains the darker pixels unchanged. If the pixels on the selected layer are lighter than the layer beneath, the lighter pixels turn transparent. On the other hand, if the pixels on the selected layer are darker, they appear unchanged.
- **Multiply:** Darkens the colors of the layers by multiplying the color with the layers beneath the selected layer. The final color in the image is always a darker color. This is the most used blending mode.
- **Color Burn:** Searches for the color information in the selected layer, and darkens the layers beneath it in the Layer panel. This blending mode increases the contrast of the image.
- **Linear Burn:** Darkens the layers beneath the selected layer by decreasing the brightness. This blending mode is similar to the Multiply blending mode but tends to turn specific portions of the image into pure black.
- **Darker Color:** Operates on all channels simultaneously rather than operating on one channel at a time (similar to the Lighter Color blending mode). When blending two colors with this blending mode, only the darker color is visible. This blending mode works in the same way as the Darken blending mode.
- **Lighten:** Inverses the effect of the Darken blending mode. In this blending mode, lighter pixels on the target layer remain unchanged; while, darker pixels are replaced with the blend color.
- **Screen:** Searches the channel information of each color and then multiples the color applied to the original colors resulting in lighter color. It is the opposite of the Multiply blending mode.
- **Color Dodge:** Decreases the contrast to reflect the blend color. It is the opposite of the Color Burn blending mode. If you blend with black, the colors remain unchanged.
- **Linear Dodge:** Reflects the blend color by brightening the base color. It is the opposite of the Linear Burn blending mode. Using blend color as black produces no change. It is primarily used for tonal and color adjustments.
- **Lighter Color:** Operates on all channels, simultaneously. The lighter color is visible when blending two colors with this mode. This blending mode works in the same way as the Lighten blending mode; the only difference is that, Lighten blending modes operate only on a single channel at a time.
- **Overlay:** Multiplies the blend colors with the base colors. You can use the Overlay blending mode if you want to preserve the shadows and highlights of an image. It is essentially the combination of two blending modes: Screen and Multiply.
- **Soft Light:** Creates a diffused spotlight effect. You can use this blending mode to correct overexposed photographs or create special effects, such as spot focus. The blend color with 50% or more brightness lightens the image and the blend color with 50% or less brightness darkens the image.

- **Hard Light:** Multiplies the colors, depending on the blend color. The effect is similar to that of shining a Harsh Spotlight on the image. If the blend color (light source) is lighter than 50% gray, the image is lightened, as if it were screened. This is useful for adding highlights to an image. If the blend color is darker than 50% gray, the image appears darker. This is useful for adding shadows to an image.
- **Vivid Light:** Burns or hides the colors by increasing or decreasing the contrast, depending on the blend color. If the blend color (light source) is lighter than 50% gray, the image is lightened by decreasing the contrast. If the blend color is darker than 50% gray, the image is darkened by increasing the contrast.
- **Linear Light:** Burns or hides the colors by decreasing or increasing the brightness, depending on the blend color. If the blend color (light source) is lighter than 50% gray, the image is lightened by increasing the brightness. If the blend color is darker than 50% gray, the image is darkened by decreasing the brightness.
- **Pin Light:** Replaces the colors, depending on the blend color. If the blend color (light source) is lighter than 50% gray, pixels darker than the blend color are replaced, and pixels lighter than the blend color do not change. If the blend color is darker than 50% gray, pixels lighter than the blend color are replaced with colors of layer beneath it in the Layers panel, which leads to darker pixels than the blend color. This is useful for adding special effects to an image.
- **Hard Mix:** Applies a posterization effect based on the selected layer's opacity value. A higher opacity value of the selected layer creates high posterization effect.
- **Difference:** Checks the color information in each channel and subtracts either the blend color from the base color or the base color from the blend color, depending on which has a greater brightness value. If you blend a layer with white, it inverts the base color; while blending the layer with black does not alter the base color.
- **Exclusion:** Produces the effect that matches the low contrast version of the Difference blending mode. Blending with white inverts the original color. Blending with black does not alter the base color.
- **Subtract:** Looks at the color information in each channel and subtracts the blend color from the base color. In 8 and 16 bit images, if the difference value is less than zero, it is clipped to zero.
- **Divide:** Looks at the color information in each channel and divides the blend color from the base color.
- **Hue:** Creates the luminance and saturation effect of the base color and the effect of the blend color.
- **Saturation:** Creates the luminance and effect of the base color and the saturation of the blend color.
- **Color:** Creates the luminance of the base color and the effect and saturation of the blend color. The Color blending mode does not change the gray levels in the image.
- **Luminosity:** Creates the effect and saturation of the base color and the luminance of the blend color. This mode creates an opposite effect that of the Color mode.

Working with Layer Style

Layer styles not only let you create special effects, but also give you the control you need to experiment over the image. In Photoshop, using layer styles, such as Bevel and Emboss or Drop Shadow, you can convert two-dimensional (2D) images to three-dimensional (3D) images. You can also use Gradient Overlay, Color Overlay, and Pattern Overlay on your document to create interesting effects. The advantage is that you can apply all these without changing the original image.

Photoshop allows you to apply layer styles on the selected layers in the active document. When you add a style to a layer, the results of the style are only applied and displayed in that layer. Each layer can contain its own style, and you can apply more than one style to a single layer. Layer styles can be applied to any layer except the Background layer. Two of Photoshop's layer styles, such as Drop Shadow and Outer Glow, require both transparent and non-transparent layer elements. For instance, to apply a Drop Shadow to a layer, it would require a transparent area within the image to hold the shadow.

Photoshop CS6 provides a number of layer styles that can be applied to normal or text layers. When you create a customized layer style, you can move that style to another layer, save the style in the Styles panel, or even move the style between two open documents. You can modify or remove the style at any time during the creative process, as layer styles do not affect the pixels of the original image. This makes working with images and texts interesting, and also provides a better control on your images since you can apply styles on the layers individually.

When you move or edit the pixels of a layer, the style applied to that layer is updated automatically. You can also save the customized layer styles for future use. When a particular style or effect is applied to a layer, an icon appears after the name of the layer in the Layers panel. Some of the commonly used styles include Drop Shadow, Inner Shadow, Inner Glow, Outer Glow, Gradient Overlay, Pattern Overlay, Color Overlay, Satin, Stroke, and Bevel & Emboss.

You can use the Layer Style dialog box to work with layer styles. There are few ways to open the Layer Style dialog box. You can access the Layer Style dialog box by using the Layer menu; you can also access it using the Layers panel. The various layer style options in the Layer Style dialog box are described as follows:

- **Drop Shadow:** Applies a soft shadow to the layer, making the layer appear to float in the air and creation an illusion of 3D. You can apply a Drop Shadow effect to an image, text, or a shape contained within the layer. Photoshop CS6 allows you to specify the color, opacity, blend mode, position, size, and contour of the effect.
- **Inner Shadow:** Applies basic drop shadows to the inside boundaries of an image, type, or a shape contained within a layer and creates a recessed appearance.
- **Outer Glow:** Applies a circle of light around an image, type, or a shape contained within the layer.
- **Inner Glow:** Creates the glow effect to the inside boundaries of a layer, selection, text, or shape.
- **Bevel & Emboss:** Applies a three-dimensional edge effect to an image, type, or shape contained within a layer. You can specify the style from the list that appears for the Bevel and Emboss option, which includes Outer Bevel, Inner Bevel, and Emboss.
- **Satin:** Adds variations in opacity by creating waves of repeated color as defined in the Contour option.
- **Color Overlay:** Fills a layer with a solid color.
- **Gradient Overlay:** Fills a layer with a gradient.
- **Pattern Overlay:** Fills a layer with a pattern selected in the Pattern option.
- **Stroke:** Creates outline using color, gradient, and pattern around an image, type, or shape contained within the layer.

In subsequent sections, you learn to add, copy, and remove layer styles. Let's begin by learning how to add a layer style.

Adding a Layer Style

To add a layer style to a layer, select that layer, and add one or more layer styles by clicking the Add a layer style button in the Layers panel. You can also select the desired layer style from the Layer menu. After you apply the layer style, it appears as a sub-element of the active layer.

You can also change the default settings for each layer style in the Layer Style dialog box. To modify a layer style, reopen the Layer Style dialog box, and make the desired changes. In addition, each layer style has its own eye icon. The eye icon is a toggle that lets you temporarily hide the layer styles. Perform the following steps to add layer style to a layer:

1. **Open** a document and **select** the layer on which you want to add layer styles. In our case, the layer with a car shape **(Car)** is selected, as shown in picture 6.3.

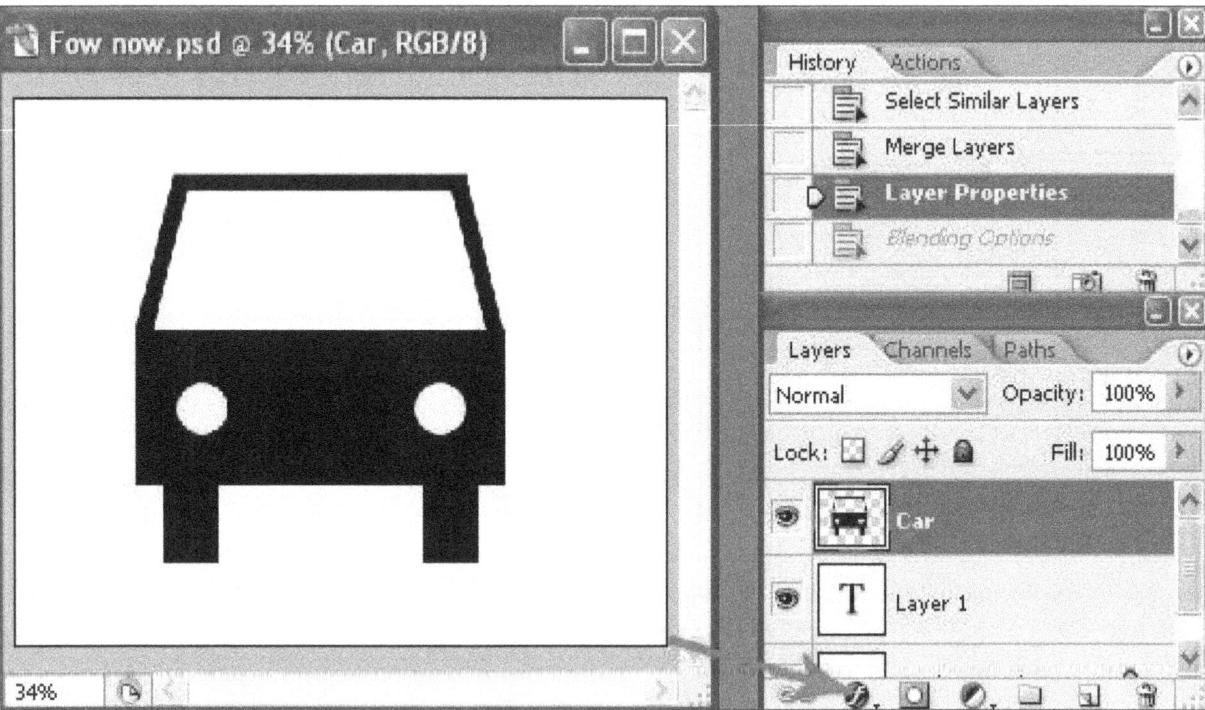

Picture 6.3

2. Click the **Add a layer style** button at the bottom of the Layers panel, as shown in picture 6.3 with the red arrow. A dropdown list appears.

3. Select the **Blending Options** option from the dropdown list. It opens the Layer Style dialog box, as shown in picture 6.4.

4. **Select** a layer style check box in the Styles pane. In our case, we select the **Bevel & Emboss** check box to add bevel and emboss. Let's proceed to modify a layer style.

5. Select the **Texture** check box under the Bevel & Emboss layer style to add texture.

6. **Double-left** click the Bevel & Emboss layer style in the Styles pane to open its options list at the right side. Then drag the **Size** slider handle in the Structure section to set to **35** px, (picture 6.4).

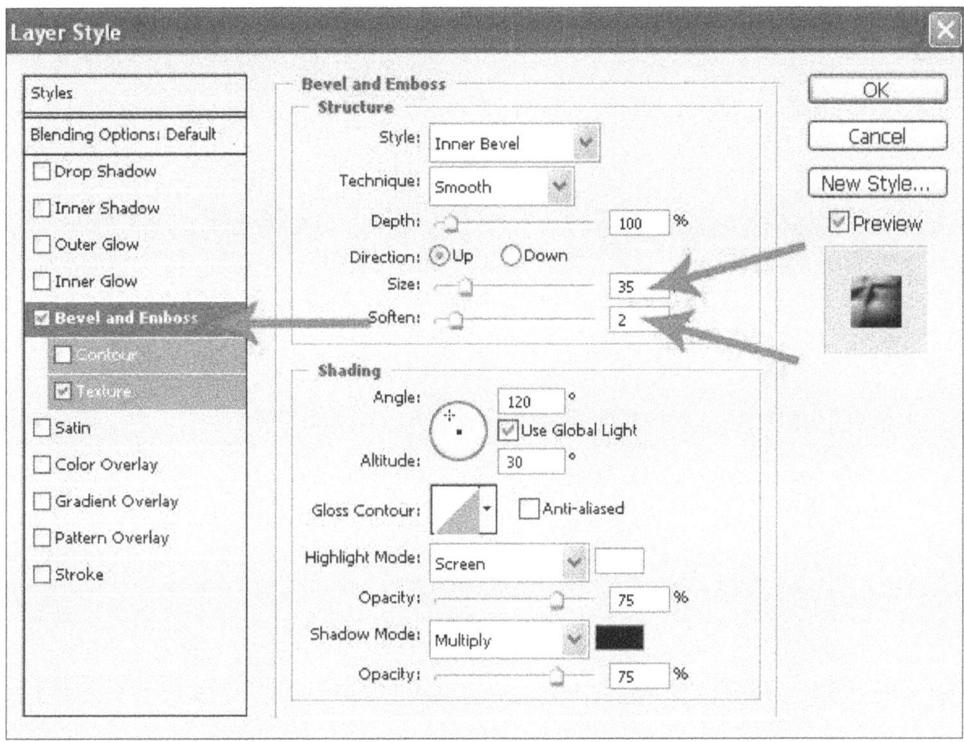

Picture 6.4

7. Drag the **Soften** slider handle in the Structure section to set to **2** px, (picture 6.4). After adding a layer style and then modifying its settings, you can click the **OK** button to close the Layer Style dialog box or add another layer style. In our case, we add one more layer style.

8. Click the **Drop Shadow** check box in the Styles pane to add drop shadow effect on your layer.

9. **Double-left** click the Drop Shadow layer style in the Styles pane to open its options list at the right side. Then drag the **Distance** slider hand in the Structure section to set to **10** px.

10. Drag the **Size** slider handle in the Structure section to set to **20** px. Then click the **OK** button to close the Layer Style dialog box.

The two layer styles appear on the Layers panel. The picture 6.5 shows the result of two effects in the Document window.

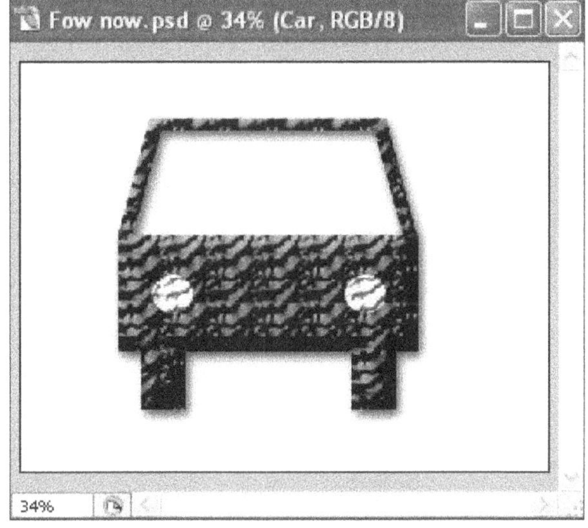

Picture 6.5

Reusing Existing Layer Style

After a layer style is applied to a layer, it can be copied and then pasted to other layers, or into another document. In most cases, it is better to save the layer style in the Styles panel. For instance, you can copy the Drop Shadow layer style with the same color, opacity, blend mode, position, and size and paste it to another layer. Perform the following steps on your computer to copy a layer style from a layer and paste it to another layer:

1. **Open** the same (previous) document, and create a **star** shape and fill it with <u>blue</u> color. Now, we want to copy layer styles from the Car layer and paste it into the Star layer.

2. Choose **Layer> Layer Style> Copy Layer Style** from the Menu bar.

3. Select the **Star** layer in the Layers panel to paste the copied layer style.

4. Choose **Layer> Layer Style> Paste Layer Style** from the Menu bar. As the result, the copied layer style is applied to the Star layer.

After copying a layer style, it remains in Photoshop's memory until you exit from the application or copy another layer style. In this way, you can copy other layer styles and paste them to the desired layers. You can also move layer styles between layers. To move layer styles, drag the layer style over another layer. In addition, you can move all the layer styles applied to the layer by dragging the Effects group instead of an individual layer style.

Removing Layer Styles

After applying different styles on a layer, you may at some point, feel that some or all of these styles are not needed. If such a case, you can temporarily disable the layer style effect by using the eye icons. Alternatively, you can remove a layer style effect permanently by clearing all of them at once, or selecting and clearing individual styles that you do not need. Perform the following steps to remove a layer style from a layer:

1. **Select** the layer with layer styles applied in the Layers panel, as shown in picture 6.6 with the red arrow.

2. **Drag** the layer style group (Effects) and **drop** on the <u>Delete layer</u> button at the bottom of the Layers panel, (picture 6.6).

Alternatively, you can select Layer> Layer Style> Clear Layer Style from the Menu bar. The Clear Layer Style option removes all the layer style applied to a layer.

If you want to remove individual layer styles, you can also drag the desired layer style to the Delete layer button. You may find this way of deleting a layer style easy. Now, let's learn to save a layer style in the next section.

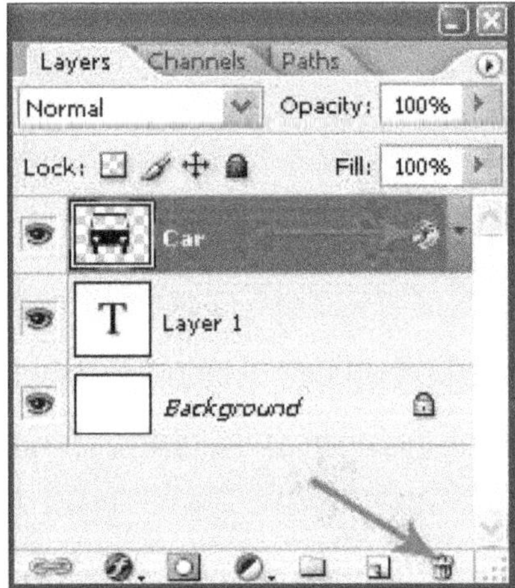

Picture 6.6

Saving a Layer Styles

Suppose you have spent a lot of effort in creating, previewing, mixing, different layer styles on an image and now want to preserve the layer style to reuse in future. In such cases, the best way is to save the layer style as a custom style in the Styles panel. Perform the following steps to save a layer style:

1. **Select** the layer in which the layer styles are applied in the Layers panel. In our case, the **Car** layer is active.

2. Click the **Styles** panel tab to show the panel, as shown in picture 6.7 with the red arrow numbered 2.

3. Click the **Create new style** button at the bottom of the Styles panel, as shown in picture 6.7 with the red arrow numbered 3. The New Style dialog box appears on your screen.

4. **Type** the desired name in the Name text box. In our case, we type **New Layer Style**.

5. Select the **Include Layer Blending Options** check box. Then click the **OK** button.

A new style icon named New Layer Style appears in the Styles panel. Next, let's learn how to mask in Photoshop to hide or display portions of an image.

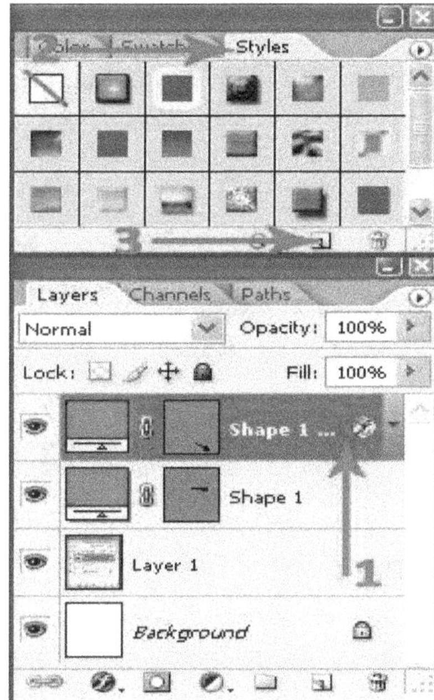

Picture 6.7

Working with Masks

Masking is a technique used to composite multiple images seamlessly into a single image. You can also use masking for tonal and color adjustments in Photoshop. Photoshop's masking option allows you to make complex and precise selections using masking. When you make a selection in an image, the unselected portion is known as the mask and primarily used to protect the unselected portion from editing. Photoshop stores masks as alpha channels that you can access using the Channels panel. You can also edit the masks with different painting tools and apply filter effects. In a mask, black represents the protected portion, and white represents the editable portion of an image.

You can modify a mask by painting either with black or white. Painting with black increases the protected area, while painting with white increases the unprotected area. Both layer and vector masks are nondestructive, which means you can re-edit your mask later without losing the original pixels. In Photoshop, you can create two types of masks:

- **Layer mask:** Refers to resolution-dependent bitmap images that you can edit using the painting or selection tools.
- **Vector mask:** Refers to resolution-independent vector shapes that you can create using a pen or shape tool.

In the Layers panel, both the layer and vector masks appear as an additional thumbnail to the right of the layer thumbnail, as shown in picture 6.8.

As shown in the picture 6.8, the layer mask thumbnail represents the grayscale channel that is created when you add the layer mask. On the other hand the vector mask thumbnail represents a path that hides the content of the layer outside the path. Keep in mind that you cannot add layer or vector masks on the Background layer.

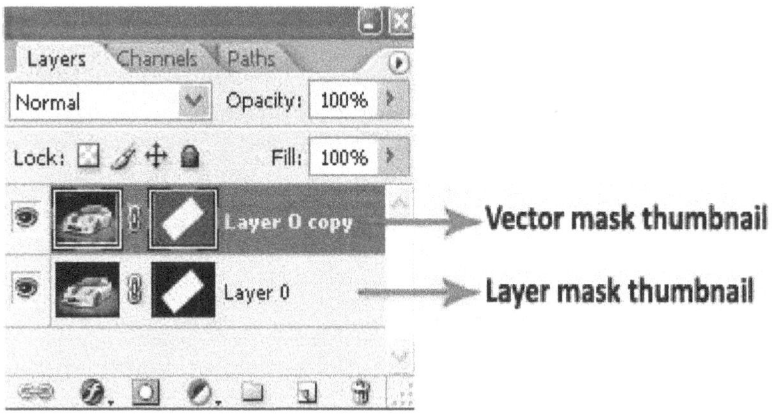

Picture 6.8

Creating a Layer Mask

A layer mask hides areas that we paint with black, show the areas that we paint with white, and shows the areas in various level of transparency that we paint in shades of gray appear. Layer masks are excellent for blending layers of different images together and creating soft transitions between images.

In Photoshop, you can create a layer mask in different ways. You can add a layer mask using either the Layer menu or the Layers panel.

To add a layer mask using the Layer menu:
- Select Layer> Layer Mask from the Menu bar.

To add a layer mask using the Layers panel:
- Click the Add layer mask button at the bottom of the panel.

Now, you are going to create a layer mask by which you can hide areas that you paint with black. Perform the following steps to create a layer mask in Photoshop:

1. **Open** a document with two images in which you want to apply layer mask. In our case, we have opened a document with two layers of different images.

In our case, we want to set the candle against a new background. That is why we have placed the background layer below the candle layer, as shown in picture 6.9.

Picture 6.9

2. **Select** the layer on which you want to add layer mask. In our case, we select the **Candle** layer.

3. Click the **Add layer mask** button at the bottom of the Layers panel, as shown in picture 6.9 with the red arrow numbered 3. A layer mask thumbnail appears attached to the Candle layer.

By default, when you click the Add layer mask button, it always reveals all layer content. That is, it is equivalent to selecting Layer> Layer Mask> Reveal All from the Menu bar. You can notice, the layer mask thumbnail appears all white, which means all pixels of the layer are visible. Now you can paint the portions with black to hide them.

Keep in mind that to hide all layer's content initially, you can select Layer> Layer Mask> Hide All from the Menu bar. If there is a selection, you can select Reveal Selection or Hide Selection options.

4. Press the **D key** to ensure the foreground color is selected as black, which is the default.

5. Select the **Brush Tool** or press the **B** key in the Tools panel.

6. **Right-click** on the Document window. A context menu appears on your screen, as shown in picture 7.0.

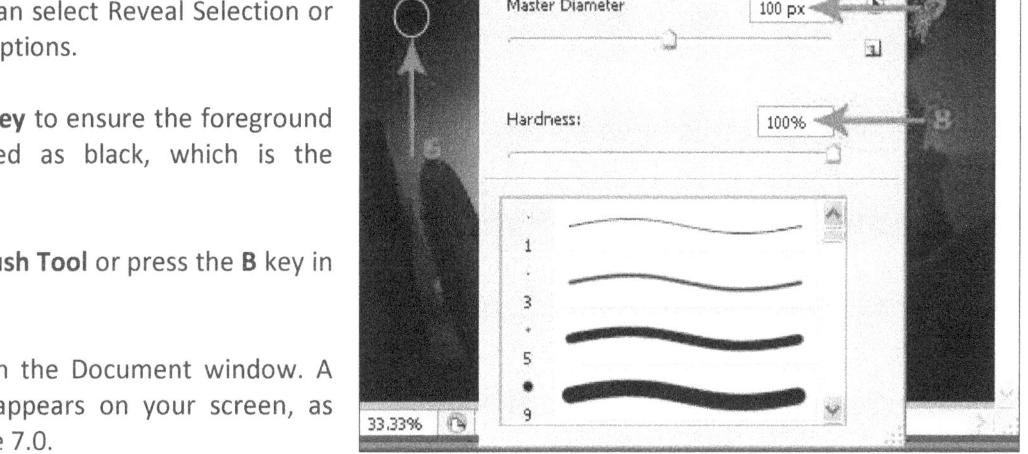

Picture 7.0

7. Set the **Size** value to **100 px**, (picture 7.0).

8. Set the **Hardness** value to **100%**, (picture 7.0).

9. **Click** inside the layer mask thumbnail in the Layers panel to activate the layer mask, (picture 7.1).

10. **Paint** the image area that you want to hide with Brush Tool (picture 7.1).

Picture 7.1 shows when you paint over the image, Photoshop reveals the content of the underlying layer.

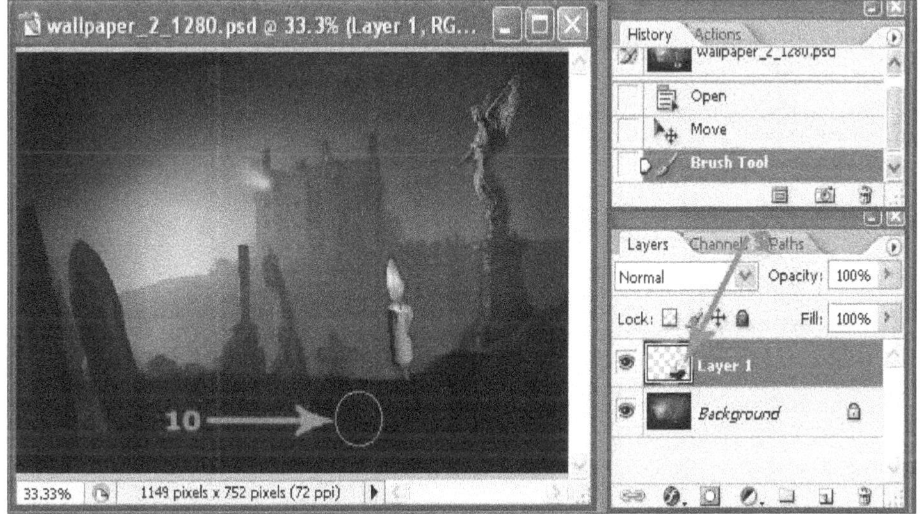

Picture 7.1

11. **Zoom in** the image area to precisely paint the area that you want to hide. Picture 7.2 below shows the finished layer mask.

You can notice the hidden area, which is the area you paint with black appears as black in the layer mask thumbnail. Later, if required you can disable the layer mask to show the hidden areas. To disable the layer mask, right-click the layer mask thumbnail in the Layers panel and select the Disable Layer Mask option from the context menu.

You can also delete and refine the mask later using the Delete Layer Mask and Refine Mask options, respectively. In addition, you can convert the mask into a selection using the Add Mask To Selection option. After creating a layer mask, you can later modify the mask by painting with black and white colors alternatively.

Picture 7.2

Creating a Vector Mask

Vector masks are resolution-independent (can be transformed to any size) and defined by a vector path on a layer created by Pen Tool, shape tools, or type tools. A vector mask creates a well-defined and sharp-edged shape on a layer, unlike the layer masks that create soft edges. A vector mask is useful if you want to add a design element with clean, defined edges. You can apply and edit one or more layer styles on the vector mask layers.

In Photoshop, you can create a vector mask in different ways. You can add a vector mask using either the Layer menu or the Layers panel.

To add a vector mask using the Layer menu:
- Select Layer> Vector Mask from the Menu bar.

To add a vector mask using the Layers panel:
- Click the Add vector mask button at the bottom of the panel.

The Add vector mask and Add layer mask button are same. When you click the Add layer mask button, the Add vector mask button becomes active. Perform these steps to add a vector mask to a layer:

1. **Open** a document to work with vector masking. In our case, we have opened the same document (with two layers) which we have used in previous section.

2. **Select** the image layer. In our case, we select the **Candle** layer.

3. Click the **Add layer mask** button <u>two times</u>. In the second time, it will create a **vector mask** for the Candle layer.

4. **Select** a shape tool to draw a shape in the Candle layer. In our case, we select **Ellipse Tool**.

5. **Select** the **Path** option as the pick mode in the <u>Options bar</u>.

6. **Create** an elliptical path surrounding the area of the image you want to be visible. In our case, we have drawn an elliptical path surrounding the candle area, as shown in picture 7.3.

You can hold down the Ctrl and Shift key together while dragging with Ellipse Tool to create a circle from center.

Picture 7.3

7. Choose **Layer> Vector Mask> Current Path** from the Menu bar. Photoshop masks the area outside the path and displays the area inside, as shown in picture 7.3.

You can also notice in the Layers panel, the visible area appears filled with white color in the vector mask thumbnail and the hidden area appears gray. After you create a layer or vector mask, you can use the Layers and Properties panels to modify it. You need to select a mask before modifying it. You can use the mask thumbnail in the Layers panel to quickly select the mask.

In Photoshop CS6, you can also use the Properties panel to modify masks. You can link or unlink, hide or show, disable or enable, and delete masks in Photoshop. In the next section, let's learn to create a channel mask in Photoshop.

Creating a Channel Mask

In Photoshop CS6, channel masks selections that you save in the Channels panel. You can create a channel mask either by clicking the Create new channel button at the bottom of the Channel panel, and then using any painting or drawing tools to create the mask; alternatively, by making a selection and converting the selection into a mask by clicking the Save selection as channel button. When you paint the channel mask, black represents the masked area, while white represents the visible areas. You can also paint with shades of gray for percentages of selection. Perform the following steps to create a channel mask:

1. **Open** a document and **select** a layer in Photoshop.

2. Click the **Channels** panel tab in the <u>Layers panel</u> group to select the panel. The Channels panel appears.

3. Click the **Create a new channel** button at the bottom of the Channels panel to create a new channel, as shown in picture 7.4 with the red arrow numbered 3. A new channel named **Alpha 1** appears.

Picture 7.4

4. Click the **Alpha 1** channel to select it, as shown in picture 7.4 with the red arrow numbered 4. The Document window fills with black.

5. Select **Brush Tool** on the Tools panel. Then click the down arrow for the **Brush Preset** picker on the Options bar. The Brush Preset picker opens in a pop-up menu, as shown in picture 7.5.

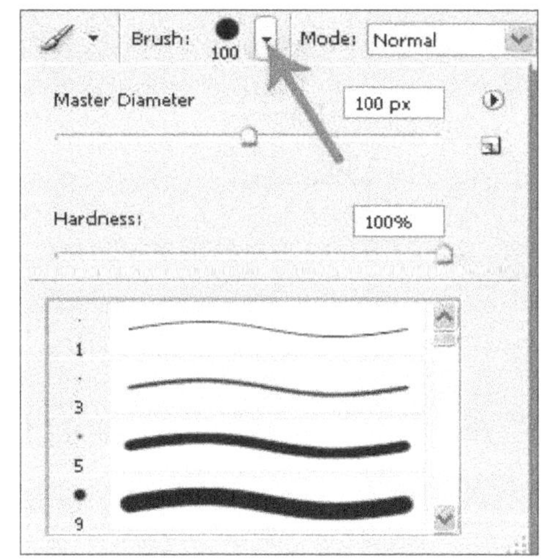

6. **Select** a brush tip (Soft Round) from the picker.

7. Click the **Show/Hide** icon (eye icon) on the <u>Blue</u> composite channel. The image is revealed in the Document window that helps to create the channel mask. Ensure that the new Alpha channel is still selected.

8. **Paint** the area of image with white using the brush to create a selection.

Picture 7.5

9. Click the **Show/Hide** icon on the <u>Blue</u> composite channel again. The image hides and reveals the mask in black and white. Similarly, you can refine the channel mask by painting with white and black colors.

Working with Quick Mask Mode

The Quick Mask Mode feature helps you to make selections using painting and drawing tools without creating channel masks. You can select Quick Mask Mode from the Tools panel by selecting the Edit in Quick Mask Mode tool. This tool toggles between Standard Mode and Quick Mask Mode.

By default, Photoshop CS6 displays image in Standard Mode. In the Quick Mask Mode, the selection appears as a red mask. You can use the painting tools to modify the mask. When you exit the Quick Mask Mode, the masked areas are converted into a selection. Perform the following steps to work with Quick Mask Mode:

1. **Open** an image, and select the entire (or a part) of the image using **Rectangular Marquee Tool** in the Tools panel, as shown in picture 7.6 with the red arrow numbered 1.

In our case, we have selected the entire image, as shown in picture 7.6.

2. Select the **Edit in Quick Mask Mode** icon in the Tools panel, as shown in picture 7.6 with the red arrow numbered 2. The selection converts into a red overlay mask.

The protected area appears covered with the red overlay. In our case, we want to remove from the selection that is increase the red overlay area.

Picture 7.6

3. Select the **Brush Tool** on the Tools panel or press the **B key** to select it.

4. Press the **D key** to select the default foreground (black) and background (white) color.

5. **Paint** the area with black to mask the image.

Keep in mind that painting with white adds more selection areas. You can toggle between Quick Mask Mode and Standard Mode until you create a precise selection.

6. Click the **Edit in Standard Mode** icon again to return to a standard selection.

In our case, the modified selection appears, as shown in picture 7.7.

Picture 7.7

When you work in Quick Mask Mode, the color for the mask is red, the opacity of the mask is 50%, and the mask represents the masked areas of the document.

However, you can modify these default settings using the Quick Mask Options dialog box that you can open by double-clicking the Edit in Quick Mask Mode or Standard Mode icon in the Tools panel, as shown in picture 7.8.

With this, we come to the end of the chapter: Working with Layers and Masks

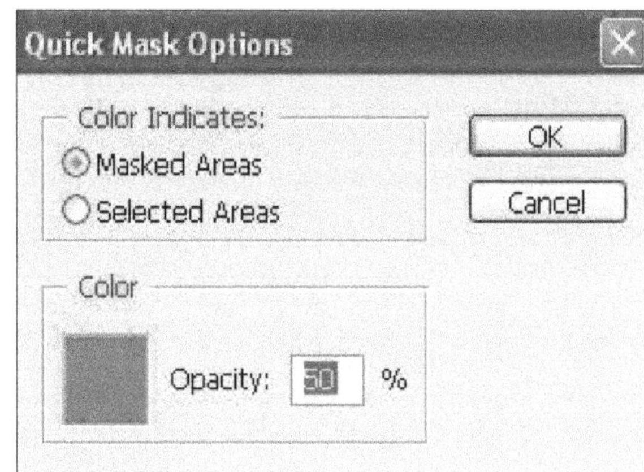

Picture 7.8

Lesson 7
Working with Text

In the digital world, text or type plays an important role in conveying information. Text is defined as a set of mathematical expressions that define letters, numbers, and characters. You can add editable text to an image to make the image interesting and informative. When combined with graphics, text allows you to create communicative designs. The two main aspects of text are its structure and presentation style. The structure refers to the arrangement of text in a document while presentation refers to the final formatted text with color and styles. Photoshop CS6 consists of four type tools, such as Horizontal Type Tool, Vertical Type Tool, Horizontal Type Mask Tool, Vertical Type Mask Tool. These tools help you to create and manage text effectively in a Photoshop document. The functionality of the horizontal and vertical type tools is similar; only the direction differs. You can select the entire text or individual characters in the text using respective type tool.

The key to Photoshop's superiority is that it produces vector-based text, which is it dos not rasterize. This implies that you can scale and transform the text without any degradation in quality. You can also use text as a mask, path, or even warp text into any shape as per your requirement. Along with existing Character and Paragraph panels, Photoshop CS6 introduces two new panels: Character Styles and Paragraph Styles that let you save customized text formatting to reuse on other text. You can select an existing text in the document to create a character style based on its formatting.

In this lesson, you will first learn about Character and Paragraph panels. Next, you will learn how to create different types of text including creating a text on a path. You will also learn to format text using the Options bar and the Character panel, warp and rasterize text. Moreover, you learn to create type mask in Photoshop. Further, you will learn to constrain the text flow within a shape. You will also learn to create a custom character style, convert type layer into a 3D layer, and apply layer styles on a type layer. In the end, you will learn to work with available text styles. Let's begin the lesson by exploring the Character and Paragraph panels.

Exploring Character and Paragraph Panels

In Photoshop CS6, you can create text using the type tools; after creating the text you can use the options available in the Options bar to edit the text. You can also use the Character and Paragraph panels to work with text. These panels provide additional options that are not available in the Options bar. In addition, you can also use the newly introduced Character Styles and Paragraph Styles panels. These panels optimize your workflow by letting you save custom styles; and reuse them in customized format on other text in the same or different document. For instance, you can save a custom text style for the headings of a document and another text style for the inside content or the body copy.

The Character panel allows you to change the font family, such as Myriad Pro or Times New Roman; and font style, such as Italic, Bold, or Condensed. You can also change other text attributes, such as font size, color, leading, kerning, tracking, language, horizontal scale, and anti-aliasing. You can open the Character panel by selecting Window> Character from the Menu bar. By default, the Character panel is not visible. Picture 7.9 shows the Character panel of Photoshop CS6:

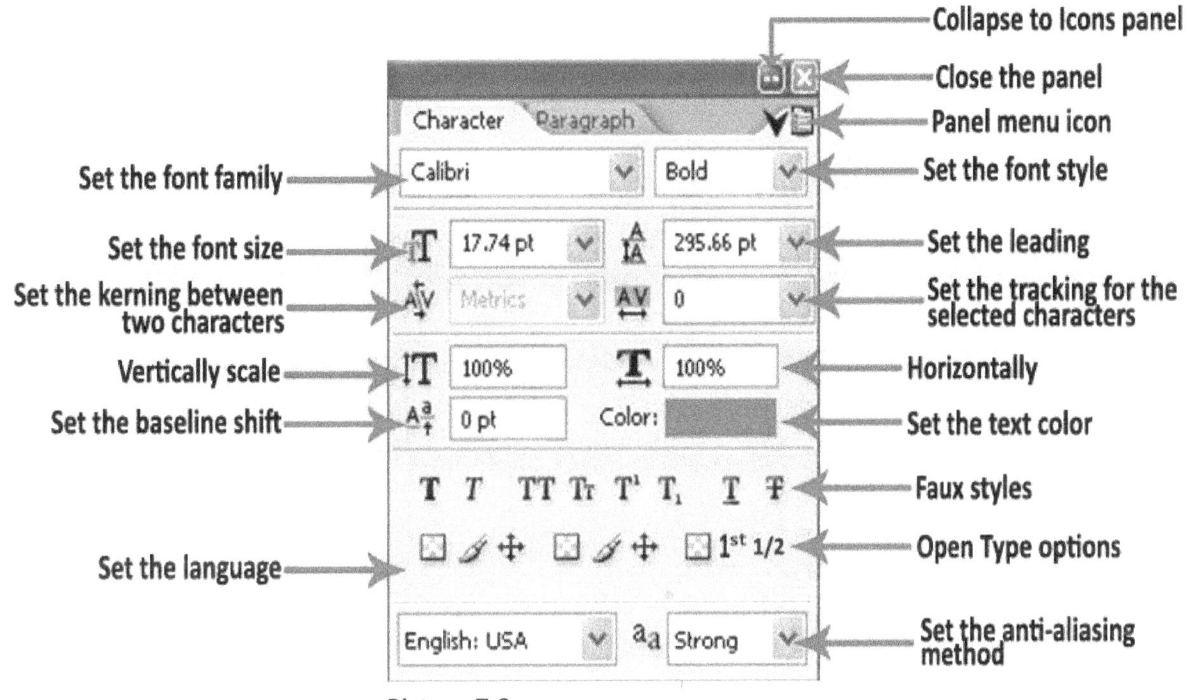

Picture 7.9

In the Character panel, when you place your mouse-pointer over an icon or an option, Photoshop CS6 displays a tooltip describing the name of the respective options. The anti-aliasing dropdown list allows you to select the anti-aliasing methods. Anti-aliasing blurs the sharp edges (square edge) by filling in the sharp edges and blending the text with the background. Photoshop CS6 uses these methods to render the edges of the font on the screen. You can select an anti-aliasing option in the Options bar or the Character panel.

Keep in mind that performing an excess anti-aliasing can result in color artifacts around the edges of the font and may produce inconsistent result when producing low resolution images.

You can access additional options from the panel menu of the Character panel. For instance, you can change the text orientation from the horizontal to vertical direction and vice versa using the Change Text Orientation option. By default, the Standard Vertical Roman Alignment option is selected. If you are preparing images for small computer screen, such as a cell phone or personal digital assistant (PDA), you can select the System Layout option in the panel menu. The default option, Fractional Widths, makes the text clear and readable. You also select the No Break option that tells Photoshop not to hyphenate the selected words. The Reset Character option resets the selected text to the Photoshop defaults, which is a very useful option. Rest of the options, such as Faux Bold, All Caps, Underline, and Strikethrough available in the panel menu can be accessed from the Character panel.

Photoshop CS6 adds new features that are available for the selected OpenType fonts. You can use this setting to adjust the features for an entire type layer by selecting the type layer in the Layers panel. Alternatively, you can use this setting on the selected text. Type layers are special Photoshop layers that contain text.

The Paragraph panel gives you precise control over the text in a paragraph. It lets you create automatic breaks between paragraphs, and align rows of text to the left, center, or right, or to justify them to the margins. You can also use the Paragraph panel to control formatting, such as hyphenation, justification, indentation, and spacing. Picture 8.0 shows the Paragraph panel in Photoshop CS6:

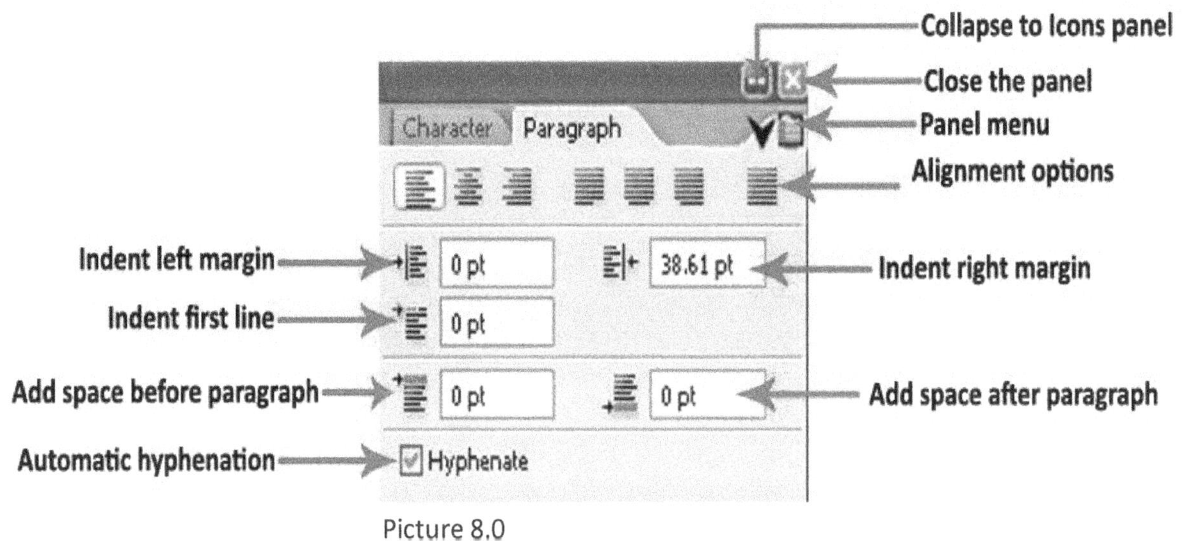

Picture 8.0

To create a paragraph text, click and drag to define a bounding box. You can type the text inside the box. When the line reaches the edge of the bounding box, a new line is automatically created. When you press the Enter key, Photoshop CS6 creates a new paragraph. You can access the Paragraph options without selecting a type layer in the Layers panel. You only need to place the insertion point inside the paragraph you want to change. However, it is not necessary to select a letter or word to apply changes. Let's now learn about creating text in Photoshop CS6.

Creating a Text

You can use the type tools for creating text or character into Photoshop document. You can either use Horizontal Type Tool or Vertical Type Tool to type text in a Photoshop document. The type tool that appears by default in Tools panel is the Horizontal Type Tool. Whenever you type some text in Photoshop, this text is created in a separate layer called the type layer. The default color for the type tool is black. You can select other type tools from the flyout of Horizontal Type Tool. The list in the next page shows the type tools in Photoshop CS6:

Photoshop CS6 Type Tools in the Tools panel

Tools Name	Purpose
Horizontal Type Tool	Creates horizontal text
Vertical Type Tool	Creates a vertical text
Horizontal Type Mask Tool	Creates a horizontal selection in the shape of type
Vertical Type Mask Tool	Creates a vertical selection in the shape of type

In Photoshop CS6, you can add text in three different ways, such as point, paragraph, and path. Both Horizontal Type Tool and Vertical Type Tool allow you to create a type object known as point type. Point types are not associated with a path. Point type text begins where you click on the Document window and expands as you type. Likewise, you can use both the tools to create paragraph text. Using either of the tools, you can define an area indicated by the bounding box to control the flow of the characters. You can also type text along an open or closed path in Photoshop CS6. Let's now learn about the different ways to create text in Photoshop CS6.

Creating Point Text

You can add text both in the horizontal and vertical orientation. To add text at a point, click at any point in the Document window and start typing the text. You can use Horizontal Type Tool to add text in a horizontal position and Vertical Type Tool to type the text in vertical position. Perform the following steps to add point text:

1. **Create** a new Photoshop document from scratch or **open** an existing document or image in which you want to add text. In our case, we have opened an image.

2. **Select** a type tool in the Tools panel. In our case, we select **Horizontal Type Tool**.

When you select a type tool in the Tools panel or press the T key to select it, the options, such as text orientation, font type, font size, text color, and alignment options specific to the type tool appear in the Options bar.

If you are using Photoshop CS6 Extended version, you can notice a 3D button that lets you convert the type layer into a 3D layer. A tick (check) mark appears in the far right of the Options bar; you can accept changes made to the text by clicking the tick mark option.

3. Select a new font size from the **Set the font size** combo box. In our case, we select **60**. After selecting a new font size, you can set other options, such as font family, font style, and font color. In our case, we use other options to their default.

4. **Click** the image where you want the text to start and **type** the desired text. The shape of mouse-pointer changes to the type tool cursor. In our case, we type: **Cromosys**.

If you continue typing, Photoshop CS6 does not create automatic line breaks and creates text in the same line even if text is not visible. If such case, you can either press the Enter key to create a new line or create paragraph text. However, you can hold the Ctrl key down to temporarily activate the bounding box on the text that you can use to replace the text in the Document window.

Creating Paragraph Text

In addition to point text, you can add text in a specific area. You can define this area using a type tool and then type the desired text inside the area. This type of text is known as paragraph text. Unlike the point text, you need to click and drag to define the area for the paragraph text. When you define an area, a bounding box appears to control the flow of text. The bounding box has small squares that let you adjust the defined area. You can type text in a bounding box in horizontal as well as in vertical positions depending on the type tool you select. When the text reaches the end of the bounding box, it is automatically wrapped to the next line. The text is confined to the defined area. When you reach the end of the bounding box, Photoshop CS6 does not expand the bounding box; instead, it shows a plus sign inside the small square indicating there is more text in the paragraph. You can later drag the small square to expand the bounding box and show the complete text in the paragraph. You can copy and paste text from other documents or another application, such as Microsoft Word. Perform the following steps to create paragraph text in Photoshop:

1. **Open** an image and **select** a type tool in the Tools panel. In our case, we select **Horizontal Type Tool**.

2. **Drag** on the image to define the area for the paragraph and then **release** the mouse button. A bounding box appears defining the area and the text cursor appears at the top-left corner.

3. **Type** the desired text inside the bounding box.

You will see on your screen that the lines automatically break when they reach at the edge of the bounding box. You can also notice a plus sign appears inside the right-bottom square handle, which indicates here is some hidden text.

4. **Drag** the right-bottom square handle outward to resize the bounding box until all the text appears. You can drag the any of the square handles to resize the bounding box in the shape you want.

Creating a Text on a Path

Until now, you have learnt to create point as well as paragraph text in Photoshop CS6. You can also create text on a path. Unlike point and paragraph text, you can create text on a path using the type options. Using the type options, you can type the text that flows along the edge of a path. You can create either an open or a closed path using shape tools. When you type the text on a path, the text follows the direction in which anchor points were added to the path. Once you type the text on the path, you can reshape the path using Direction Selection Tool, and the text will change to fit the new form of the path. The path does not appear when the document is printed. Perform the following steps to create text on a path:

1. **Create** a new Photoshop document or **open** an existing document.

2. Select **Pen Tool** from the Tools panel or press the **P** key on the keyboard.

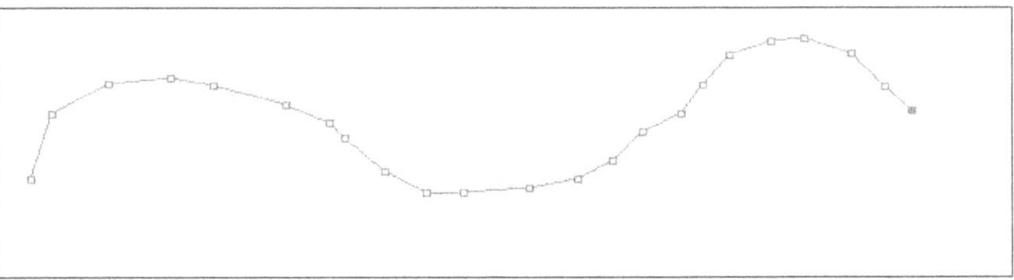

Picture 8.1

3. **Draw** a path on which you want to add the text, as shown in picture 8.1.

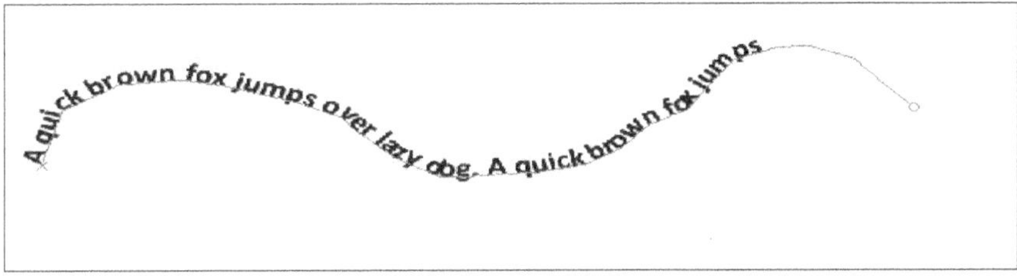

4. **Select** a type tool on the Tools panel. In our case, we select Horizontal Type Tool.

Picture 8.2

5. **Place** the mouse-pointer over the start point of the path, and then **click** once. The path now has an insertion point added to the line.

6. **Type** the text you want to add. As you type, the words flow along the curve of the path, as shown in picture 8.2.

After creating the desired text, you can modify the text using the Options bar or the Character panel. You learn to format the text using the Options bar in the next section.

Formatting Text using the Options Bar

In most cases, you create the text with the default settings and later edit the text with the settings that match your requirement. In other words, it is rather difficult to assume the text settings that match the rest of the design elements. Photoshop CS6 always remembers the last used settings for the type tools unless you restart Photoshop. When you select a type tool, Photoshop CS6 displays related settings/options on the Options bar. Perform the following steps to format text using the Options bar:

1. **Open** a document and **type** the text that you want to format. A new layer is created in the Layer panel.

2. **Double-click** the type layer thumbnail to select the text in the Document window.

3. Drag the **Set the font size** icon to set a new font size. In our case, we set the font size to **18 pt**.

The method of dragging the icon to change the font size is useful as it simultaneously updates the font size in the Document window. You can also select predefined size or type the font size in the Set the font size combo box.

4. **Select** a desired font family from the **Set the font family** dropdown lit. In our case, we our case, we select **Papyrus**.

5. Click the **Set the text color** swatch in the Options bar. The **Color Picker (Text Color)** dialog box appears.

6. Select **red** color for your text. The text in the Document window simultaneously updates with the selected color.

7. Click the **OK** button to close the dialog box. Then select **Move Tool** to select the text. Let's now learn to format a text using the Character panel.

Formatting Text using the Character Panel

The Character panel provides the options, such as font family, font style, and other text attributes, such as font size, color, leading, kerning, tracking, language, horizontal scale, and anti-aliasing. You can modify these settings to format the selected text. You can open the Character panel by selecting Window> Character from the Menu bar. Perform the following steps to use the Character panel to format the text:

1. **Select** the type layer in the Layers panel and choose **Window> Character** from the Menu bar to open the Character panel.

2. **Select** the text you want to modify. Then **select** the desired font family in the **Set the font family** dropdown list. In our case, we select **Segoe Print**.

3. **Select** the desired font size in the **Set the font size** combo box. In our case, we have selected **20 pt** for our text.

4. **Select** the desired tracking in the **Set the tracking for the selected characters** dropdown list. In our case, we select **140**.

5. Select the desired baseline shift in the **Set the baseline shift** dropdown list. In our case, we have selected **-8 pt**.

6. Select the desired horizontal scale in the **Horizontally scale** dropdown list. In our case, we have selected **120%**.

7. Deselect the text by clicking **Move Tool** or selecting another layer in the Layers panel. Let's now learn to edit text in Photoshop CS6.

Working with Text

In Photoshop CS6, after creating the text, you can work with the text as per the requirement. You can edit the text by warping text. The warping options allow creating a heading within a Photoshop document. You can also check for spelling mistakes in your type layers. Further, you can convert a type layer to a standard raster layer. By converting a type layer to a raster layer, you can apply filter effects as well as painting effects. Let's now learn to warp text in Photoshop.

Warping Text

In Photoshop CS6, you can create text in almost any size and shape. In addition to straight horizontal and vertical text, Photoshop also allows you to created warped text. Warping options give you the control to present your text creatively. Warping text does not require converting the text into raster data. That means you can change font family, font size, and color of the warped text.

You can access the warp text options from the Options bar. Click the Create warped text button to open the Warp Text dialog box. In this dialog box, you can select different warp styles from the Style dropdown list. Note that the Create warped text button is available only when there is a text selected or the insertion mode in active. Perform the following steps to warp text in Photoshop:

1. **Type** the text in a Photoshop document. Photoshop creates a new layer.

2. **Double-click** the type layer thumbnail in the Layers panel to highlight all text in that type layer.

3. Click the **Create warped text** button on the Options bar. The Warp Text dialog box appears.

Picture 8.3

4. **Select** the desired warp text option from the Style dropdown list. In our case, we select **Bulge**. The options related to the Bulge options, such as Bend, Horizontal Distortion, and Vertical Distortion appear in the Warp Text dialog box.

5. Drag the **Bend** slider handle to set the value to **+50%**. Then drag the **Horizontal Distortion** slider handle to set the value to **+60%**.

6. Drag the **Vertical Distortion** slider handle to set the value to **+15%**. Then click the **OK** button to apply the changes on the selected text.

7. Select the **Move Tool** in the Tools panel to deselect the text. The warped text appears in the Document window, as shown in picture 8.3.

Checking for Spelling Mistakes

While typing text, you might misspell a single or multiple words. Such spelling mistakes are likely to occur when the typing is done in haste. Spelling mistakes are not quite appreciated and accepted on a professional front. Photoshop includes a fully functional spell checking system, which lets you ensure all of your words are spelled correctly. Photoshop continues to highlight misspelled words until the document is completely scanned. Perform these steps to check spelling mistakes in your text:

1. **Open** the document that contains the text. You can open a document with one or more type layers.

2. **Double-click** the type layer thumbnail to select the text in the Document. Then choose **Edit> Check Spelling** from the Menu bar to open the Check Spelling dialog box.

The **Check Spelling** dialog box appears when Photoshop does not find a word in its dictionary. If there are no mistakes, Photoshop displays a Spell check complete message box.

3. Select an option in the Suggestion list box. Then click the **Change** button to change the word to the currently selected option and **move** to the next word that is not found in Photoshop's dictionary.

When Photoshop does not find a word in its built-in dictionary, it displays that word in the Not in Dictionary text box. You can choose one of the following options in the Check Spelling dialog box:

- **Ignore:** Ignores the word once.
- **Ignore All:** Ignores all instances of the word.
- **Change:** Lets you replace the incorrect word with a new word of your choice.
- **Change All:** Replaces all similar occurrences of the incorrect word with the suggested word.
- **Add:** Appends the word to Photoshop dictionary

4. Click the **OK** button to close the message box and the Check Spelling dialog box. Let's now learn to convert a type layer into a normal raster layer.

Rasterizing Type Layers

The advantage of using the type tool is that you can modify these options as per your requirement either before or after typing the text. You can choose a font from the font family dropdown list. In Photoshop CS6, some tools and commands are not available for the type layers. For instance, you cannot apply any filter effects or use the point tools on type layers.

To use the painting tools or filter effects, you first need to rasterize the type layer, which implies converting the type layer into a normal layer. You can select Layer> Rasterize> Type from the Menu bar to convert. However, after you convert a type layer into a normal layer, you cannot apply text formatting options, such as font size, and font style. This is because Photoshop treats the layer as an image layer. Rasterize command converts type layers, shape layers, vector masks, or smart objects into raster images. Perform the following steps to rasterize a type layer:

1. **Open** a Photoshop document containing one or more type layers.

2. **Select** the type layer that you want to convert in the Layers panel.

3. Choose **Layer> Rasterize> Type** from the Menu bar. As the result, the selected type layer is converted into a standard layer.

Working with Type Mask

Photoshop CS6 has two type mask tools that let you create mask: Horizontal Type Mask Tool and Vertical Type Mask Tool. You can use the type mask tools to create selections that match with the shape of the text. When you create text using Horizontal Type Tool and Vertical Type Tool, the text appears in the current foreground color. However, when you use the type mask tools, Photoshop creates a mask in the size and shape of the selected font with the mask appearing as a red overlay.

When you create type masks, the mask appears in the active layer. Unlike normal type layer, Photoshop does not create type layers. You can also modify the mask similar to a normal type layer after creating it. Perform the following steps to create a type mask:

1. **Open** a document with good background image in Photoshop to create a type mask, as shown in picture 8.4.

2. Select **Horizontal Type Mask Tool** from the Tools panel. Then **click** inside the Document window and **type** the text. In our case, we type: **TYPE MASK**. It is shown in picture 8.5.

Picture 8.4

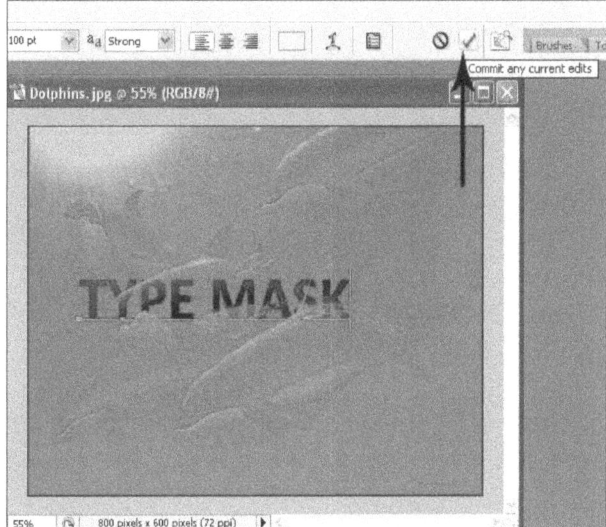

Picture 8.5

As you type, Photoshop creates a mask in the size and shape of the current font. Also note that, type mask must be selected before applying any of the changes.

3. After typing the text, you need to **select** the text by dragging from right to left and change the font size to **100 pt**.

4. Click the **Commit any current edits** button on the Options bar, as shown in picture 8.5 with the black arrow. Photoshop converts the mask from a red overlay into a traditional selection.

One of the advantages to a type mask is that you can create type using any fill you desire. For instance, you can create a type mask with any word and then use the image of any kind and mask to create a unique fill.

5. Press **Ctrl+J** keys together to copy the selection into a new layer.

6. **Open** a new white document, and **drag** and **drop** this masked layer in the new document. Your new document will look as shown in picture 8.6.

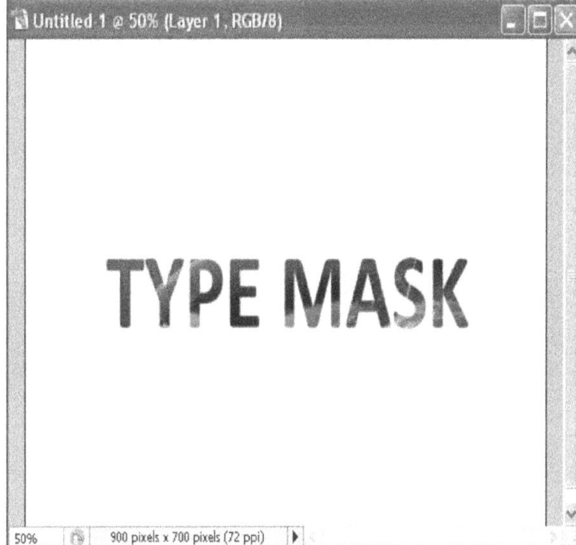

Picture 8.6

Constraining Text to a Shape

You can add a textual element to an image using a work path. It is a great way to add creative text style in your image. You can select an object in your image of any shape and add the text within that shape. This way the text can be merged seamlessly into your image rather just placing the text over the image.

To achieve this effect, make a selection of the shape of the object using any of the selection tools. After the selection, you need to convert the selection into a work path. You can use this work path to constrain the text flow. Perform the following steps to create text effect by constraining the text flow:

1. **Open** an image and **make** a selection using any of the selection tools.

2. **Right-click** inside the selection and select the **Make Work Path** option from the context menu, as shown in picture 8.7.

3. In the <u>Make Work Path</u> dialog box it opens, click the **OK** button in the default tolerance value.

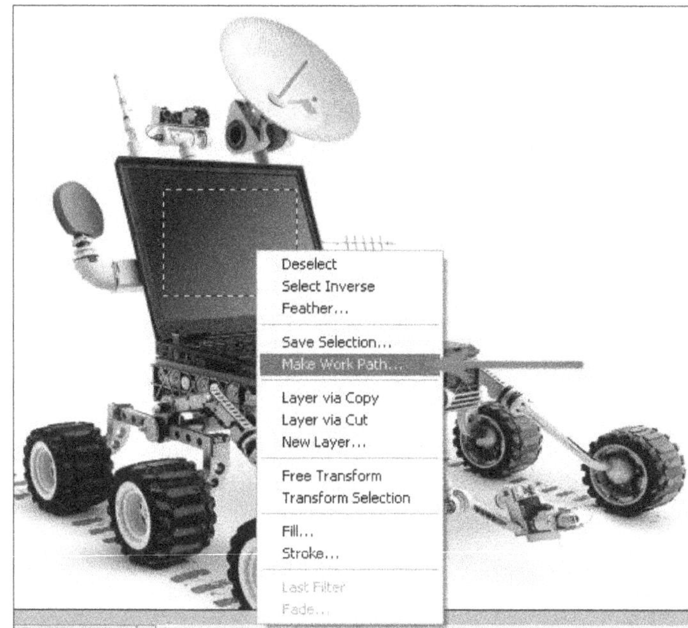

Picture 8.7

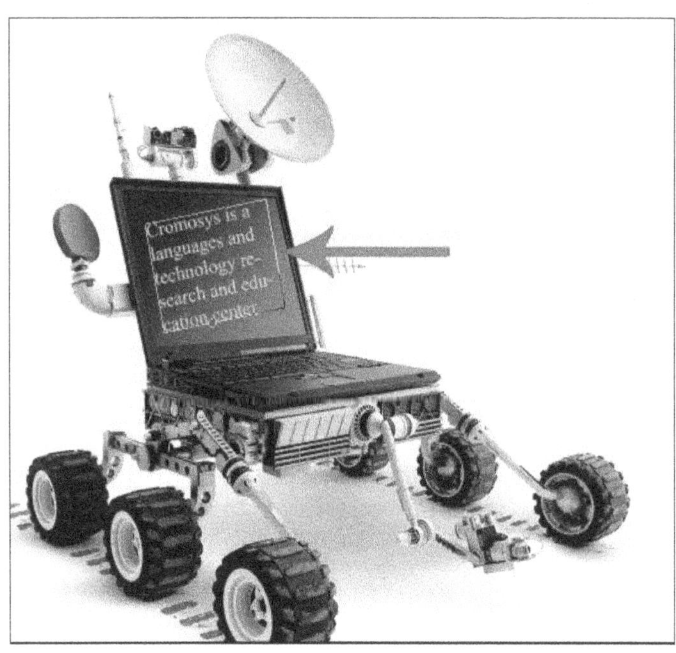

Picture 8.8

A new path is created in the Paths panel, which is automatically displayed in the Layers panel group.

4. **Select** a type tool on the Tools panel. In our case, we select **Horizontal Type Tool**. Then **click** inside the work path to pick a starting point.

Ensure to click inside the work path, else Photoshop creates text on the work path. A dotted circle appears around the type tool cursor indicating the text will appear inside the work path.

5. **Type** the text. The text constrains within the shape of the work path, as shown in picture 8.8.

Working with Character Styles

As discussed earlier, Photoshop CS6 introduces two new panels: Character Styles and Paragraph Styles. You can use these panels to create and save type styles, which are the popular features in Adobe InDesign. These features advance the type editing capabilities in Photoshop. A group of formatted text attributes is collectively called a type style. There are two types of type styles: character and paragraph; that are briefly discussed as follows:

- **Character style:** Refers to the group of attributes, such as font size, color, kerning, and leading of the character.
- **Paragraph style:** Refers to group of both character and paragraph attributes, such as indents and spacing, alignment, and hyphenation.

In Photoshop CS6, the Character Styles and Paragraph Styles panels allow you to create character and paragraph type styles. You can also save the character and paragraph style as presets. Presets allow you to quickly apply the predefined text formatting in the existing as well as new document. They also allow you to organize text formatting and optimize the text editing workflow. Let's now learn to create a custom character style.

Creating Custom Character Style

To create a custom character style, you can format some text the way you want using the Option bar or the Character panel. After formatting the text, select the New Character Style option from the Character Styles panel menu or click the Create new Character Style button at the bottom of the Character Styles panel.

By default, Photoshop CS6 names a new character style as Character Style 1. You can rename the character style by double-clicking it in the panel and then typing a desired name in the Style Name text box of the Character Style Options dialog box. You can also use the Character Style Options dialog box to further edit the character style. Once you save the style, you can simply select the type layer in the Layers panel, and then click the style name from the list in the Character Styles panel. You can apply the new style on a single or groups of characters. Perform the following steps to create a custom character style:

1. **Open** an existing document or **create** a new document. Then select a **type tool** and type the text in the Document window.

The text you type is created using the default type settings. Now, you can format the text as per the style you want to create. Before formatting text, ensure that you select the text.

2. **Double-click** the type layer thumbnail to select all text in the Document window.

3. **Format** the text using the <u>Character panel</u>. In our case, we format our text by changing its font size, font family, font color, and horizontal scale.

4. Choose **Window> Character Styles** from the Menu bar to open the Character Styles panel. The Character Styles panel appears in the Photoshop window. This panel stores the character styles and you can organize character styles using this panel.

5. Click the **Create new Character Style** button at the bottom of the panel. A new character style is created with the default name **Character Style 1**, and appears selected.

6. **Double-click** the new character style in the Character Styles panel. The Character Style Options dialog box appears. In this dialog box, you can further format the text, if required and rename the new character style.

7. **Type** a new name for the newly created character style. In our case, we rename it as **Heading 1**. Then click the **Faux Italic** check box to change the font style.

8. Click the **OK** button to save the changes and close the dialog box. The new character style appears in the Character Styles panel.

Next time you create a text in the existing document, the text appears with the new character panel. You can either select another character style or override the character style. The Clear Override option lets you reverse the changes to the preset's default value. Let's now learn to apply a character style to a text.

Applying a Character Style

The new character style feature saves lot of time while working with text in Photoshop. You can save a character style and reuse as many times you want. When you create a new type layer, Photoshop always applies its default text settings on the type layer. Photoshop names the default character style as None. You can modify the default character style as per your requirement. However, you can create and apply custom character styles. To apply a custom character style, create the type layer and select the custom style in the Character Styles panel. Perform the following steps on your computer to apply a custom character style:

1. **Type** the text with default settings in your document. Before typing the text, ensure that **None** is selected in the Character Styles panel.

2. **Click** the character style in the Character Styles panel. In our case, we click **Heading 1,** and this character style is applied to the selected type layer.

In this section, you have learnt to create and apply character styles. You can also create paragraph styles in Photoshop CS6 using the Paragraph Styles panel. You can use the Paragraph Style Options dialog box to create and manage the paragraph style presets in Photoshop CS6. The method of creating a paragraph style is similar to the method of creating a character style. Let's now learn to create 3D text in Photoshop CS6.

Creating 3D Text

Photoshop CS6 allows you to create 3D text from 2D text. The 3D feature is available only in the Photoshop CS6 Extended version. While working with text, you can convert a 2D text to 3D text using the Update 3D associated with the text option present on the Options bar. After converting a text into 3D, you can work with it as a 3D object using various options in Photoshop CS6. You will learn to work with 3D objects later in this book. In this section, you will learn to create 3D text by converting a 2D text into 3D. Perform the following steps to create 3D text in Photoshop CS6:

1. **Create** a new document and **type** the text. Then **double-click** the type layer thumbnail to select the text in the Document window.

2. Click the button **3D** present on the Options bar. A message box appears seeking the permission to switch to the 3D workspace.

3. Click the **Yes** button to switch to the 3D workspace. The 3D workspace appears with panels related to work with 3D objects.

In the 3D workspace, you can modify the 3D text using various options in the 3D and Properties panels. You can change the color, apply texture, and render the 3D objects in Photoshop CS6 Extended version. The 3D Mode options on the Options bar let you work with the 3D view. In the next section, let's learn how to use layer styles on the type layers.

Adding Layer Styles on Type Layers

Layer styles are built-in special effects that you can apply in all kinds of layers. They are non-destructive and they remain editable if you save the document in PSD file format. You can also add layer styles to the type layers to make them stand out in your design. Layer styles are the popular choice among designers to create amazing typographic effects. Perform these steps to add layer styles on type layer:

1. **Type** the text using a type tool in a document. Then **double-click** an empty area on the type layer in the Layers panel. It opens the Layer Style dialog box.

In the Layers panel, when you double-click the type layer thumbnail, the text in the Document window highlights. Double-clicking the type layer name allows you to rename the type layer.

2. Select the **Stroke** check box in the Styles pane. Then type the value **8** in the Size text box in the Structure section.

3. Select the **Bevel & Emboss** check box in the Styles pane. Then select (enable) the **Texture** checkbox under the Bevel & Emboss option.

4. Click **OK** button with default settings. The layer style appears on the text on your Document window. Similarly, you can experiment with different styles and their settings to create interesting text effects.

Lesson 8
Painting and Retouching in Photoshop

Photoshop CS6 offers many creative capabilities, such as painting and retouching tools to create new images or modify existing images. This type image editing with the use of computers, where digital tools are used to perform all the traditional painting techniques is known as digital painting. For instance, you can use Photoshop's brush tools instead of conventional paintbrush. In Photoshop CS6, painting involves changing the colors of the pixels that make up any digital image. Using Photoshop's painting tools, you can paint with soft edges. Photoshop CS6 provides several painting tools, such as Brush Tool, Clone Stamp Tool, Pattern Stamp Tool, History Brush Tool, and Art History Brush Tool. These brush tools help in the creation of images using digital brush strokes.

Retouching is the most popular aspect of Photoshop. You can enhance digital images using the retouching tools including Healing Brush Tool, Patch Tool, Red Eye Tool, Burn Tool, and Dodge Tool. A typical workflow consists of importing raw images into Photoshop from your digital camera and then retouching them using various retouching tools. For instance, you can enhance a photograph by reducing excess noise from it or you can lighten and soften a person's skin tone and texture.

In this chapter, you will first learn to modify images using various painting tools in Photoshop including Gradient Tool, Brush Tool, Mixer Brush Tool, Color Replacement Tool, and Clone Stamp Tool. Towards the end, you will learn about the array of retouching tools, such as Healing Brush Tool, Patch Tool, Blur Tool, Sharpen Tool, and Dodge Tool. Let's begin the chapter by working with the painting tools.

Working with Painting Tools

Photoshop CS6 provides several tools to paint images and edit their color. For instance, Brush Tool works similar to a real world painting tool and can be used to apply color with brush strokes. Similarly, Gradient Tool and Paint Bucket Tool are used to apply color to large areas of an image or selection.

In the Options bar for each tool, you can set the way you want the color to be applied to an image and also select a brush size from the Brush Presets picker. In the subsequent selections, you learn about Gradient Tool, Paint Bucket Tool, Brush Tool, Pencil Tool, and Color Replacement Tool. Now, let's begin with Gradient Tool.

Using Gradient Tool

A gradient is a type of fill that is made up of two or more colors blended together. Gradient Tool is used to fill an area with smooth or sharp transitions (ascending or descending) from one color to another. In Photoshop, you can fill an area with linear, radial, angle, reflected, diamond and multi-colored gradients. A gradient fill can be applied to a selection or an entire layer. The starting point (where the mouse button is clicked on an image) and ending point (where the mouse button is released) affect the gradient's appearance, depending on the pattern selected by the user. Gradient Tool cannot be used on images in the Bitmap or Indexed Color modes.

You can apply gradients by using the preset selection of colors or you can create your own gradient. When you select Gradient Tool on the Tools panel, the Options bar displays the related settings. Before applying a gradient fill, you can select the type of gradient you want to create on the Options bar. The five types of gradient fills that can be applied to a selection or a layer are:

- **Linear Gradient:** Applies the gradient from the start point to the end point in a straight or diagonal line
- **Radial Gradient:** Applies the gradient in a circular pattern
- **Angle Gradient:** Applies the gradient at a defined angle
- **Reflected Gradient:** Applies the linear gradients on both sides of the starting point
- **Diamond Gradient:** Applies to create a starting point in the outward diamond pattern

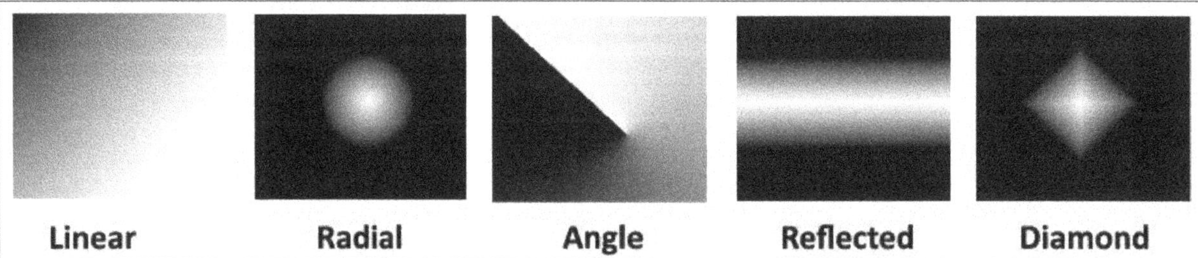

Picture 8.9 illustrates all the gradient fill types

In addition to gradient fill types, you can also adjust other options of the Gradient Tool in the Options bar. Besides the gradient types, the available options on the Options bar are:

- **Gradient picker:** Allows you to select a preset gradient fill.
- **Mode:** Allows you to select any of the Photoshop's blending modes for the gradient fill. The default blending mode for gradient fill is Normal.
- **Opacity:** Allows you to set the transparency of the gradient fill. You can set an opacity value ranging from 0% to 100%. By default, the opacity value is set to 100%.
- **Reverse:** Reverses the order in which the colors in the gradient are applied. By default, this option is unchecked.
- **Dither:** Adds noise or random information. This option is selected by default.
- **Transparency:** Allows you to add transparency to your gradient using gradient mask. By default, the Transparency check box is selected.

After knowing about the gradient options on the Options bar, perform the following steps on your computer to apply and modify a gradient fill to an image:

1. **Open** an image in which you want to apply the gradient fill. Then select **Gradient Tool** from the Tools panel, as shown in picture 9.0 with the red arrow numbered 1.

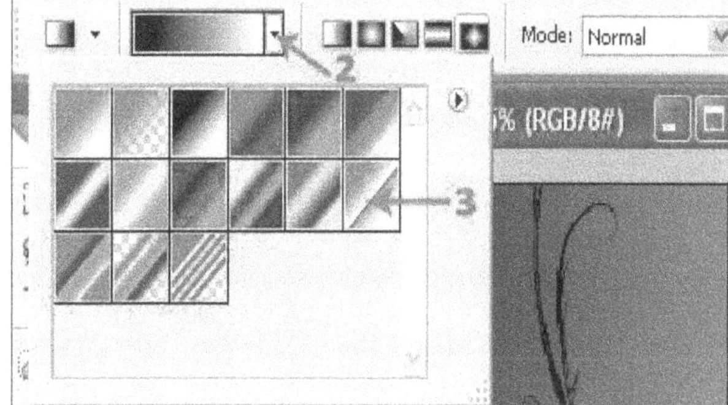

Picture 9.0   Picture 9.1

2. **Click** the down-arrow next to the gradient sample in the Options bar. A pop-up window called the **Gradient picker** opens, as shown in picture 9.1 with the red arrow numbered 2.

3. **Select** the gradient preset in the Gradient picker. In our case, we have selected the **Chrome** preset as the gradient (shown in picture 9.1 with the red arrow numbered 3).

4. Select the **Radial Gradient** fill type on the Options bar (shown in picture 9.2 with the red arrow numbered 4).

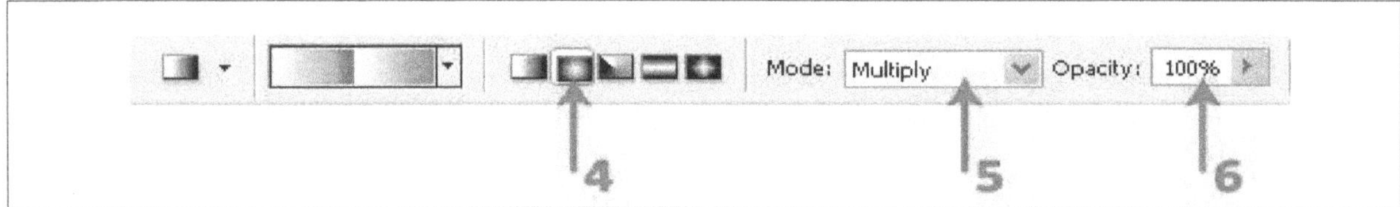

Picture 9.2

5. **Select** a blending mode in the <u>Mode</u> dropdown list. In our case, we have selected **Multiply** (shown in picture 9.3 with the red arrow numbered 5).

6. **Type** a transparency value in the <u>Opacity</u> combo box. In our case, we have kept the default value **100%** (shown in picture 9.2 with the red arrow numbered 6).

You can notice on your screen that the preview of the Chrome gradient fill changes as you change the settings on the Options bar.

7. **Click** and **drag** the mouse-pointer from center of the image to top-left corner of the image, as shown in picture 9.3 with the red arrow numbered 7.

Picture 9.3   Picture 9.4

The radial gradient fill effect applies on the image, as shown in picture 9.4. You can click and drag in any direction or any length with Gradient Tool; each time you will get a different result. You can try different angles and settings to decide the best effect for your design. Similarly, you can select any other gradient presets from the Gradient picker pop-up window and apply them on the images or selections. You can also modify the gradient presets by changing the color in the Gradient Editor dialog box. You can access the Gradient Editor dialog box by clicking the gradient sample in the Options bar.

8. You can **click** the gradient sample for the selected preset on the Options bar, as already shown in picture 9.2 with the red arrow numbered 4. The **Gradient Editor** dialog box appears on your screen.

You can click below the gradient spectrum (bar) to add a new color stop and drag a color stop away from the gradient bar to remove it. You can also adjust the amount of each color by dragging the color stop left and right. Similarly, to add transparency, select a color stop and then specify a value for the Opacity option.

9. You can click the **OK** button in the Gradient Editor dialog box after you have modified the gradient settings.

10. Press **Ctrl+Z** keys together once to undo the previous gradient fill.

11. **Click** and **drag** the mouse-pointer from center of the image to top-left corner of the image to apply the modified gradient.

Using Brush Tools

Brush tools, as the name suggests, works similar to paintbrushes that you use in the real-world. These tools paint smooth strokes with the foreground color of an image. You can also use a brush tool to paint textures or part of an image using Pattern Stamp Tool and Clone Stamp Tool, respectively. By default, the mouse-pointer appears as a circle icon when a brush tool is selected, and indicates the current position of the brush.

You can also change the brush pointer to a cross-hair by pressing the Caps Lock key on the keyboard. You can save a set of brush settings as a brush preset. Brush presets allow quick access to frequently used brush characteristics. By default, Photoshop CS6 includes several sample brush presets. You can start with a preset and then modify it to produce a new brush effect. You can quickly choose presets from the Brush Preset picker on the Options bar. The Brush Preset picker also allows you to create new brush presets and modify brush settings, such as size and hardness.

By default, brush tools paints brush strokes with soft edges. When you paint diagonal brush strokes, you draw jagged lines. However, by default Photoshop applies anti-aliasing to diagonal brush strokes to create soft edges. When you select Brush Tool, several options specific to the tool appear in the Options bar, as shown in picture 9.5.

Picture 9.5

The list below explains in detail about the options that you find in Options bar when you select the Brush Tool:

- **Mode:** Allows you to change the blending mode for the brush strokes. Behind and Clear are the two additional blending modes that are available for Brush Tool.
- **Opacity:** Controls the transparency of the brush strokes. You must set the transparency value before painting a brush stroke.
- **Flow:** Controls the rate at which a brush tool applies the paint. By default, the Flow option is set to 100%.
- **Airbrush:** Activates the airbrush mode. This mode produces the spray effect. The longer you hold the mouse-button, the more the paint pumps out, and the wider the airbrush effect spreads.

The typical workflow of a Brush Tool consists of selecting a color, setting options, such as brush size, hardness, and flow; and then painting over the area. You can also zoom in the image to precisely point small areas and corners. You can press the [or] key to decrease or increase the brush size respectively. Perform the following steps to paint an image using Brush Tool:

1. **Open** a drawing in which you want to paint using Brush Tool. Then select **Brush Tool** on the Tools panel or press the **B key**.

2. Select a color in **Set foreground color** that you want to paint with. In our case, we have selected **red** color.

3. Click the **Brush Preset** button on the Options bar to open the Brush Preset picker. Then select the brush size **35 px**.

4. **Select** the hardness value **20%** for the brush. Then **paint** over the parts of the drawing that you want to paint with the foreground color (red).

Similarly, you can paint over other areas with the color you want. Photoshop CS6 contains a library of brush presets, from which you can use to paint your drawing. The Brush Presets panel displays different types of brush tips that can be applied with Brush Tool. The Brush Presets picker stores saved brush tip settings, such as brush size, hardness, and airbrush, as well as the brush options available in the Brush panel. You can load various brush libraries using the Brush Presets panel.

The Brush Presets panel includes the Size option, which temporarily changes the brush size until you do not select any other brush or tool. You can drag the Size slider or enter a value to specify the size of the selected brush. The Brush Presets panel menu lets you select brush libraries. Let's learn about Mixer Brush Tool.

Using Mixer Brush Tool

Mixer Brush Tool was introduced in Photoshop CS5 and is a step forward in achieving realistic painting effects. It is a highly sophisticated painting tool with Bristle Tips options. Mixer Brush Tool allows you to combine two or more colors on a single brush tip. On the canvas, you can either mix colors with the underlying colors, or use a dry brush to blend the colors. Mixer Brush Tool lets you control paint wetness, load rate, mixing rate. After each stroke, Mixer Brush Tool lets you define whether the brush is cleaned or refilled. The new Bristle Tips option enables you to paint textured brush strokes. Perform the following steps to use Mixer Brush Tool to convert an image into a painting:

1. **Open** an image in Photoshop in which you want to use Mixer Brush Tool. Then select **Mixer Brush Tool** on the Tools panel.

2. Click the **Brush Preset** button on the Options bar to open the Brush Presets picker.

3. Select the **Round Fan Stiff Thin Bristle** brush tip.

4. **Set** the brush size to **85 px** in the Size text box. A thumbnail representing the Bristle Tip appears on top-left corner of the Document window.

You can change the Size value in three different ways in Photoshop:

    A. Type the exact value in the Size text box and press the Enter key.

    B. Highlight the Size text box and press the Up Arrow or Down Arrow keys to increase or decrease the values respectively.

    C. Drag the slider handle towards right to increase and towards left to decrease the value.

Similarly, you can follow one of the above ways to change values in other options.

5. Choose **Window> Brush** from the Menu bar or press the F5 key to open the Brush panel. The Brush panel appears with the settings for the selected brush tip, as shown in picture 9.6.

6. Select **Flat Curve** shape in the Shape dropdown list.

7. Set the **Bristles** value to **93%**. Then, set the **Length** value to **295%**. And then, set the **Thickness** value to **13%**.

8. Set the **Angle** value to 13^0. Then set the **Spacing** value to **6%**.

The modified brush thumbnail appears on top-left corner of the Document window.

You modify bristle characteristics to create realistic brush strokes. In the Brush panel, you can set the following options for the Bristle Tips:

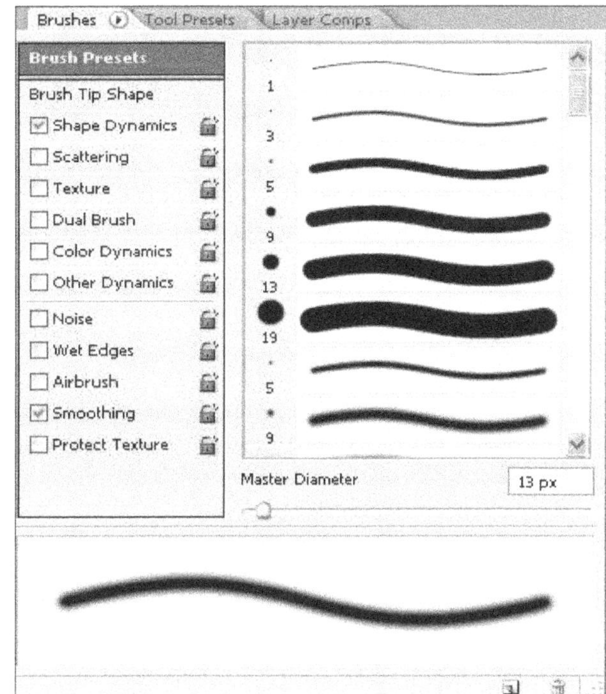

Picture 9.6

- **Shape**: Allows you to specify bristles arrangement.
- **Bristles**: Allows you to specify bristle density.
- **Length**: Allows you to modify the bristle length.
- **Thickness**: Allows you to specify the width of individual bristles.
- **Stiffness**: Allows you to specify the bristle flexibility.
- **Angle**: Allows you to specify the brush tip angle.
- **Spacing**: Allows you to specify the distance between the brush marks in a stroke.

9. Press the **F5 key** on the keyboard to hide the Brush panel, with all other options to their default settings.

10. **Paint** over the areas that you want to convert to a painting. In our case, we have converted an image into a real-world painting.

While painting, you need to click and drag multiple times to paint with different brush sizes and settings, which can be changed in the Brush panel. One of the most important options for the Mixer Brush Tool is the Wet option. This option appears on the Options bar when Mixer Brush Tool is selected. The Wet option lets you control the amount of paint the brush picks up from the canvas.

Using Color Replacement

Color Replacement Tool allows you to manually paint color, hue, saturation, and luminosity values with a brush. It preserves the original texture unlike Brush Tool. It simplifies the process of replacing specific colors in an image. You can paint over an image or a selection and replace its original color with a new color. You cannot use Color Replacement Tool on images in Bitmap, Indexed, and Multi-channel color modes. Perform the following steps to use Color Replacement Tool to change the color of a selection:

1. **Open** an image and **make** a selection of the object you want to change. In our case, we create a path using Pen Tool and then convert the path into a selection.

2. Select the **color** in the foreground color box. In our case, we select **red** color.

3. **Hold down** Brush Tool on the Tools panel and then select **Color Replacement Tool** from the flyout. Once Color Replacement Tool is active, you can set various options, such as Mode, Limits, Tolerance, and Anti-alias, specific to this tool in the Options bar.

4. Click the **Brush Preset** down arrow to open the Brush Preset picker.

5. **Set** the brush size as **35 px** in the Size text box. Then, set the brush hardness value as **71%** in the Hardness text box. And then, set the spacing value as **50%** in the Spacing text box.

6. **Paint** over the areas in which you want to replace the color to red. In our case, the color is now replaced with red color.

As you can see on your screen, Color Replacement Tool preserves the some texture and paints a red color over it. When you click and drag to paint with Color Replacement Tool selected, Photoshop picks a sample color and analyzes the pixels below the tool and determines the pixels that match the sample color, and paints only those color. It does not completely replace the image with the red color as you paint with a brush tool.

Using Clone Stamp Tool

Clone Stamp Tool is the perfect tool for replacing part of an image. This tool is also used to clone or duplicate selected areas of an image and paint the area over another part or image. You can sample the part of the image that you want to duplicate and paint over another part of the same image or another image. However, note that you can only paint the sampled pixels over another image that has the same color mode as the sampled pixels you can also paint part of one layer over another layer. For an example, picture 9.7 shows the image on which we applied Clone Stamp Tool, and the result is shown in picture 9.8. We really enjoyed removing the hammer and the broken pieces from the source image which is picture 9.7.

Picture 9.7

The Aligned option allows you to paint with the current sampling point whenever you resume painting. However, if you want to paint each stroke from the initial sampling point, deselect the Aligned option on the Options bar. For precise control over the size of clone area, you can use different brush tips. You can control the behavior of the brush tip using the Opacity and Flow settings available in the Options bar.

Photoshop CS6 provides a preview of the sampled area within the brush tip when you sample pixels. Perform the following steps to use Clone Stamp Tool to duplicate selected areas:

Picture 9.8

1. **Open** an image in Photoshop in which you want to use clone. Then select **Clone Stamp Tool** on the Tools panel.

2. Click the **Brush Preset** picker button on the Options bar. The Brush Preset picker appears on your screen.

3. Drag the **Size** slider handle to **150 px** to set the diameter of the brush. Then, drag the **Hardness** slider handle to **15%** to set the brush hardness.

4. **Click** the image while holding the Alt key down to sample pixels. Then move the mouse-pointer over the area where you want the sampled pixels (clone) to appear. The preview of the sample pixels appear inside the brush tip.

5. **Drag** to clone of sampled pixels. As you drag, the clone of the sampled pixels appear gradually on your screen. When you drag, limit the area to the shape of the object you are cloning. This avoids unnecessary areas to be added in the process.

Using Pattern Stamp Tool

Pattern Stamp Tool works in the same way as Clone Stamp Tool, except that the Pattern Stamp Tool clones from predefined pixels, such as a pattern, rather than from a source point in the image. You can select this tool by clicking and holding the mouse-button on Clone Stamp Tool. When using Pattern Stamp Tool:

    A. You first have to select an existing pattern from the Options bar, or Define a new pattern by using the Define Pattern option in the Edit menu.
    B. Clone this pattern by using Pattern Stamp Tool on an image.
    C. After selecting the pattern, click and drag over the area you want to replace with the pattern.

You can select a blending mode from the Options bar to merge the pattern with the existing pixels. Until now, you have learnt about various painting tools. Let's learn about retouching tools in Photoshop in the next section.

Working with Retouching Tools

Besides painting tools, Photoshop CS6 provides different retouching tools, which can be used to enhance images by performing various corrections. You can use these tools to fix any kind of imperfection, such as patches, scan lines, or red eyes. You can remove these and other defects from your images with the help of the retouching tools. In the following sections, you learn about the most commonly used retouching tools including Spot Healing Brush Tool, Healing Brush Tool, Patch Tool, Eraser Tool, Blur Tool, Sharpen Tool, Smudge Tool, Dodge Tool, Burn Tool, and Sponge Tool. Some commonly used retouching tools are discussed in the subsequent sections.

Using Spot Healing Brush Tool

Spot Healing Brush Tool primarily used to rapidly retouch imperfections in an image. Unlike Healing Brush Tool, it does not allow to pick a sample area. Instead, it automatically samples pixels from the surrounding area and matches elements, such as texture, lighting, transparency, and shading of the sampled pixels, and paints the targeted pixels with the characteristics of the sampled pixels. This tool is very effective where the surrounding area is free of imperfections.

You can set different options on the Options bar, such as Mode, Type, and Sample All Layers. The Mode option lets you select a blending mode for the tool. The Type option allows you to set a type for the pixels to be filled. For instance, the Content-Aware option compares surrounding image content with the imperfection pixels and seamlessly replaces the pixels and retains key details, such as shadows and object edges. The Sample All Layers option samples pixels from all the visible layers, when working with multiple layered documents. Perform these steps to remove blemishes using Spot Healing Brush Tool:

1. **Open** an image with imperfections that you want to remove, (picture 9.9 with red arrows). Then select **Spot Healing Brush Tool** on the Tools panel.

Picture 9.9

Picture 10.0

2. **Click** the Brush picker down arrow to open the Brush picker pop-up window. Then **set** the brush tip size to **170 px**, as per the size of blemish you want to remove.

Preferably, you should select a brush tip larger than the spot you want to remove from your image.

3. **Place** your brush tip over the area you want to remove from your image.

4. **Click** the area you want to remove, as shown in picture 10.0. Photoshop automatically replaces the pixels with surrounding pixels.

In case, you are using a large image or replacing a large area, Photoshop displays a progress bar. The Progress message box tells you that to replace the area; Photoshop computes the texture using the Content-Aware Fill feature.

The result of the Spot Healing Brush Tool is shown in picture 10.1. Now, let's learn how to use Healing Brush Tool.

Picture 10.1

Using Healing Brush Tool

Healing Brush Tool allows you to remove imperfections by merging them into the surrounding area and making them disappear. Similar to the Spot Healing Brush Tool, the Healing Brush Tool matches the sampled pixels to the sources pixels to blend seamlessly into the rest of the image.

However, you need to pick sample pixels when using Healing Brush Tool. To sample pixels, click the image area while pressing the Alt key. Perform the following steps to use Healing Brush Tool to remove imperfections:

1. **Open** an image with the imperfections. Then, hold down **Spot Healing Brush Tool** on the Tools panel and select **Healing Brush Tool** from the flyout.

2. **Right-click** inside the Document window and **set** the size of the brush tip to **78 px** in the context menu. You can leave other options to their default values.

3. **Hold-down** the Alt key and **click** the surrounding area to sample the pixels you want to replace over the blemishes.

In the Options bar, ensure the Sampled radio button is selected. Alternatively, you can select the Pattern radio button, if you want to replace blemishes using the predefined Photoshop patterns or user-defined patterns. In our case, we are using the default settings for this retouching operation.

4. **Click** and **drag** the mouse-pointer over the area you want to retouch. A plus (+) sign appears in the area from where the pixels are picked as sample.

Similarly, you can remove the other blemishes in the image. You can click to sample pixels multiple times when removing larger object in an image. When healing in a separate layer, you can use the opacity and blending mode settings to control the healing process.

Using Patch Tool

Patch Tool is also used to retouch imperfections by taking samples from the correct area and matching the texture, transparency, and shading of the imperfect area. You can also use Patch Tool to clone areas of an image. Patch Tool selects similar to the Lasso Tool.

To make a selection using Patch Tool, select the tool from the Tools panel and drag around the imperfections or the area you want to replace. Now, place the mouse-pointer inside the selection. A small selection icon appears below Patch Tool. Click and drag the selection to the source area.

Source area is the pixels that you want to replace the existing selection. You can also use the Destination option, alternatively. Select the Destination radio button on the Options bar to drag the pixels you want to replace, over the imperfection pixels. Perform the following steps on your computer to use Patch Tool in Photoshop:

1. **Open** the image in which you want to retouch using Patch Tool. Then, **click** and **hold-down** Spot Healing Brush Tool on the Tools panel and select **Patch Tool** from the flyout.

2. **Make** a selection around the area you want to replace with Patch Tool. In the Options bar, make sure the Source radio button is selected.

3. **Place** Patch Tool cursor inside the selection and **drag** the selection over the source area. When you drag, the pixels at the source area are displayed inside the destination selection.

4. **Release** the mouse button when you are satisfied with the area you want to replace with.

When dragging the selection, you can see, two marquee selections; one over the area where you made the first selection with Patch Tool; and other selection is attached to the mouse-pointer. The first marquee selection displays a preview of the area under the marquee attached to the mouse-pointer when moved. If you select the Destination radio button in the Options bar, then you need to select the source first and then move the source over the area you want to replace.

Using Content-Aware Move Tool

In Photoshop CS6, a new content-aware feature is introduced as a separate tool called Content-Aware Move Tool. You can find this tool in the Spot Healing Brush Tool flyout. The Content-Aware Move Tool allows you to move or extend the selected pixels of your image. You can make selections using selection tools or any other methods.

After making the selection, you can drag it to a new position; Photoshop erases the earlier selection and moves the selection to your desired location. This happens when the Move option is selected for the Mode setting on the Options bar. This mode setting provides two options: Move and Extend, which are briefly explained below:

> **Move:** Fills the empty area with pixels based on the surrounding areas to create a realistic background.
> **Extend:** Extends the selection and fill the empty area with the surrounding pixels.

By default, the Mode setting is set to Move. You can also select an option for the Adaptation setting. By default, this setting is set to Medium. You can select options, such as Very Strict, Strict, Medium, Loose, and Very Loose for the Adaptation setting. Perform the following steps to use Content-Aware Move Tool to extend a selection:

1. **Open** an image to use Content-Aware Move Tool. Then, **hold down** Spot Healing Brush Tool and select **Content-Aware Move Tool** from the flyout.

2. **Make** a selection of the object that you want to extend using Content-Aware Move Tool.

3. Select **Extend** from the Mode dropdown list on the Options bar. Then, select the **Very Strict** option from the Adaptation dropdown list on the Options bar.

4. **Drag** the selection upward to extend it. After that, **release** the mouse button. As a result, the empty area created when you move the selection is filled by the Content-Aware algorithm.

For better results, move the selection by a smaller distance while holding the Shift key down. Using the Shift key constrains the movement into straight line. You can extend the selection cleanly using smaller movement multiple times.

Exploring Eraser Tool

Eraser Tool works similar to an ordinary eraser; that is, it removes portions of an image and replaces the deleted portion with the current background color or transparency.

If you are working on a Background layer, Eraser Tool erases pixels and fills with the background color. If you are working on a normal layer, Eraser Tool erases to transparency, that is, the pixels are removed and as a result the underlying layer in the Layers panel is exposed. However, if the layer transparency of a normal layer is locked, the pixels changes to the background color.

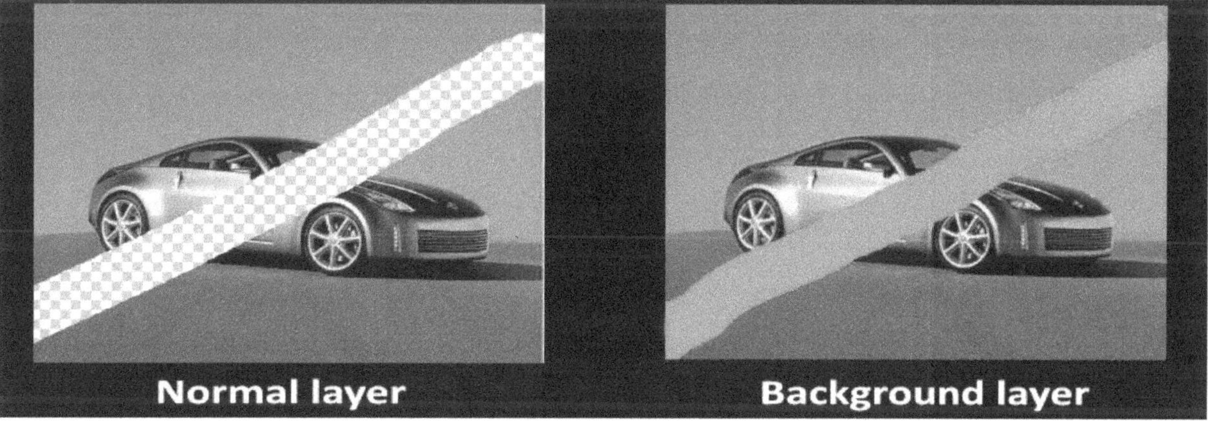

Picture 10.2

Picture 10.2 above shows how the Eraser Tool removes and fills pixels on a normal layer and a Background layer. As shown in this picture, Eraser Tool fills the current background color (green) in case of Background layer; and fills transparency in case of a normal layer. Let's now learn about Background Eraser Tool.

Using Background Eraser Tool

Background Eraser Tool erases pixels of an image and makes it transparent. In multi-layered images, the pixels of the Background layer are erased. As you click the image and drag the mouse-pointer, Background Eraser Tool automatically converts the Background layer to a normal layer with a transparent background.

When you select Background Eraser Tool, the cursor turns into a circle with a crosshair in it. This tool samples colors as you drag it on the image. The crosshair indicates the color that Background Eraser Tool samples and starts deleting the color as you drag. For instance, if you click the crosshair on a white background, it will only remove white color as you drag. However, if you move the crosshair over a different color, it begins to remove the color instead of the white. Perform the following simple steps to use Background Eraser Tool to remove a background:

1. **Open** an image with solid background. Then select **Background Eraser Tool** on the Tools panel. In our case, the image appears as a Background layer in the Layers panel.

2. **Set** the brush tip size to **60 px** in the Brush Preset picker. Then, **move** the brush tip over the edge of the object and ensure the crosshair stays over the background, which is white in our case.

3. **Drag** the brush tip near the edge of the object to remove the background. The background starts erasing without affecting the object.

You can also select various options on the Options bar for Background Eraser Tool. The three types of sampling options provided are:
> **Continuous:** Allows you to set different samples continuously as you drag over an image. This is helpful when you have to erase pixels of different colors from adjacent areas.
> **Once:** Limits the erasing action to the pixels similar in color to the portion where you clicked first (that is, where you clicked the first time to select the pixel).
> **Background Swatch:** Erases the portion that contains the current background color.

Similarly, the Limits option for Background Eraser Tool provides the following three options:
> **Discontiguous:** Erases similarly colored areas from non-adjacent areas
> **Contiguous:** Erases similarly colored areas from adjacent areas
> **Find Edges:** Erases pixels from similarly colored adjacent areas while preserving the edge contrast so that the edge boundaries of the image remain unaffected.

Exploring Magic Eraser Tool

Magic Eraser Tool can be compared to Magic Wand Tool, which is used to select similarly colored areas in an image based on the tolerance setting. Magic Eraser Tool erases pixels that are similar with the pixels that you click. By modifying the tolerance value, you can define the range of pixels that will be removed when you click with Magic Eraser Tool.

The tolerance value, on the Options bar, determines the range of colors of the pixels to be erased. The Opacity value determines the strength of the erasure. For instance, 100% opacity completely erases the pixels from an area of an image; while 50% opacity performs partial erasing.

If the Contiguous check box is cleared in the Options bar, the pixels of the color similar to the sampled area (the portion of the image you clicked the first time) are erased from the entire image or selection. In addition, if the Anti-aliased check box is selected, Magic Eraser Tool preserves the smoothness of the edges in the erased area.

Exploring Blur Tool

Blur Tool softens an image or makes it blurry. It works by reducing the contrast between pixels. Blur Tool is used to highlight an area in an image by blurring the rest of the image, or to smooth jagged edges. You can use Blur Tool to remove minor imperfections and smooth out wrinkles. The professional graphic designers use this tool at the finishing point of making an image ready. After the Blur Tool is used on an image, some minor mistakes in designing cannot be found. You can use the Lighten and Darken blending modes with Blur Tool to avoid over blurring the image.

The pixels that you modify using Blur Tool are permanently altered. You cannot convert the pixels back to their original state. However, you can use Sharpen Tool to sharpen the blurred image. To blur an image, select Blur Tool and paint over the area you want to blur.

Exploring Sharpen Tool

Sharpen Tool works opposite to Blur Tool and is used to increase the contrast and clarity of blurred images with soft edges. Sharpen Tool allows you to create defined edges in an image. Most images taken from a digital camera or scanner require some amount of sharpening. Remember that sharpening cannot correct a severely blurred image. Consider the following tips while sharpening your image in Photoshop:

- Sharpen the image on a separate layer.
- Use Luminance as the blending mode while sharpening to avoid color shift along the edges.
- Sharpen the image in multiple stages.

Exploring Smudge Tool

Smudge Tool is a powerful tool in Photoshop as it drags out the image pixels and creates the effect of smudging wet paint with a finger. Smudge Tool is used for painting or retouching. For instance, you can remove minor imperfections. It can also be useful for blending out the jagged edges that can sometimes occur when sizing up an image.

Exploring Dodge Tool

Dodge Tool lightens the pixels in an image. You can paint over an area with Dodge Tool to lighten the area. This way, the unnecessary dark portions of an image can be made lighter. The Options bar of Dodge Tool offers the Range option.

The additional options associated with the Range option are:
Shadows: Affects the darker areas of the image.
Midtones: Affects the middle range of the gray portions of an image.
Highlights: Affects the lighter areas of the image.

Exploring Burn Tool

Burn Tool is opposite in function to Dodge Tool in that it darkens the pixels. In graphic designing, this tool is used quite often. Using this tool, you can darken a specific area of an image. Sometimes, excessive diffusion of light can also spoil the quality of the image. For instance, an excessively lightened image may not be very pleasant to look at. In such a case, you can use Burn Tool to darken the pixels of the image to make it more pleasing to the eye.

The Options bar of Burn Tool is similar to the Options bar of Dodge Tool. You can select the Shadows, Midtones, and Highlights options from the Range dropdown list to burn the image. You can also set the level of exposure in the Exposure dropdown list in the Options bar. Exposure determines the extent to which the area is to be darkened.

Exploring Sponge Tool

Sponge Tool delicately modifies the color saturation of an area in the image. While working in the Grayscale mode, Sponge Tool increases or decreases the contrast of an image. You can use Sponge Tool to select a part of an image or the entire image. However, for beginners, it is commended to make a selection in the image before using Sponge Tool. This reduces the chances of working outside the required area in the image.

There are several tools in Photoshop to work with. In graphic designing, each tool plays an important role which helps us to design the image to meet the market demand. Each tool has its advantages and can be used to achieve certain effect. Sometimes, you can achieve similar effects using two separate tools in Photoshop, but over a period of time you get used to certain type of tools and use it more often than others.

Lesson 9
Using Filters and Automate Commands

Filters help you to create special effects in Photoshop. They also provide you the controls required to experiment and modify the filter for the desired result. For example, you can use the Liquify filter to push, pull, reflect, pucker, and bloat an area of the image. Using this filter you can create interesting effects on your image. You can run filters on image layers, masks, channels, smart objects and shape layers. Photoshop CS6 a new filter called Oil Paint, which turns an image into an oil painting and three Blur filters: Field Blur, Iris Blur, and Tilt-Shift.

In this fast paced designing environment, Photoshop's automation commands become more than just necessary. You can use automate commands for repetitive image processing tasks performed on a daily basis. These commands save time and enable you to deliver consistent quality results. For instance, you can process hundreds of image files with the click of a button through batch file processing, using the Batch command.

In this chapter, you will first learn about Photoshop's special effects known as filter. You will also learn about the Smart Filters and Filter Gallery. In addition, you will learn to apply various filter effects. Next, you will learn about actions wherein you will learn to create and play actions. Towards the end, you will learn to use automate commands including Batch and Crop and Straighten. Let's begin the chapter by understanding Photoshop filters.

Understanding Filters

Filters are the special effects that you can apply on any image. For instance, you can make an image appear as a hand drawn sketch using the Graphic Pen or Chalk & Charcoal filters. You can also use filters to retouch images or transform by applying unique distortions. In addition, you can make changes in a filter as per your requirements. Specify the values for the options associated with the filter to make changes in a filter. Some commonly used filters include Sharpen, Gaussian Blur, Motion Blur, Lens Correction, Despeckle, Liquify, and Vanishing Point. The Filter menu contains both standalone filters and filters in filter group:

- Filters with common effects or tasks, such as Artistic and Distort, appear under separate groups. Such a collection of filters is known as a filter group.
- Filters that do not fall under any filter group stand alone in the Filter menu, such as Liquify and Adaptive Wide Angle.

At the top of the Filter menu, the name of the last used filter appears. This option is used to quickly apply the last filter again on a selected layer. This option is followed by the Convert for Smart Filters and Filter Gallery options.

Photoshop CS6 introduces the Adaptive Wide Angle filter, which allows you to quickly straighten curved objects in panoramic images. Panoramic images are created when you shoot using cameras with fisheye or wide-angle lenses. In addition, Photoshop CS6 includes three blur filters: Field Blur, Iris Blur, and Tilt-Shift. You will learn more about these new features later in this chapter.

When you select a filter, a corresponding dialog box appears displaying the options related to the selected filter along with a preview pane. For instance, if you select the Lens Blur filter, the Lens Blur dialog box opens with the options related to the Lens Blur filter. Alternatively, you can select a filter and view its options by selecting a filter name in the Filter Gallery box. To open the Filter Gallery dialog box, you need to select Filter> Filter Gallery from the Menu bar. Let's now learn about Smart Filters in Photoshop.

Working with Smart Filters

Smart objects are non-destructive objects in Photoshop CS6. Smart objects are useful as they can remain fully editable with their original characteristics. You can modify the characteristics at any point of time. A Smart Filter is a filter that you apply on a smart object. Smart Filters are nondestructive and appear as sub-layers in the Layers panel under the smart object layer. The Smart Filter icon appears to the right of the smart object layer in the Layers panel. To expand or collapse a Smart Filter, click the triangle next to the icon. You can show or hide Smart Filters independently by clicking the eye icon.

To apply a Smart Filter, you need to first convert a layer into a smart object layer. In Photoshop, you can import files as smart objects as well as convert normal layers to smart object layers. You cannot apply filters, such as Extract, Liquify, Pattern Maker, and Vanishing Point to a smart object layer. Likewise Photoshop's adjustment layers, Smart Filters allow you to modify their settings after an effect is applied. Perform the following steps to work with Smart Filters in Photoshop CS6:

1. **Select** a smart object layer (**Layer 0**) in the Layers panel, as shown in picture 10.3 with the red arrow. Then choose **Filter> Stylize> Tiles** from the Menu bar to open the Tiles dialog box.

2. In the <u>Tiles</u> dialog box, you can specify the number of tiles and an offset value in percentage. We click the **OK** button with the default settings. The Tiles filter effect is applied on the smart object, as shown in picture 10.4.

Picture 10.3

Picture 10.4

As you can see on your screen, the Tiles filter effect appears in the Layers panel under the smart objet layer and named as Smart Filters. After adding the Smart Filter, you can modify it later.

3. **Select** a type tool and **type** the desired text. In our case, we type **MOSAIC** and applied a layer effect (**Stroke**), as shown in picture 10.5.

4. **Select** the smart object layer (**Layer 0**) again in the Layers panel. Then **double-click** the Tiles filter in the Layers panel to modify it. The Tiles dialog box appears again.

5. **Type** the new value for the <u>Maximum Offset</u> as: **40**. Then select the **Inverse Image** radio button to fill the empty area that is created due to the specified offset value, with the inverse of the image.

6. Click the **OK** button in the Tiles dialog box. The smart object with modified settings appears in the Document window.

Picture 10.5

Using the Filter Gallery

The Filter Gallery enables you to preview many of the Photoshop's filters at one place. Using the Filter Gallery, you can apply one or more filters on the selected layer, toggle filter visibility, and change the stacking order of the filters. It also provides a large preview of the result of the applied filter effects.

You can access the Filter Gallery by selecting Filter> Filter Gallery from the Menu bar. In our case, we have categorized the Filter Gallery dialog box into three sections: Image Preview, Filter Selection, and Filter Controls, as shown in picture 10.6.

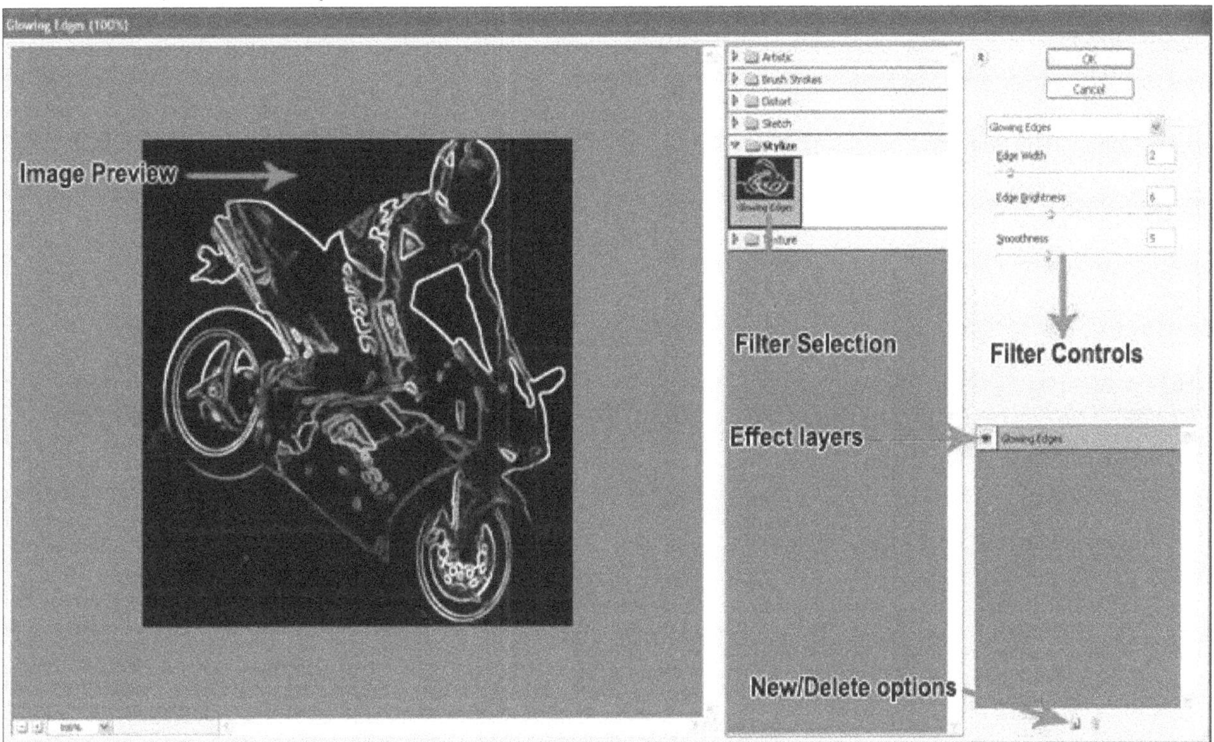

Picture 10.6

This picture shows a preview of the Glowing Edges filter available under the Stylize category. The options specific to the Glowing Edges effect are displayed on the right side of a filter category and change according to the selected filter effect or category. Clicking a filter category name in the Filter Gallery dialog box displays the thumbnails of the filters available under the selected category. After modifying the settings, you can click the OK button to apply the effects on images.

In the subsequent sections, you learn about different types of filter and filter groups, such as Pixelate, Blur, Vanishing Point, Liquify, and Render filters on an image. Let's now learn about the Mosaic filter under the Pixelate filter group.

Applying the Pixelate Filters

The Pixelate filters are used to create pixelation effects. These effects can be used in special cases. For instance, you can use the Color Halftone filter to create a newspaper effect that has lots of tiny visible dots. There are seven different Pixelate filters, such as Color Halftone, Crystalize, Facet, Fragment, Mezzotint, Mosaic, and Pointilize. Some of the filters, such as the Fragment filter do not include dialog box where as other filters include dialog boxes. The Filter Gallery does not include these filters.

In this section, you are going to learn about the Mosaic filter that lets you create pixelated effect similar to the effect that appears when you zoom in an image. Perform the following simple steps on your computer to apply the Mosaic filter effect:

1. **Select** the raster layer in the Layers panel. In our case, we have selected **Layer 0**, as shown in picture 10.7.

2. Choose **Filter> Pixelate> Mosaic** from the Menu bar. The Mosaic dialog box appears with the Cell Size option and a preview pane.

Picture 10.7

Picture 10.8

3. **Type** a new value as per your requirement to pixelate the image. In our case, we set the Cell Size value to **12**.

4. Click the **OK** button at the top of the box to close the Mosaic dialog box.

The **Mosaic** filter effect appears on the selected layer, as shown in picture 10.8. You can see on your screen that the image appears pixelalted.

After learning about Mosaic filter effect, let's learn to use the Blur filters that allow you to blur images in many ways.

Applying the Blur Filter

The Blur filters allow you to blur images in a number of ways. The filters under this group are used to retouch and repair images in Photoshop. For instance, the Radial Blur filter creates a blur in a circular direction. There is also a Shape Blur filter, which blurs in a shape selected in the custom shapes option. You can apply the blur effect either to the whole image or to a specific area defined by a selection marquee.

Photoshop CS6 has introduced three new Blur filters: Field Blur, Iris Blur, and Tilt-Shift that make the blurring process much easier. These filters use a new workspace where the controls appear on the Document window which helps you to determine blur's placement, size, and strength. In our case, we use the new Tilt-Shift filter that lets you control the part of the image that is in focus. For instance, you can use this filter to blur images that have distracting backgrounds. Perform the following steps to apply the new Tilt-Shift filter to an image:

1. **Open** an image on which you want to apply a blur effect.

2. Choose **Filter> Blur> Tilt-Shift** from the Menu bar. The Tilt-Shift controls appear that you can use to modify the default settings.

3. **Drag** the solid line upward to increase the blur area. Then **drag** the blur ring at the center clockwise to increase or anticlockwise to decrease the Blur amount.

Photoshop also allows you to rotate the effect of the filter. To rotate, you need to place the mouse-pointer over the roundness handle (white dot) at the center of the solid line, and then the rotation arrow appears.

4. **Drag** the arrow head to rotate the blur effect. Then click **OK** button on the Options bar to apply the blur effect. Similarly, you can use other Blur filters.

Exploring Render Filters

Render filters are used to create special effects, such as cloud patterns and simulated light reflections in an image. One of the filters available under the Render filters group is Lighting Effects that lets you produce a number of lighting effects on your images. You can choose from 17 light presets, three light types, and various light properties, such as Color, Hotspot, Glass, and Ambience. You can also use create 3D effects using bump maps, which are grayscale files.

The Difference Clouds filter allows you to create clouds patterns. To produce a cloud pattern, this filter uses random values that are generated because of the difference between foreground and background colors.

The Render filters are not available in the Filter Gallery. You can access these filters by selecting Filter> Render from the Menu bar. Let's briefly discuss the different types of Render filters:
- **Clouds:** Uses foreground and background colors to create the cloud effect and replaces the original images.
- **Difference Clouds:** Uses foreground and background colors and also blends them with the existing pixels to create the cloud effect.
- **Fibers:** Uses foreground and background colors to create the fiber effect and replaces the original image.
- **Lens Flare:** Creates realistic lens flare effects. You can use flare effect presets and place accordingly.
- **Lighting Effects:** Adds lighting effects to create vivid effects. You can create different types of lights and place them in the image.

Exploring the Vanishing Point Filter

The Vanishing Point filter lets you clone, paint, and transform image objects at the same time retains the visual perspective by automatically adjusting the perspective planes. When you select the Vanishing Point filter, the Vanishing Points dialog box appear where you can define the perspective planes in the image. You can use the Create Plane Tool and click on the image to define the four points of the perspective grid.

After you define the perspective grid, you can edit the image using Marquee Tool, Stamp Tool, or Brush Tool. Editing in the Vanishing Point dialog box allows you to maintain consistent perspective throughout the image. Instead, you work dimensionally on the perspective planes in the image. Let's now learn to use the Liquify filter.

Using the Liquify Filter

The Liquify filter uses several tools to push, pull, rotate, reflect, pucker, and bloat the pixels of any image. You can use the Liquify filter for various purposes from photo retouching to artistic effects. The Liquify filter now uses the GPU; however, it depends whether your video card supports it. This enables the filter work much faster and more efficient to use.

However, you cannot apply the Liquify filter to a smart object. You can select Filter> Liquify from the Menu bar to open the Liquify dialog box that enables you to modify your image. In the Liquify dialog box, you can pull and warp using Pucker Tool, Bloat Tool, and Push Left Tool to change your image. In the Liquify dialog box, you can see the following sections:

- **Tools panel:** Appears on the left of the screen, and includes various tools, such as Forward Warp, Reconstruct, Twirl, Pucker, Bloat, Push, Mirror, Turbulence, Freeze/Thaw Mask, Hand, and Zoom.
- **Image preview area:** Displays the image or the object you are editing.
- **Options panel:** Displays all the options of the selected tool. The options are grouped according to specific behavior of the selected tool. Perform the following steps to use the Liquify filter:

1. **Open** the image that you want to modify using the Liquify filter. Then choose **Filter> Liquify** from the Menu bar to open its dialog box, as shown in picture 10.9.

Picture 10.9

2. Select **Pucker Tool** in the Liquify Tools panel on the left side, as shown in picture 10.9 with the red arrow numbered 2.

3. **Set** the desired brush size in the <u>Brush Size</u> combo box in the right pane. In our case, we set the brush size to **905**, as shown in picture 10.9 with the red arrow numbered 3.

As you click and drag with Pucker Tool, the pixels are moved towards the center of the brush area. This is useful when you want to inflate something. In addition, if you want to move pixels away from the center of the brush, use Bloat Tool.

4. **Click** or **drag** on the image to inflate it. In our case, the image appears inflated, as shown in picture 11.0.

5. Click the **OK** button when you are satisfied with the effect.

Similarly, you can use other tools available in the Liquify dialog box and experiment to perform creative image manipulation in Photoshop.

In the next section, we are going to learn about actions in Photoshop CS6.

Picture 11.0

Working with Actions

An action is a series of recorded Photoshop commands that can be played back repeatedly at any time. Actions are important for consistency and efficiency. For instance, you are importing 100 raw images from your digital camera, and each image needs to be converted to a specific size and resolution. Now, instead of repeating the import process 100 times, you can perform the process once, and save it as an action in Photoshop.

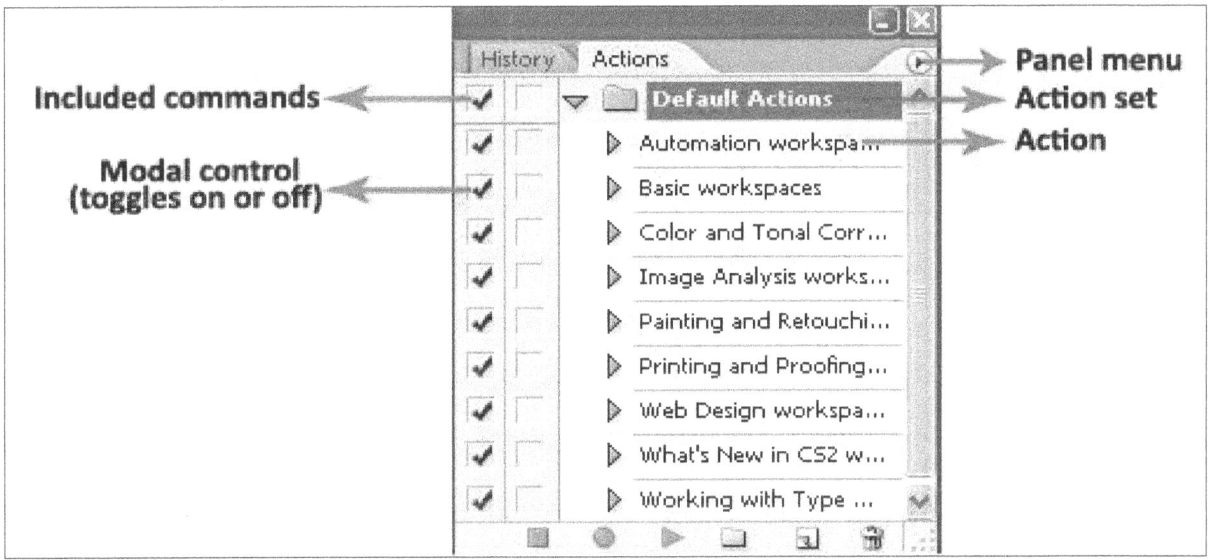

Picture 11.1

You can apply an action to any number of image layers. Photoshop CS6 also allows you to modify existing actions, and save them as a custom action. To apply an action, select the layer on which you want to apply the action and open the Actions panel. In the Actions panel, select the action and then click the Play selection button at the bottom of the panel.

You can open the Actions panel by selecting Window> Actions from the Menu bar (or pressing the F9 key). The picture 11.1 in the previous page shows the Actions panel with the default actions. The Actions panel displays the default action set (Default Actions) when opened for the first time. In Photoshop CS6, a new action called Mixer Brush Cloning Point Setup is added to the default action set. Besides the default action set that appears by default in the Actions panel, you can select additional action sets, such as Frames, Image Effects, Text Effects, and Video Actions from the panel menu.

By default, the Actions panel is displayed in the list mode. You can also display it in the button mode by selecting the Button Mode option from the Actions panel menu. The Actions panel has three columns:

- **Left column:** Allows you to include or exclude actions. It also allows you to select steps within an action. Those selected actions are applied when you play the action.
- **Middle column:** Allows whether or not the action display dialog boxes. When you click this column, an icon appears that indicates when the action played it displays a dialog box.
- **Right column:** Lists the names of actions or action sets. By clicking the right-arrow, you can expand or collapse actions and action sets.

The Actions panel allows you to create new actions, modify existing actions, and save an action. You can create an action from commands, filters, or adjustments, including blending mode changes to layers. You can also enhance actions by creating a droplet.

A droplet allows you to apply multiple actions without launching Photoshop. You can drag the image files that you want to modify over the droplet, which appears as a file on the hard drive. The droplet applies all the actions that are part of it on the images and saves in a specified folder. Let's now learn to load a built-in action set.

Loading a Built-in Action Set

Photoshop CS6 provides several built-in action sets, such as Commands, Frames, Image Effects, LAB – Black & White Technique, Production, Stars Trains, Text Effects, Textures, and video Actions. All these built-in action sets can be accessed from the Actions panel menu. In addition, you can also download and install actions from the various third-party vendors. After you load the action, you can apply the action by playing the action. Perform the following simple steps on your computer to load a built-in action in Photoshop CS6:

1. Select **Window> Actions** from the Menu bar to open the Actions panel. In the default workspace (Essentials), the Actions panel is not visible.

2. Click the **Actions panel menu**. The panel menu appears on your screen.

3. **Select** a built-in action set you want to load. In our case, we select the **Stars Trails** action set. The Star Trails action set appears in the Actions panel below the Default Actions action set.

After loading the action set, you can expand or contract the actions by clicking the right-pointing arrow before the name. You can also remove actions from the Actions panel. To remove an action set, drag and drop it over the Delete button at the bottom of the Actions panel.

Using a Built-in Action

To use a built-in action in Photoshop, you need to select the action and then click the Play selection button. When you click the Play selection button, all the recorded commands within that action are executed one by one on the image. You can execute an action on a selection or an entire image or layer. However, to execute some actions you need to make a selection. While playing an action, you can exclude specific commands that you do not want to execute.

In addition, you can specify values or use tools if the action contains Modal controls. Modal controls are settings that appear in a dialog box only when the middle column in the Actions panel is selected and you play an action. Now you can perform the following simple steps on your computer to play an action on an image:

1. **Open** the document and **select** the image layer in the Layers panel. In our case, we select the **Background** layer in the Layers panel.

2. **Select** an action in the Actions panel. In our case, we select the **Quadrant Colors** action in the Default Actions action set.

3. Click the **Play selection** button at the bottom of the Actions panel. As the result, the Quadrant Colors action plays automatically and the resulting effects appear after few seconds.

You can also notice a new layer is created in the Layers panel. The Quadrant Colors action performs various steps to get the final result. All the commands are played in descending order. For instance, the first command (Make snapshot) is played first and then the Convert Mode command is played and so on. You can start from any of the commands listed in the action.

To play, select Levels and click the Play selection button. The middle column (Modal control) toggles on or off depending on whether an action displays dialog boxes, when it is played. Let's now play the Quadrant Colors action with the Modal control selected for the action.

4. Click the **Toggle dialog on/off** button for the Quadrant Colors action. A message box appears.

5. Click the **OK** button. Small icons appear for the commands that have Modal control.

6. Select the **Background layer** again in the Layers panel. Then click the eye icon of the **Background copy** layer to hide.

7. **Ensure** the Quadrant Colors action is selected in the Actions panel and then click the **Play selection** button again. The **New Snapshot** dialog box appears.

8. **Type** a name for the snapshot in the Name text box. In our case, the new name typed is **Quadrant Colors**.

9. Click the **OK** button which opens the **Duplicate Layer** dialog box. Then click the **OK** button with the default name **Background copy 2**.

You can see the commands without Modal control dialog boxes are applied to the image in the Document window and the Levels dialog box appears. You can use the Levels dialog box to modify the default settings.

10. Click the **OK** button in the Levels dialog.

Niranjan Jha Showman
Trainer, Author, Physician, Entrepreneur, Filmmaker, Activist
Cromosys Corporation
Education and Technology Research Center
www.facebook.com/cromosys
+91-9561450045
Nallasopara (W), Mumbai, India

NIRANJAN JHA SHOWMAN

Founder - Niranjan Jha Showman

Education and Technology Research Center

Patankar Park, Nallasopara (W), Mumbai. +91-9561450045

Education, Technology, Publication, Healthcare, Newsmedia, Realtor, Filmmaking

www.facebook.com/cromosys

Cromosys Publication
Teach
Yourself
German
NIRANJAN JHA SHOWMAN

Cromosys Publication
Teach Yourself French
NIRANJAN JHA SHOWMAN

Cromosys Publication
Teach
Yourself
Spanish
NIRANJAN JHA SHOWMAN

Cromosys Publication

English
Voice
Accent and
Pronunciation

NIRANJAN JHA SHOWMAN

Teach Yourself Autodesk MAYA

Cromosys Publication

NIRANJAN JHA SHOWMAN

Cromosys Publication

Teach
Yourself
Autodesk
3ds Max

NIRANJAN JHA SHOWMAN

Cromosys Publication
CRIMINAL FACTORY
NIRANJAN JHA SHOWMAN

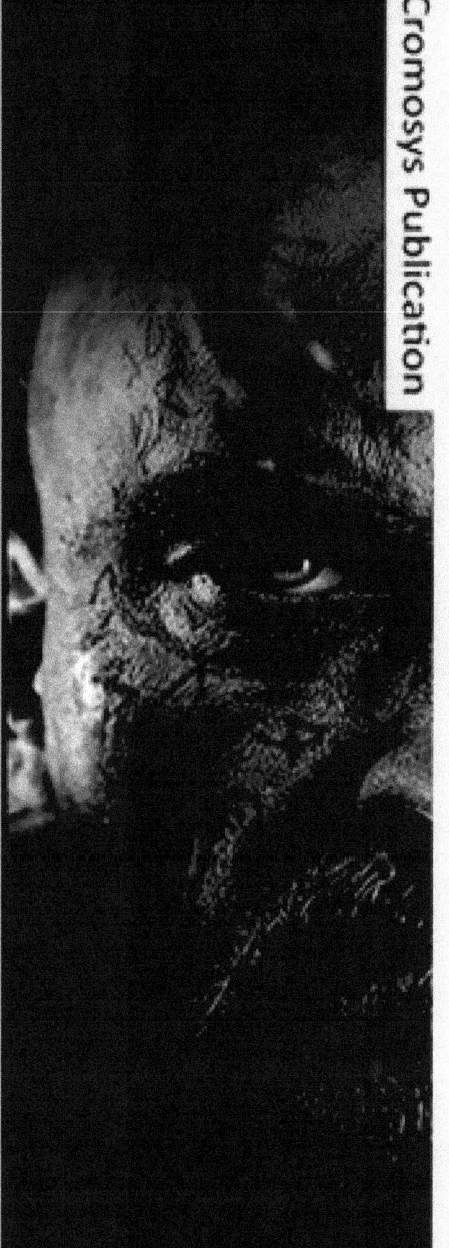

Cromosys Publication
FOCAL DISASTER
NIRANJAN JHA SHOWMAN

Cromosys Publication
Your talents will not help you succeed without your skill of using them.
NIRANJAN JHA SHOWMAN
BE MILLIONAIRE LIKE ME

Copyright Office
Government of India

सत्यमेव जयते

Extracts from the Register of Copyrights

Dated : 16/08/2022

1.	Registration Number	: **T-86782-2022**
2.	Name, address and nationality of the applicant	: NIRANJAN JHA SHOWMAN, CROMOSYS PUBLICATION, 001, JAYSATYAM, PATANKAR ROAD, NALLASOPARA (W), MUMBAI, MAHARASHTRA - 401203. INDIAN
3.	Nature of the applicant's interest in the copyright of the work	: AUTHOR
4.	Class and description of the work	: LITERARY / BOOK
5.	Title of the work	: **Teach Yourself Photoshop**
6.	Language of the work	: ENGLISH
7.	Name, address and nationality of the author and if the author is deceased, date of his decease	: NIRANJAN JHA SHOWMAN, CROMOSYS PUBLICATION, 001, JAYSATYAM, PATANKAR ROAD, NALLASOPARA (W), MUMBAI, MAHARASHTRA - 401203. INDIAN
8.	Whether the work is published or unpublished	: UNPUBLISHED
9.	Year and country of first publication and name, address and nationality of the publisher	: N.A.
10.	Years and countries of subsequent publications, if any, and names, addresses and nationalities of the publishers	: N.A. SAME AS ABOVE
11.	Names, addresses and nationalities of the owners of various rights comprising the copyright in the work and the extent of rights held by each, together with particulars of assignments and licences, if any	:
12.	Names, addresses and nationalities of other persons, if any, authorised to assign or licence of rights comprising the copyright	: N.A.
13.	If the work is an 'Artistic work', the location of the original work, including name, address and nationality of the person in possession of the work. (In the case of an architectural work, the year of completion of the work should also be shown).	: N.A.
14.	If the work is an 'Artistic work', whether it is registered under the Designs Act 2000 if yes give details.	: N.A.
15.	If the work is an 'Artistic work', capable of being registered as a design under the Designs Act 2000.whether it has been applied to an article though an industrial process and ,if yes ,the number of times it is reproduced.	: N.A.
16.	Remarks, if any	:

Diary Number : 8423/2020-DF/T
Date of Application : 25/07/2020
Date of Receipt : 25/07/2020

DEPUTY REGISTRAR OF COPYRIGHTS